LEWIS WEINBERGER

L.WEINBERGER, BA

D0984106

Assembling My Father

Assembling My Father

A DAUGHTER'S DETECTIVE STORY

Anna Cypra Oliver

HOUGHTON MIFFLIN COMPANY | BOSTON NEW YORK 2004

For information about permission to reproduce selections from this book,
write to Permissions, Houghton Mifflin Company, 215 Park Avenue South,
New York, New York 10003.

Visit our Web site: www.houghtonmifflinbooks.com.

Typeset in Eureka

Library of Congress Cataloging-in-Publication Data
  Oliver, Anna Cypra.
  Assembling my father : a daughter's detective
story / Anna Cypra Oliver.
    p. cm.
  ISBN 0-618-34152-8
  1. Weinberger, Lewis, d. 1974. 2. Suicide victims — New Mexico — Taos —
Biography. 3. Suicide victims — New Mexico — Taos — Family relationships.
4. Oliver, Anna Cypra. 5. Fathers and daughters — New Mexico — Taos —
Biography. 6. Fathers — Death — Psychological aspects. I. Title.
  HV6548.U52T367 2004
  362.28'092—dc22 [B] 2003067790

Printed in the United States of America
MP 10 9 8 7 6 5 4 3 2 1

The names of some of the individuals in this book have been changed.

for my father

and

for Stephan,
without whom this
and so much more
would not have been possible

Acknowledgments

This book is, in many important ways, a collaboration, and I must express my deepest appreciation to all the people who contributed their stories and their voices: Stephan Marc Klein, Irwin Sollinger, Miriam Stoll, Robert Stoll, Joseph Weinberger, the late Rose Oliver, John Oliver, Anna London, Norman London, Daniel S. Cohn, Stephan Weinberger, Suzanne Hinman, Margo Cutler, Donald Singer, Roland "Jay" Finch, Barry Fishkin, Roberta Blender Maltese, Kenneth Schatz, Jeremy Grainger, Jerome Yavarkovsky, Lee Driver, Mara Andover, Art Ross, Annie Dugan, Tracy McCallum, Rick Klein, Rollo Silver, Beverly Pollack Silver, the late Bill Gersh, and last but far from least, Peter Oliver, best of all possible brothers, and my mother, Teresa Oliver Arledge, who, despite her fears about what I might say, encouraged me to tell the truth as I saw it. Her pride in me and in this book means more than I can articulate.

Many others contributed over the years to the creation of this work, offering their insights and critical support. Stephan Klein, again, has to be acknowledged for his rigorous analysis of and incisive commentary on every aspect of this project, as well as his matchless skills as a researcher: you are my Continental Op. My gratitude goes to professors (and authors) Patricia Hampl, M. J. Fitzgerald, and Charles Sugnet, who nurtured the first small seeds into a full-blown book; to Elissa Raffa, comrade in writing and keen critic; fellow scribblers Carolyn Crooke, Teresa Whitman, Marcia Peck, and Mark Powell; my cousin Jane Perlmutter; Stephan's and now my dear friend Joel Marsh; everyone in Writing X, but especially Michael Hawley, Marc Gaetani, and Jan Schmidt, who were there through every step of the long slog, and Eric Darton, valued friend and mentor, without whose support and extraordinary gift for free association I would never have come so far. My special thanks to Betsy Lerner and Richard Todd for their generosity toward a young writer; to Madelon Sprengnether, Terry Tempest Williams, and Susan Orlean for their invaluable encouragement; and, further back, to Nancy Jenkins, peerless high school humanities teacher, to whom a good part of any success I ever achieve, as a writer and as a person, has to be attributed. Gratitude is owed to my first husband, who, despite our troubles, was among the first and most ardent supporters of this book.

My profound thanks to the New York Foundation for the Arts for its financial support—not to mention acknowledgment—of my work and the work of so many others artists.

And thanks to Tammy Gobert in the archives department at Rensselaer Polytechnic Institute for all her help; Frederick T. Courtright, at the Permissions Company, for tracking everything down; Tony, Terrence, and Epi at Century Copy for their unfailing good will toward my cut-and-paste manuscripts; and Carol and the rest of the booksellers at Three Lives and Company, always a refuge.

My editor, Elaine Pfefferblit, cannot be adequately repaid for the sharpness of mind and erudition she brought to my manuscript or for her commitment to the story it told. Thanks also to Jayne Yaffe Kemp, whose deft manuscript editing brought marvelous precision and depth to the final draft. And to everyone at Houghton Mifflin: you offer heartening proof that literary publishing is still very much alive.

Finally, overwhelming gratitude goes to my agent, Kathleen Anderson, risk taker and generous spirit, who saw shape in the murk and, hand over hand, dragged the words I was reluctant to form to the surface.

Assembling My Father

"A man who dies at the age of thirty-five," said Moritz Heimann once, "is at every point of his life a man who dies at the age of thirty-five." Nothing is more dubious than this sentence—but for the sole reason that the tense is wrong. A man—so says the truth that was meant here—who died at thirty-five will appear to *remembrance* at every point in his life as a man who dies at the age of thirty-five. In other words, the statement that makes no sense for real life becomes indisputable for remembered life.

—WALTER BENJAMIN, "THE STORYTELLER"

On April 9, 1974, a man lays newspaper on the floor of his rented room in Taos, New Mexico. He puts a gun in his mouth. He pulls the trigger. He is thirty-five years old.

A middle-class Jew raised in Queens, a New Yorker to the core, an architect, an intellectual, finds himself alone in a dirt-walled rented room. His wife has left him. He sees his son, age seven, and his daughter, age five, only at his ex-wife's whim. His parents are dead. His business is bankrupt. His house is sold. He dies flying on coke.

No mystery really: a man on drugs, paranoid, delusional, comes to the end of his rope. Except, as Nabokov says, "detail is always welcome."

And so, skin pasted to muscle wrapped around bone, joint slipped into joint, I reconstruct him. I—the five-year-old daughter in the story —struggle to remember a man I don't remember, a man who is for me at every point in his life a man who dies at the age of thirty-five.

Buds and Thorns

Ordinarily we do not see a *picture* of a thing but receive an impression of the thing itself, of the entire form including the sides we cannot see, and of all the space surrounding it. . . . In the same way we know that we have seen a church when we have merely received an impression of a tall building combined with a steeple. And if we are not interested in knowing more we usually notice no more. But if we are interested we go further. . . . The mental process that goes on in the mind of a person who observes a building in this way is very much like that which goes on in the mind of an architect when planning a building. After having roughly decided on the main forms he continues by adding details which shoot out from the body like buds and thorns. . . . He mentally prepares the materials and combines them in one large structure. It gives him pleasure to work with the different materials, to see them change from an amorphous mass of ordinary stone and wood into a definite entity, the result of his own efforts.

—STEEN EILER RASMUSSEN, *Experiencing Architecture*

NIGHT WATCHMAN

Ojo de Dios. Eye of God. I don't know who taught me how to make one. It might have been the Sunday school teacher at First Methodist. Or maybe I saw one at a school friend's house or in the back window of a pickup truck. I just remember sitting under a tree on our property in Taos, on the bench seat left over from some old Chevy, winding yarn around and around two crossed sticks until it formed a colored diamond, green and yellow bands radiating from a brown eye of yarn in the center. I was nine. My mother must have gotten the yarn for me, or had it in her scrap bag. When it was finished, I hung the *ojo* on the wall above my bed in the plywood shack we lived in then.

It was just a thing you made from two sticks and colored yarn, but I believed in it. I had heard that if you hung one in your house, the eye of God would always watch over you. He would make sure your quilts did not slide off the too high bed at night, so you would not wake up shivering after the stove had gone out. He would prevent the cat from standing on your neck, choking you while you slept. He would keep the vampires away, so you could fall asleep with your face in the sweet air, instead of buried in the covers to protect the tender area where fangs were most likely to sink into the skin.

It was my first conception of God.

And when the quilts did indeed stay on and the cat, at least for a few days, curled up at my side instead of on my jugular, I was convinced that it worked. My faith was easy and adaptable. It did not demand large proofs. It seemed good in those days to have God there, always watching.

CONVERSATIONAL TERRORISM

My mother went out west to be a hippie. My stepfather beat her. My father killed himself. My mother, born Jewish, became a fundamentalist Christian when I was twelve.

These were the things I said about myself, always, in any conversation, almost immediately, when I was eighteen and on my own for the first time, an exile from bohemian Taos to mainstream Middle America, a disorienting land of mini-malls and all-night grocery warehouses. These facts defined me. They set me apart from the suburbanites and Iowa farm kids I found myself among at college in Minneapolis. Their histories, even when traumatic, rarely consisted of so fantastic a combination of elements.

I never knew what not to tell people.

Whenever I spoke, I played a game of double vision with myself. I'd speak and judge myself speaking at the same moment. The words, the shades of meaning, the tone: aggressive, condescending, arrogant, or rarely, but sometimes, hitting just the right note of friendly interest and camaraderie. I didn't relax into conversation and parse it later, wishing I could take back certain words and add others. I wished I could take them back even as they emerged.

I used to say to people, straight out, "My father killed himself." People I barely knew. At a bar, say, when a bunch of us went out after class, someone would ask, "And your father? Where is your father now? What does he do?"

"My father died when I was a child." Pause. "He killed himself."

It was promiscuous. It was like fucking on a first date.

Not that I knew anything about that. In those years, my late teens and early twenties, I was already respectably married. I was a Christian. I'd never slept with anyone besides my husband.

"Oh, I'm sorry," the person would say.

Things happen, I'd shrug. Get over it. Aloud, I'd say, "Don't be, it was a long time ago. I hardly knew him."

It was not an invitation to intimacy, but a fending-off. Cold shoulder by total exposure. I enjoyed, I admit, the shock on my acquaintance's face. I did not say, He put a bullet through the roof of his mouth. He blew his brains out. But that's what I wanted to convey. The full grisly horror of it.

My father killed himself. And then there was nothing more to say.

REMAINS: AN INVENTORY OF MY FATHER

1. A handful of photographs of him, including his high school graduation portrait and some taken in Florida by my mother.

2. A silver belt buckle.

3. Photographs taken by my father of my mother in her twenties, and of my brother and me when we were children.

4. *Architectural Record*, Vol. 145, No. 6: "Record Houses of 1969."

5. *Miami Herald*, "Dwelling Is Designed for Family Living," May 25, 1969.

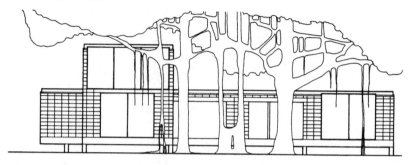

The first house my parents owned was featured in *Architectural Record's* "Record Houses of 1969" as one of the twenty "trend-setting winners" of that year. An article ran in the home section of the *Miami Herald*, Sunday, May 25, 1969, under the headline: "Dwelling Is Designed for Family Living."

I spread the magazine and the crumbling newspaper on my dining room table to study them. I had just been born when we moved in; my brother, Peter, was two years old. Our parents had been married nine years. My father, Lewis Weinberger, built that house, or had it built, working as a developer and contractor in Dade County.

"The house," the *Herald* says, "seems to float in a 'cage' of shimmering greenery."

Donald Singer, whose name and photograph appear in the magazine spread, was the architect. This information strikes me as peculiar because my father was also an architect. I've known his profession for as long as I can remember, though almost nothing else. He got a degree from Rensselaer Polytechnic Institute in Troy, New York, a fact I discovered only after a question on my own college applications asked me to describe my parents' educational background; I had to ask my mother where he'd gone. The syllables of the school's name impressed me. *Rensselaer*, I would repeat quietly to myself, *Rensselaer Polytechnic Institute*. Why then did he not design the house himself?

"Like a big sculpture perched alone in a rain forest," Donald Singer is quoted as saying in *Architectural Record*.

Maybe Donald Singer was a friend. He seems not to have charged my parents for his plans, or if he did, his fee is not included in the figure cited by *Architectural Record*: $22,400: "[excluding] the architect's fee or builder's profit, as Mr. Weinberger was contractor."

"Mr. Weinberger": my father. And "Mrs. Weinberger": my mother, only twenty-nine years old. My mother, who was "pleased," the *Herald* says, "to discover she could dispense with drapery treatments" because the eighty-foot banyan tree on their property, a former nursery, prevented neighbors from peering through the two-story-high windows that formed one side of the house. A statement reported so confidently in its time that it completely conceals the seed sprouting in her even then: a disdain, which at any moment might give way to revulsion, for such niceties as drapery treatments.

RELIABLE INFORMATION

My mother's grandparents owned an elegant apartment on Central Park West and an enormous summer house on Lake Mahopac, a resort town an hour or so from New York City. At the dinner table, years after the summer house was sold, the family used to argue about whether it had sixteen rooms or twenty. My mother, "born again" by then, would insist upon the smaller number because, as much as she loved that house, she somehow found fewer rooms less embarrassing.

My mother's parents lived in a less splendid but comfortable house in Queens, where they moved from Brooklyn in 1952. My grandmother was Jewish and a leftist intellectual; my grandfather, whom my mother adored, a Chilean lapsed-Catholic artist. My mother had one younger brother named John and a spaniel named Dinky. She went to Jamaica High School and then to Barnard College, where her mother had gone before her.

In 1960, smiling joyously, or so the photographs make it seem, my mother married my father in her parents' living room. She was nineteen. Six years later the two of them adopted my brother, then six weeks old, and in 1968, my mother became pregnant with me. My parents had already settled in Florida, and two weeks after I was born they moved into the house designed for them by Donald Singer. My father worked for his father, a developer, in Miami.

In 1969, my mother and father abandoned that house to travel across the country with my brother and me for a year. They returned to Florida, sold the house, sold or gave away their belongings, and went to live in a cabin on a mountainside in New Mexico. Not long after, my mother left my father, deciding, as she told me when I was in high school—regretfully, in one of her not infrequent sad moods—that she "just didn't want to be married anymore." She took my brother and me and moved to New Buffalo, a commune just outside Taos.

My mother divorced my father.

A year and a half later, my father committed suicide.

THE DAY MY FATHER DIED

My mother, brother, and I were living in a crumbling old house in southern Colorado with my mother's boyfriend (and Peter's and my de facto stepfather), Wayne. It had no electricity or running water, and its only sources of heat were the wood-burning cookstove and a converted oil drum that turned dangerously red when fully stoked. I was in kindergarten, Peter in second grade. In exchange for minding his cows, we lived for free on Elias Lucero's land in the foothills of San Luis.

I was always last off the school bus. I would scoot sideways under the swinging metal gate, knees up, feet and hands negotiating the rungs of the cattle guard. Dry hills bordered one side of the dirt road, a willow-lined pasture the other. The road wound for a mile toward the pile of adobe Elias had offered us. The house, abandoned until we arrived, sat on a hill, its two stories melting like a waxen face into the ground. The next year I would be old enough to go to the new elementary school across town with my brother, but for now I rode back and forth by myself to the kindergarten alongside the main highway. Left at our gate in the afternoon, I sometimes loitered until Peter showed up on the big bus; other times, anticipating the thick warmth of wood heat and slices of newly baked bread, I would set off on the shortcut through the hills and twisted piñon on my own.

But on the day my father died, the bus driver did not drop me at my usual stop. He made me get off at Dick and Pam's house instead. My mother had called the principal, the bus driver said. That was all he knew.

Dick and Pam were friends of my mother and Wayne. When the driver said Dick's name out loud, the other children snickered. I had no idea what was so funny, but their snide laughter was nothing new. Their daddies did not like my daddy, and they did not like me. "Hippie," they'd hiss in the schoolyard. "Dirty gringo." I came home more than once with torn clothes, teeth marks, my scalp smarting from having my hair pulled. *Words are better than fists*, my mother would say, dabbing Mercurochrome on my cuts. *The one who wins is the one who walks away.* But she never actually scolded me for fighting. Both she and Wayne knew it was unavoidable. Grown-up hippies got picked on, too, sometimes with just a dirty look or a shove at the grocery store, sometimes with a bullet fired into a doorpost, or a bottle of gasoline with a lit rag for a fuse thrown through a window. The house belonging to a friend of ours had burned down one night while he and his old lady were in Denver.

Because it was springtime and the road was muddy, the bus driver could pull only a little way into Dick and Pam's driveway. I clumped down the stairs, dragging my jacket and a clutch of papers, my bangs in my eyes, the buckles on my black galoshes clacking. The doors slapped shut behind me. The short, square bus was hard to maneuver on the narrow road. As the driver scraped it between the fence and the wild plum bushes and pulled slowly away, the children piled against the back window, hot breath and noses to the glass, tongues out, fingers wagging in their ears. I hated them. Every stick or stone in the driveway was one of their mean bodies, and I gave them a rubbery thump with my toe, the galoshes flapping against my legs.

Peter was there, I recall, when I came to the door, although that doesn't quite make sense, since he had farther to go. Pam gave us milk and honey-carob cookies, and I remember eating the cookies with Dick's mottled cat perched on my lap. I knew from other occasions that the cat liked to drink beer, lapped it in great gulps from its water dish, then walked away with a slurred sideways motion, as if its paws had become stiff and irregular as adobe clods. I don't remember how Pam acted when I came to the door or what words she used, after we had eaten our cookies, to tell us that our father was dead. I don't remember wondering what it meant to be dead: I seemed to have understood.

My brother's face crumpled up. When he was five, Peter had spent the summer traveling with Lewis from Taos to Seattle. Thinking of it now, I can see them together, two guys cruising in the car with the windows down. My brother falls into a sweaty sleep with his head against Lewis's hip, eats cheeseburgers, steamy and warm through their paper wrappers, at a concrete table beside a Tastee-Freez in Arizona, Nevada, Utah. Lewis gives him his first swimming lesson in some overchlorinated roadside pool, a bath in the skittery neon glare of one motor motel or another. During the long stretches when Lewis doesn't talk, when he stares into the shimmering haze above the highway, Peter punches buttons on the radio. A father-son road show.

I, on the other hand, could not even remember what Lewis looked like. He once came to visit my brother and me at Morningstar commune, where we lived with my mother and Wayne. He might have come to take us with him for the weekend. He was standing in the doorway, and I looked up at him, but the sun was behind him: I couldn't see his face. I was four at most. He seemed to be a tall man, but that must have been a trick of New Mexican architecture. My mother tells me that he was only five nine or maybe five ten, an average height.

Peter sat across the table from me at Pam's, a round-faced boy with cracked lips and shaggy brown hair, hunched into himself, nose running, tears spilling over onto his cheeks, red with the effort not to cry. I didn't cry. Instead, I thought clearly and in words: *He must not have known we loved him.* I hadn't had my turn with Lewis yet; I was supposed to spend that summer, only two months away, with him in Taos. Maybe he didn't know I was coming. Maybe he didn't know how much I wanted to come.

Lewis died, I thought then and for years after, because he didn't know we loved him.

My mother rarely referred to him as anything else. Not "your father" or "your dad." My mother's own name was Teresa, after her Chilean paternal grandmother, but I never would have called her that, or Terry either, as most people did: it seemed shockingly disrespectful and strangely unintimate to me when friends called their parents by their first names. And yet, my father was always called Lewis.

If asked, my mother would tell me snippets of their life together —the apartment they lived in when they were first married, the book-shelf whose boards and blocks they stole one night from a nearby con-struction site, his droll sense of humor, how Lewis went into the bedroom one afternoon to "fold laundry" and how, after a half-hour of silence, my mother found him lying on the bed, sound asleep on top of the heaped clothes. After that, "I'll be inside, folding laundry" became their code phrase for taking a nap. Little things, inane but sweet.

Unless specifically prompted, my mother hardly ever talked about him, though at rare times, when I was a teenager, she would say, "You have your father's face. Your expressions are just like his," and I would feel the thrill of a connection that was explicitly, exclusively, between him and me. The way I cocked my eyebrow. The way the corner of my mouth tucked in when I frowned. Just an impression. She couldn't put her finger on it exactly. But I know from his high school gradua-tion portrait that had I been a boy, I would have looked just like him —dark bushy eyebrows, round jaw, square nose, freckles.

Other than our resemblance, my most tangible connection to Lewis was a plush blue and yellow teddy bear I'd named Sydney. I'm not sure where the bear came from. I'm convinced my brother brought it back from their trip to Seattle, but I also recall pulling it from a wire bin in a brightly lit toy store. Lewis was standing nearby, on the edge of my vision, smiling. I recently tried to clear up the mystery of the bear's origins by asking my mother, but she doesn't remember the bear or the trip, only that Lewis left Peter in Florida with my uncle Joe, my father's older brother, for part of the summer.

Not long after my father's death, we learned that our house was next on the locals' list for firebombing. We left overnight.

For all I know, Sydney is still in the attic.

1. The apartment in Manhattan where she lived with Lewis when they were first married.

2. The Dodgers. She loved Brooklyn, where she had been born, and baseball. She knew the lingo, and as a kid could hit a ball as far as any boy. She felt betrayed when the Dodgers moved to L.A. She never spoke about Queens, where she lived from the time she was twelve until she went to college.

3. The Mahopac house.

4. *The Lords of Flatbush*, a movie about a street gang, like those who ruled her Brooklyn neighborhood when she was an early adolescent. She adored Vinnie Barbarino, the sweet thug played by John Travolta on the sitcom *Welcome Back, Kotter* because he, too, reminded her of those sexy local boys in their leather jackets and duck's-ass haircuts.

5. The feather beds in the inns where my mother and Lewis stayed on their monthlong honeymoon in Europe. The rooms were so small and the beds so big that you had to crawl over the pouf to get into the room.

6. Kennedy's assassination.

7. Murdoch, the Great Dane my parents had in Florida. They gave the dog away when my brother grew to be a toddler, after it bit another little boy who came to visit.

8. How she offered my brother a spoonful of peanut butter when he was two years old. She mimicked the face he made when it stuck to the roof of his mouth. "Goob," he said.

9. How my brother used to sneak out of the Florida house when he was supposed to be napping and scamper down the path to see his friend Brooksie. My mother was afraid he would fall into Brooksie's pool.

10. How my brother reached out for a can of bacon grease on the stove and accidentally spilled hot fat on his hand. My mother whisked him to the bathtub and ran cold water over his skin for a long time. It didn't blister. She was terrified but in control.

11. How, on the trip around the country my parents took the year after my birth, their mood sank so low that even my brother sensed it. "Chirk up, guys," he said. "Chirk up." They laughed at that. He was three years old.

I first learned to form my letters and to read in San Luis. Using the workbooks and primers Grandma Rose had sent me from New York, I would sit on a tree stump at the kitchen table and practice writing letters in the orange glow of the kerosene lamp. I was five years old and already avid for words.

Grandma told me once, a long time ago, that you were like that, too. Voracious when it came to the written word. In a box of slides, I found a picture of you wearing army green shorts and a white T-shirt, lying on a bed in Florida with my newborn brother next to your bare legs. Only the lower half of your face is visible, your head propped against the wall on a pillow; you are smoking a cigarette, a newspaper is pressed to your stomach, and beside Peter on the bed is a copy of The New York Review of Books.

There were few books in our house; in fact, there were none that I specifically recall, nor any bookshelves, magazines, or, in those years of isolation in the foothills of the Colorado Rockies, any trips to the town library, if there even was one. Wayne was never a reader, and I guess in those days Mom fancied herself a nineteenth-century farm wife, gardening, baking, sewing, hauling water. For stories, we relied on Wayne and Mystery Theatre on AM radio; we listened to it in the dark while piled on Mom and Wayne's bed or driving somewhere—assuming Wayne wasn't drunk—in the rust-bucket Dodge pickup. The books I remember were from later years, and all of them came from Grandma: Curious George, Doctor Dolittle, *and my all-time favorite,* Mandy. *Grandma gave Peter* The Story of Babar *and* Charlie and the Chocolate Factory. *Because they were his, I had to wait until he was done before I could lay my hands on them.*

When I was about twelve, after Wayne died and Mom married Curtis Sande (whom others in Taos remember, without affection, as the "Sheriff of Morningstar," given a tin badge to wear around the commune because he was considered the meanest, most controlling person on the mesa), I began to take a notebook into the plum thicket on our property, a secret study perfect for writing stories. I wasn't one of those kids with fantasies about having been lost at birth; I didn't dream I was really a princess or a movie star's misplaced daughter, but the stories I was writing, I realize now, were full of foundlings and orphans. They were always disappearing, à la Narnia and The Wind in the Willows, *into magical forests populated by flute-playing satyrs and tree fairies. After Mom and I read* David Copperfield *and* Oliver Twist *together,* my waifs acquired British accents. I loved reading those novels aloud; it was winter and we would sit on the sofa, our voices spinning out into the darkened house. "Barkus is willing," we used to quip to each other all the time, "Barkus is willing." That was before Mom gave up reading novels because they took her attention away from the Lord.

In high school, I developed a penchant for melodrama. I filled notebooks with observations, song fragments, long declarative sentences. I stood at the sink, washing dishes, declaiming lines of dialogue that popped into my head. In drama class, I performed melancholic monologues I had written myself.

And then in college, my senior year, I did what many young writers do when they decide to consider themselves writers in earnest. I sat down to write a book about my childhood:

My mother went out west to be a hippie. My stepfather beat her. My father killed himself.

"FLUTTERING HEART"

Until I reached my midtwenties, I had little interest in knowing anything about my father. For ten years, Tucker and Nellie, friends of Lewis and my mother from their hippie days, kept a trunk full of photographs belonging to Lewis in a storage closet. They lived down the road from the house my mother eventually built in Talpa, on the outskirts of Taos. For ten years, the trunk sat there, a quarter of a mile away, within easy walking distance. We talked—or my brother did, mostly—on and off about going down the road to get it, but we never did. And then we moved away: my brother to college in California, me to Minnesota, and my mother to upstate New York.

My brother would mention the photos from time to time. "If you're in Taos, get the photos," he'd say. "Call Tucker, find out if he still has the photos."

Why don't you get them yourself? I would wonder, but never asked out loud.

It wasn't that I didn't want to see my father's photographs. It was just that I didn't think they'd be anything new. Nellie mentioned pictures of me and Peter and my mother and friends of Lewis: we already had envelopesful that he took of us as children. But then, I didn't want the trunk to be lost either.

One summer, a few months before my twenty-fifth birthday and a month after my fifth wedding anniversary, I returned to Taos for a weeklong visit. When I left home for college, I told my mother I was never coming back, but after so many years in the Midwest, I was hungry to see the mountains and the rich light of New Mexico again. My husband, who had been born in Minneapolis, loved Minnesota and didn't want to move anywhere else, but its trimmed hedges and dandelion-free lawns grieved me. I needed to remind myself of the wild place from which I had come.

I decided to give Tucker a call about my father's trunk. I didn't think about why I wanted it, or even that I wanted it; it was just there, this thing of my father's. My own indifference shamed me a little. What must Tucker think of us for having abandoned it? It seemed indecent to leave it floating around like so much driftwood.

"I told you when you asked me the last time," Tucker said. "I gave the photos to Bill Gersh."

Last time? I didn't remember asking him before.

I called Bill Gersh. I knew who he was, but we had never spoken. Tall, thin, with large eyes, a hooked nose, and dark unruly hair, he had a mad look about him that always made me nervous, even from a distance. Everyone called him, simply, Gersh.

When he answered the phone, I said, "This is Lewis Weinberger's daughter." In that instant, my heart gave a surprising lurch. I always felt anxious when I had to call someone I didn't know well—something about the disembodied voice unsettled me, the inability to assess the effect my words were having—but this palpitation was something new. It was the first time I had said those words to anyone. There was a small silence, a hitch in his breathing, and mine, as the sound of that name, twenty years out of the past, resonated between us. I felt as if I had spoken my father into the world.

Gersh was known in town for being, if not crazy, something of a wild man. All the years we lived in Taos, my mother would have nothing to do with him. Not that her attitude could be taken as evidence against him: after my mother's conversion to fundamentalism, there were a lot of people from her past with whom she broke ties—and they with her. So when Gersh invited me to come up to Magic Tortoise on Lama Mountain, the cooperative community north of Taos where he had been living for the past twenty-odd years, I asked my friend Fielding to come with me; whether for company or protection, I was not sure.

It was a clear July day, and Fielding and I took our time getting to Lama. We passed all the familiar landmarks: the moss-colored pastures of El Prado, the blinking light at the turnoff to Arroyo Seco and the Ski Valley, the sagebrush mesa and barbed-wire fence that stretched for seven miles between the blinking light and the hills that swooped down into the unexpected green gash of Arroyo Hondo. Every familiar bend excited me: the road that took me to Briggs, a boyfriend of mine for one overheated month in high school; Celso's bar, where there were once as many beer can flip-tops as pebbles strewn on the gravel parking lot; the dirt road along the Hondo River which led to a single huge cottonwood tree and a gully carved into the road by a spring at the cottonwood's foot. Beyond the cottonwood began the treacherous switchbacks up to Morningstar commune. We used to navigate them in a truck so big and so wide that a wheel always seemed about to go over the edge. The colors of the desert were surreal: ocher rock and orange soil, black trunks of piñon trees, the aqua tint of sagebrush blending into the blue horizon.

Fielding and I had known each other since grade school. Because my mother had sold our house and moved away, I was staying with Fielding at her mother's place in town. On the way up to Lama, we reminded each other, as we always did when we hadn't seen each other for a while, of the times we raided her mother's closet for tea-party dress-up clothes. We spent whole afternoons transforming ourselves, wreathed in her artist-mother's gorgeous scarves and outlandish hats, although we never got as far as staging an actual tea party. We dissolved on the bed long before that in a froth of chiffon and crinkled silk.

We were more tentative when talking about our present lives. I felt peculiar about having already celebrated my fifth wedding anniversary: it was normal in the church to have married so young, but the bizarreness of it always struck me in the company of anyone secular. I had met Stuart when I was an entering freshman and he was a sophomore at North Central Bible College in Minneapolis. I'd transferred several times since then, finally graduating from the University of Minnesota, and was currently in my second year of an MFA program on the same campus. I also owned a dog and a house in the suburbs, a fact of which I was vaguely ashamed. I disparaged the floral-print wallpaper in the pictures I showed her. "I had such a thing for wallpaper for a while," I said.

As for Fielding, she had been with the same man for a few years but didn't know what step to take next. Her lover was a Peruvian Indian. They had met in Italy and usually spent a good part of every year near Cuzco with his family. She was golden-haired fair; he was black-haired dark. Everything about them seemed bohemian and exotic.

I wanted to tell her that I had changed, that I was not the prude I used to be. I drank wine; I read everything; I watched steamy movies. I said "fuck" sometimes. I was not, I wanted to assure her, a fundamentalist. That had been my mother in me. I was not even sure I believed in God anymore. Which God? Whose God? But there was too much to explain, and I couldn't give voice to the dissatisfaction creeping up my throat. By the time we turned onto the road to Lama, we had both grown quiet.

A moment after we pulled up, Gersh, as thin and wild-looking as ever, strolled slowly out to the car. The yard, like most in northern New Mexico, was packed dirt with patches of dark weeds. A sweep of deep green pine framed the adobe house. Just down the road, I could see the circular house in which my mother's oldest friend, Beverly, lived. Beverly had left Queens before my parents did and, after she settled in Taos, invited them to come west to visit her. She was another person with whom my mother didn't have much to do anymore.

When I got out of the car, Gersh said, "You look just like your father."

I knew this, but it felt strange to be recognized. "Do I?" I asked.

Gersh glanced across the car roof at Fielding. "And you're Willi's daughter, aren't you?" His eyes, too large for their sockets, gave his long face a disturbing intensity. It was hard to hold his gaze as he spoke.

"Yes," Fielding said in her sweet, sometimes little-girl voice. "We've met before."

She was delicate and fair and lovely in an I-don't-care-how-I-look way. Next to her, I felt clumsy and plain.

"Come inside," Gersh said. "I'll show you the house."

We followed him silently. In the past, I had avoided going to Lama. I associated it with active New Age spirituality, which for me meant anything from faith in crystals to white Westerners practicing Buddhism, and found it a disquieting place to visit. Cynical as I was, I felt vibes there, a peculiar pulse. My upbringing had left me with a powerful suspicion of all non-Christian religions, of which Taos had more than the average small town's share. A confluence of old world and new, sacred mountains and color-saturated light, Taos drew mystics and philosophical eccentrics of all sorts. Among the white population alone were Buddhists, Hanuman worshippers, animists, and witches, not to mention the peyote-eating Pueblo Indians and the Hispanics, their dark churches filled with *santos*. People who practiced other religions, including Catholicism, were either to be converted, or, failing that, fervently prayed for from a distance. Despite my church's injunction to "hate the sin and love the sinner," it was clear that, should they refuse to repent, our doctrine condemned these willful souls. Beverly was condemned. Gersh was condemned.

And yet, even when I was a fundamentalist, I had had no sympathy for fundamentalism's fire-and-brimstone intolerance, the forces of light battling the forces of darkness. Nor had I ever cared much for the hoodoo pervading Taos: white people "co-opting" (as postcolonial theory courses in graduate school had taught me to say) the religions of nonwhite cultures. Still, there were places that even to me felt inhabited by spirits, places that emanated something: a sense of electricity in the air. As I crossed the yard to Gersh's front door, my stomach clutched. No matter how rational I educated myself to be, the beliefs of my adolescence were seared into my soul.

We didn't say much as Gersh showed us around. The house was

a maze of rooms, all built at different times. My father, Gersh said, had helped in the construction of some of them. A collection of colorful masks and Gersh's artwork—oil portraits and fabulous New Mexico–style shadow boxes brimming with paint-splashed toys—enlivened the pinkish walls. Light poured through the windows. I relaxed a little. It wasn't weird. A few props and a good plank floor, and it could have been a spread in *House Beautiful*. Gersh didn't try to make small talk or put us at ease, but he didn't act like a crazy man either. There was no reason for alarm.

He finally led us to a workshop next to the house, a small room, a story and a half high. Multipaned windows spilled light onto a desk; shelves filled entirely with record albums lined one wall. The lower floor was jammed with boxes. Gersh had already pulled out Lewis's belongings. The trunk, a large upright rectangle of red metal, which Gersh said was army-issue, sat in the middle of the floor. It was open, a heap of photographs visible inside. He must have been looking through them before we came.

Gersh pointed to a wooden case and a small wooden chest stacked on top of it. "Your father made these," he said. "Did you know he was into woodworking?"

I shook my head. "I knew he made jewelry." He had been stationed at Fort Dix, New Jersey, shortly after he and my mother were married. He made jewelry during his two years of service. Why this was, my mother had never explained.

The case was made of honey-colored wood, the lid smooth and perfectly fitted. Weathered two-by-fours, like the boards of an old barn, formed the lid and sides of the chest. It looked like a folk art find. I was impressed, and proud. *My father made these.* I ran my fingers over their satiny surfaces. Their existence was a gift.

"And this is the camera he used to take all these pictures." Gersh opened the smaller, square case to reveal a medium-format camera: an old Graflex 4x5. He tapped a finger on the chest. "If you don't mind," he said, "I'd like to keep this one. Your father was a good friend."

"Of course," I said, without hesitation. I owed him something for preserving these pieces, for their safekeeping. I didn't even ask him to open it to see what it looked like inside.

Gersh began to pull lidded boxes of the kind used for storing legal documents out of the army trunk. About a dozen were crammed with photographs. Negatives spilled out the sides. Most of the photographs were portraits; a few were nature scenes—serene shots of water, whorls of wood, empty seed pods.

"I'd like to look through the pictures with you," Gersh said, "and tell you who some of these people are."

Inexplicably, my throat tightened. I had expected to take the photographs and go. Gersh's involvement unnerved me. "Sure," I said. "That'd be great."

There were photographs of me and Peter when I was one and he was three, and dozens of my mother, often nude. Nothing, as I'd suspected, that I hadn't seen before. Some of the other pictures were from Lama, and a couple were taken during my parents' travels across the country in their VW bus. There were also several of my brother and me as shaggy-haired children of about six and four—after the breakup, I realized—as well as a few of my father, his hair as ragged as ours. He appeared healthy and lean, handsome, younger than in any of those taken during the Florida years. In earlier pictures, his face and body

were heavy, puffy. His close-cropped hair and little mustache gave him an aggressively 1950s, middle-aged-family-man look. The resemblance to me in these later photographs, as in his high school graduation portrait, was pronounced.

"Oh, look at you," Fielding said, pulling my attention away from my father's sunburnt, freckled face. She held up a picture of me as a baby.

I leaned forward to look at the photograph in her hand: I was about two years old, naked, my hair and skin so dirty that it looked as if I hadn't been bathed in weeks. It had the poignant, heart-stopping aspect of a Farm Security Administration photograph—some migrant worker's daughter in the Depression South.

I recognized a few people from the old days: Beverly; her husband, Rollo; others looked vaguely familiar, but I couldn't name them. Gersh identified the completely new faces, and then I instantly forgot who he said they were. They didn't mean anything to me. They came from a world for which I harbored only distrust: of hippies and communes and all manner of bizarre behavior. I was not prepared to learn their names. I didn't know what could be gained by remembering them. Nor did it occur to me to ask Gersh any questions about my father. It was my mother, I'd always heard, who wanted to leave their middle-class life and venture west. If I had come looking for my father —and I had not, not then, not yet—I would not have thought to look for him at Lama.

Gersh sat above us on a stack of boxes. Photographs were scattered in piles around Fielding and me on the wood floor. The faces stared up at us in the dim room. After almost an hour, we'd finished going through the lidded boxes. Relieved, I shifted to get up, but before I could rise, Gersh said, "Listen, there's something I want to tell you. This is pretty far out, but I wasn't on drugs."

My suspicion of Gersh and of Lama surged up with tidal force. I glanced at Fielding. She raised a delicate eyebrow at me, looking amused. Whatever unfolded was theater to her.

"You know Lewis was living at Lama," Gersh said. "He had a cabin way up in the hills above this place. Do you remember that? Your mom and you kids all lived there before she took off."

I nodded, reluctant, but too polite not to acknowledge what Gersh had to say. The one-room cabin was the first of our homes with a dirt floor, no electricity, and no running water. My father drilled a hole in the metal spinning wheel of my mother's Singer electric sewing machine so that with a chopstick inserted in the hole to turn the wheel, she would be able to sew clothes. I didn't remember the cabin, but my mother had pictures of the place. She'd made it sound romantic. That was the beginning of her pioneer life, and the end of her relationship with my father.

"After that," Gersh continued, "he lived there by himself for I don't know how long. He was into the scene for a while: goats, chickens, gardening—that's what we were doing up here—and building. He was helping put up some of the houses. But then he got the idea to move into town. He was pretty freaked out at the time—into some heavy shit. Maybe you've heard about that. We invited him to stay with us, me and Iris, my wife, but he'd found this house in Taos to rent. A person has to choose his own way, you know? There's only so much you can do."

I knew that house. It sat on the verge of Kit Carson Road, two blocks from the plaza, just before Kit Carson swept down a hill and into Cañon. When my brother was about twelve and I was ten, he pointed it out to me as the place where our father had died. Someone had told him, he said, but he couldn't remember who. I had passed it often, close as it was to the center of town and near friends. Kit Carson was a tourist street, lined by galleries and shops, the Kit Carson Home and Museum. A high adobe wall surrounded the house, separating it from the public sidewalk, masses of lilacs spilled over the wall every spring. Each time I passed it, I would slow down, but I never tried to look over the top. I would just keep walking and think: *That is the house in which my father killed himself.*

"Then one evening, not long after he split"—Gersh fixed me with a stare. "He died in April, right?"

"I guess," I said. I didn't remember and had never asked.

"It was definitely spring. I remember the mud."

I nodded. Though I had not thought of it in a long time, I could see the short square bus trying to negotiate Dick and Pam's rutted driveway in San Luis, the tops of my galoshes flapping against my legs.

"I was on my way back from milking the goat around dusk. Everything was kind of purply, you know, not quite dark. I had the bucket full of milk in my hand. The path from the pens to the house had bushes on all sides, and as I'm walking along, all of a sudden, I see something up ahead of me. Fluttering." Gersh held out his hand. "Right here. Chest-level. I couldn't make it out. I kept trying to get closer, but every time I moved, it moved. It maintained exactly the same distance between me and it, and just hovered there. And then, I knew." Gersh's eyes bulged at me. "It was your father."

Fielding and I simultaneously released a breath. I hadn't realized I was holding mine.

"My father?" I asked, sounding, to my surprise, only mildly skeptical.

"His heart," Gersh said. "Not with wings, or any shit like that. Just like the doctors say. A pumping fist. He was trying to speak. He wanted to tell me something. Then the heart disappeared. Just like that. I walked the rest of the way down the path, calling his name and looking for him, but he was gone."

The faces in the photographs stared up at me from the floor. I felt cold.

"The thing of it was," Gersh said, "I hadn't heard yet that he was dead." He paused a moment to let this sink in.

I didn't look at Fielding, but I could tell from her stillness that she was transfixed, too.

"That same night," Gersh continued, "Iris and I were in bed when we felt something trying to crawl under the covers between us. I'm not bullshitting you. We both felt it. And we both knew it was Lewis. He had gone over to the other side and was trying to get back. I sat up in bed and spoke to him. 'Hey, man,' I said. 'You can't stay here. You made your choice, and whatever's waiting for you, you have to go. You have to go.' And so he went. The next morning, I found out he'd shot himself." Gersh shook his head in wonder. "He laid newspaper on the fucking floor first because he didn't want to make a mess."

I was too shocked to ask Gersh how he knew this detail. A fist of air had lodged itself in my throat. I felt stricken at the thought that my father might have regretted his decision to kill himself after he was already dead.

LIMBO

I brought the camera case and the huge, unwieldy trunk of photographs home to Minneapolis on the airplane. There were hundreds of pictures and negatives in the red metal army trunk. I sifted through everything carefully, making a pile of photos for me and a pile for my brother, who was working in commercial real estate in San Diego, where he had gone to college. I held negatives to the light and examined slides, dividing the images according to which of us was featured, sharing the family shots, giving each of us one of any that were similar. My fingertips dried out from handling the fibrous photo paper. My nails scratched against the wax paper negative sleeves.

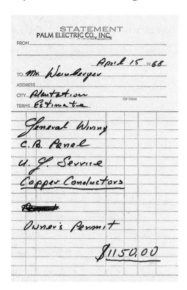

I was looking for anything that might tell me something about my father: notes on the back of photographs, letters, slips of paper with his writing on it. I found no personal scribblings, just transaction receipts, including one for electrical wiring and another from the Causeway Lumber Company for 166 feet of steel to be delivered to my parents' house in Florida. I found their divorce decree, dated September 11, 1972, and, most interestingly, a postcard to my father from a woman named Lynn, dated July 5, 1972. The card showed a couple in a colorized woodland, he with a straw boater balanced on a rock beside him and she in a long, deep red dress. They were kissing. "Men may come," the caption said, "and men may go, but this goes on forever." The stamp was upside down: the high school code for "love."

"I'm in limbo," Lynn writes from a rooftop in Chatham, Cape Cod. "I can't be with a man because I want you—and it feels good." She signs it, "Goodnite love. The stars in your sky are the stars in mine."

I resented Lynn. I disliked her for being the other woman, although my mother had long since left my father's life by then.

The photographs sat on the floor in neat and not-so-neat piles all around the trunk. One afternoon, when I forgot to close the nearby window before a rainstorm, one pile got wet. The piles drifted. I couldn't figure out which set was for me and which was for Peter. I left the pictures on the floor for a month, then I put them back into the trunk—all of them. I tossed in the postcard from Lynn and the divorce decree. I hauled the heavy trunk upstairs. It had a lid that clamped down on all four sides, popping off when released like the lid on a biscuit tin. Someone had used the top as a workbench: its surface in places was splotched white, yellow, and green like a painter's drop cloth. I set it against the wall.

The photographs were at once too much and too little to absorb. I went on with my life.

WALLPAPER

Change the sheets, sweep and mop the kitchen, wash the counters, the stove, the vegetable drawers in the refrigerator, scrape the soot off the glass doors of the fireplace with Windex and newspaper. Every Saturday, first thing in the morning, I clean the house. This is something I know how to do well, having been required to help my mother clean our house every weekend when I was in high school. It is a ritual I usually like. I put one of the few albums I own on my husband's stereo —Nanci Griffith or Paul Simon's *Graceland*—and then I set to work. I don't vacuum the entire carpet or dust everything at one time; I progress from room to room, finishing one top to bottom before moving on to another. This progressive transformation gives me a sense of satisfaction. It's like the kid's room in *Where the Wild Things Are*, turning carpet thread by carpet thread into a forest, except here the process develops in reverse, the forest turning back into a bedroom, leaf by leaf, until the wallpapered walls are set solidly in place again.

And yet.

On this particular Saturday morning, a sunny spring day in 1995, almost two years after my visit to Gersh, I am not cleaning the house. A welter of rags covers the kitchen table; the Hoover, with its headlamp, sits upright, plugged in, but silent, in the middle of the living room carpet. The stereo is silent as well. Stuart is outside, mowing, as he does every other Saturday beginning in April—just before the dandelions go to seed and well after the neighbors have started to scowl at our ragged half-acre lawn. He does not help me clean the house, but he maintains the yard and our two cars, and he does the laundry, a chore I detest. There is nothing different about this Saturday, nothing to distinguish it from all the others, except that instead of cleaning I am standing at the picture window in the living room, arms at my sides, looking out into the luxuriant yard at the trees. The zzz-zz-zzz of the mower comes to me from the side of the house.

Everything is in bloom. A crab apple, luscious with pink blossoms, nearly fills the vista, but my eyes are drawn past it to a ring of pines and narrow-trunked white birches at the far end of the lawn. Of the whole property, I like this corner best. The trees grow so densely there that the ground underneath them is bare. A huge boulder makes an inviting seat in the sun-flecked shadows.

A line about trees drifts through my head: *They are that that talks of going / But never gets away.*

Robert Frost's "Sound of Trees," a discovery I'd made as a sophomore in college. Only a year out of high school, where I'd gone around chanting bits of Eliot and Blake and Gerard Manley Hopkins, and I had already almost forgotten how much I loved poetry, the leap and jolt of it, the way a line could cut to the heart of human longing with a single hard-edged slash.

We chose this house for the trees. There are fifty-two on our property: mostly oak, a scattering of maple, three flowering pink crab, and a tall smooth-barked kind that I have never identified which in late summer clogs the grass with dark berries. Our first winter, three deer, a buck and two does, pulled fronds of evergreen from the shrub under our bedroom window.

A hummingbird darts into the crab apple tree. My hands at my sides feel heavy.

I had wanted, I thought, to get out of the city, to be surrounded by green, to be able to see the sky meet the horizon as I could in New Mexico, though the countryside was too flat and the clutter of civilization too great for that to be possible. Land and a house built in the early 1950s were cheap in Blaine, thirty minutes north of Minneapolis, where patches of oak forest still survive, as well as a few farms, though most of the fields have begun to sprout subdivisions.

With my mother and Peter and my stepfather Wayne, I had lived in an abandoned adobe house, on the beach in Hawaii, in a bug-infested trailer, and a plywood shack, but never in a house with wallpaper. During the early months of our courtship, long before we gave any thought to being married, Stuart and I would ride our bicycles through the neighborhoods of Minneapolis, picking out the houses we liked. That one with the wraparound porch. There, with the dormered window. This one here with the glow of lamplight through the curtains.

A red cardinal alights on a branch in the crab apple. My throat constricts, as if I've swallowed something that won't go down.

We had met on my second day at North Central Bible College, before classes even began, at a picnic for new students in Elliot Park. Stuart was the photography editor of the yearbook, and he was there to take pictures of the event. He noticed me because of my camera: a Nikon F2 with a telephoto lens. It was not the kind of thing women in that denomination, the Assemblies of God, usually carried around with them. My mother, always generous with a gift, had bought it for me the year before so that I could shoot for the high school newspaper.

Everyone at the picnic appeared the same to me. The boys were clean-cut and preppy, the girls alarmingly well made-up. Everyone seemed to be blond. I prided myself on being from a place that was known for its natural beauty and funky individuality. Their hair-sprayed dos and mascara-clotted eyelashes astonished me. I looked with scorn on the fussiness of their carefully coordinated outfits.

Stuart didn't have their polish, either. He was blond like them, true, with gray-blue eyes, Germanic or Scandinavian like almost everyone in the Midwest, but his hair brushed his collar. He wore a faded flannel shirt and outsized hiking boots. He was older than the others —eight years older than I, it turned out—and seemed as out of place as I did. I told him about my father, with more emotion than I usually expressed, and he listened, unperturbed, radiating sympathy. By the second semester, Stuart and I were together every spare minute.

That summer, I stayed in Minneapolis instead of going home to Taos. Stuart worked more than sixty hours a week. I had no job, no other friends. We went to church together on Sunday and out to eat or for a walk around the lake whenever he was free. Other than that, I did nothing, went nowhere, and yet I was tired all the time, so weary my bones ached. I spent most of my time furnishing my apartment. It was the beginning of a pattern: rooted in place, bound by walls and the promise of love, I bought furniture. Immobilized by fatigue, a haze of sadness whose source I could not identify, I moved pictures, fluffed pillows, arranged and rearranged tchotchkes.

This house is the second we've owned. We bought the first in south Minneapolis right after we got married—a small two-story stucco built in 1920 in one of the city's first subdivisions. A girl raised on adobe, I fell instantly in love with the maple floors and cabinets. Money left to me by my mother's family and by my father paid for that house as well as this one. I was nineteen years old.

This is what fundamentalist women did. They married young because they believed that godly women were first and foremost wives and mothers, and because the temptation to sleep with their boyfriends or anyone else had to be averted. I had other models, such as my liberal grandparents and my friends from high school, but still I couldn't wait to set up house and start producing children of my own. The desire to be cared for and protected—and to care for and protect as I had never been—was irresistible.

I feel a buzzing in my head, the lightness that comes from not getting enough air.

We have not gone to church regularly since moving to Blaine. The church we had been attending was south of Minneapolis, now an hour's drive away. We tried a few churches in the neighborhood, but meeting new people was always hard for me and I found something distasteful about each church we visited. It was easier one Sunday, and then another and another, to stay home. My anger at the strictures of fundamentalism had been building for some time.

Stuart was raised as a fundamentalist Christian, too. Born into it, he belonged to the third churchgoing generation in his family. Equally disenchanted with "charismatic" religion, but less reactionary than I, he sometimes went to the hip Catholic church down the road. He asked me to join him at first, but we agreed, after a time or two, that it would be better for both of us if he went alone. I can't sit through a service. Any hint of evangelical influence—a guitar, a chorus, a hand raised during singing—nauseates me; any reference in the sermon to sacrificing myself on the altar of God, or any of a dozen other self-abnegating imperatives that have been hammered into me, and my stomach clenches with fury.

Now I bake and sew and clean. I like knowing how to do these things; such skills, rare among my contemporaries, seem to me a matter of self-reliance as much as homemaking. When we first moved here, Stuart and I pulled dark paneling off the walls and put up wallpaper. I made curtains for the kitchen windows. We bought furniture. That held my attention for a while. We spent our evenings watching television or walking the dog around the development behind us or through the woods across the road. Once in a while, we attended a photography exhibit at the Minneapolis Institute of Arts.

Behind the house, the mower chugs and then cuts out. The static of leaves and branches, their volume suddenly punched up, rushes into the silence. I take a deep, slow breath, trying to force air into my lungs around the obstruction in my throat.

After the first winter in Blaine, I applied to graduate school to keep from going out of my mind. I still bake and clean and sew, but the change in routine makes the chores bearable. And in between, I write. I go to school. I read books that I wouldn't have read when I was a Christian, a few years ago. I read Derrida; I read *The Second Sex*; I read *Discipline and Punish*, and think, My god! Then I write a paper on the "production of docile bodies" in the fundamentalist church.

Stuart supports me in these pursuits. He accepts the gradual transformation of my beliefs and point of view from Christian to adamantly secular, but even so our two ways of looking at the world rarely converge. His is visual; mine is literary. I go to lectures and readings, most often alone. When I come home late from school, he has dinner prepared, coffee brewing, a dish of strawberries waiting for me, the fire crackling. He kisses me hello.

From the backyard comes the clink of metal on metal. The dog barks. The heavy wooden gate slams shut. A moment later, the mower starts up again. A smell of cut grass wafts through the open windows.

I think of Robert Frost. He is not one of my favorite poets. I like stranger works—more fragmented and ambiguous. Even so, of the handful of poems I know by heart, three are his: "Mending Wall,"

"Desert Places," and "The Sound of Trees." The themes that preoccupy him are American ones: the tension between fence and frontier, between the desire for security and the urge to light out for the territories. He speaks to the heart of a displaced daughter of upper-middle-class hippies. Frost writes over and over about the boundary, as the literary critic Richard Poirier puts it, between home and wandering. Like so many of his poems, "The Sound of Trees" is about the need for home, stability, comfort, which in a moment can become stifling: "They are that that talks of going / But never gets away; / And that talks no less for knowing, / As it grows wiser and older, / That now it means to stay." The balance, so hard to strike, is between suffocation and chaos, the desire to remain and the longing to leave the known.

My eyes fall on the wooden camera case my father made; I've placed it under the living room window and piled my few coffee table books on top of it.

He wanted stability, I've been told. My mother wanted adventure and change. But look where her urges got them both.

"FUCK FOU"

Wayman "Wayne" Reynolds was a big man. He wasn't tall, but he was beefy, with powerful arms, thick thighs, and a barrel chest. Even the beer belly that sagged over the waistband of his button-fly Levi's—the only pants he ever wore—couldn't  diminish the sense of his strength and solidness. A high school dropout and self-proclaimed redneck, he had a vampire gap where his four front teeth, punched out in a navy brawl, should have been. He twisted his thick red hair into a braid that swung between his shoulder blades, and never went out without his brown Stetson on his head. In winter or on his motorcycle, he wore a black leather jacket with Harley-Davidson wings soaring across the back.

If my mother was trying to shed her upbringing, its privileges

and refinement, the education it valued, the achievement it emphasized, the art and fine living it prized, she could not have made a
better choice than to take up with Wayman Reynolds. He was a beer-
swilling, pot-smoking, foulmouthed, uncouth, ignorant lout.

My mother's parents were appalled. Her mother hated him. Peter,
who remembered Lewis, never forgot that Wayne was not his father.

I was less discriminating. Wayne had been my "pop" since I was
two. The only world I knew was the one he occupied. He may have
been boorish and a brute by the standards of my mother's upbringing, but to me, he was charged with life. There was something indis-
tinct about my mother, something watery and insubstantial. My memories of her in those years are few—in fact, the image that comes most
immediately to mind is not a memory at all, but a photograph she
took of herself in San Luis, not long after my father's death. Using a
Brownie box camera that had
once belonged to him, my
mother captured her own face
staring into a round hand
mirror that hung in a window
frame of our house. A terrible
brooding stillness masks the
usual beauty of her long oval
face, its deep-set eyes and
voluptuous mouth not so much
sad as utterly impassive.

Wayne, on the other hand,
was colorful, vibrant, huge. A
jack-of-all-trades, he worked
hard, building crude furniture, animal pens, fences. He tilled the soil
for our garden, irrigated, gathered and chopped cords of firewood,
hunted for food, tanned hides, made bullets, repaired cars, rebuilt engines, and, now and then, broke horses. When my mother bought land
in Talpa, he constructed a plywood-and-tarpaper shack on the property so that we could move out of the dilapidated trailer we'd been
renting in Ranchos de Taos. He also intended to build a house. In
preparation for it, we mixed mounds of dirt and straw into adobe

bricks, then dragged enormous pine vigas out of the mountains to use for ceiling beams.

When he wasn't drinking, Wayne was extremely funny and warm, even charming in a rough-hewn way. He taught us how to play poker and gin rummy for raisins and chocolate chips and drove us into the mountains for picnics. At night, tangled together on his and my mother's bed, he kept us in hysterics with stories of his hoodlum youth in Bakersfield, California. He told us that he once showed up at Bakersfield High wearing blue jeans, an insolent act in the 1950s, when boys were allowed to wear only chinos or dress slacks to school. A teacher said that he'd have to take them off if he wanted to attend her class, so he obediently complied—by unbuttoning the fly and dropping the offending garment where he stood.

Whether he actually dropped out or was expelled from high school, neither my mother nor I remember for sure, but in his late adolescence, he and his buddies spent their time stealing hubcaps and car radios. They eventually graduated to the whole car. As Wayne described it, it was all a lark and a big "fuck you" to everyone and everything. Even his arrest at age seventeen for grand theft auto was part of the high jinks. It might, he admitted, have been a blessing. The judge gave him a choice: he could march down to a recruiter's office and sign up for one of the armed services, or he could go to jail. That's how he wound up in the navy. We thought his rebelliousness magnificent and brave. He was our own James Dean.

Even so, we were always mindful of how dangerous he was, and how easily angered. He was a man without control, who gave in to his every impulse, especially when he was drinking. No matter how attuned we were to his moods, we could never anticipate what would make him explode. One night, he came home to our trailer in Ranchos to find my mother watching *Roots* and became so furious at her for letting black people, whom he hated along with "spics" and "wops" (and "kikes"?), enter his living room that he smashed an iron skillet through the television set, leaving a jagged black hole in the screen.

For a man who despised authority as much as he did, Wayne was also a strict, if entirely arbitrary, disciplinarian—what might be laughed at one day could get you into a world of trouble the next.

He hit my brother with his thick black leather belt, pulling it from the loops around his waist while Peter fled, stumbling and crying, away from him. But he didn't often spank me. I was his sweetheart. He recognized that I loved words, loved to write stories, loved the look of my own handwriting on a page, so he devised a punishment for misbehavior especially for me. When I was bad, I had to write out a sentence that described my crime: "I will not forget to feed the rabbits." "I will not leave my clothes in a heap on the floor." "I will not be a smart-ass to my mother." Then I had to copy the sentence, as children used to do on the blackboard at school, over and over again. I wrote in pencil on Big Chief tablets. The number of times depended on the seriousness of what I had done: a hundred times for something of minimal severity, five hundred or more for something heinous. Any sort of back talk or sass fell into this category.

I will not be a smart-ass to my mother. I will not be a smart-ass to my mother. I will not be a smart-ass to my mother, five hundred times.

Sometimes Wayne would revise my sentence: *I will not be a smart-ass to my mother, who takes care of me, puts a roof over my head and food in my mouth.*

It often took several days to scrawl the required number of words. By the time I was finished, my fingers were so tightly clenched around the pencil that I could barely uncurl them.

HOUSE ON THE HILL

Moron. Sissy. Slob. Drunk or sober, these were the names that Wayne called Peter all the time. He badgered him constantly: stop slouching, get your hands out of your pockets. Once, just for the hell of it, he put his booted foot through the bottom of a Lincoln Log fort that my brother was building on the plank floor of the San Luis house. He lifted the logs with a laugh and scattered them everywhere.

My mother never protested his behavior. Even when Wayne held his hand over Peter's mouth at the dining table and told him to "breathe through your fucking nose, that's what it's there for," she didn't intervene. Wayne's hand was huge, the fingers so wide they plugged Peter's nostrils too. His face turned red, then white. He struggled in the chair, his legs and arms flailing, trying to pry Wayne's hand away.

As children, Peter and I spent a lot of time alone together. I never minded the solitude, always preferring dolls and books to people. But Peter was a lonely kid. Except for Psyche and Adam Siddhartha, friends from Morningstar who would come on occasion to spend a week with us, we mostly had each other for companionship. When Peter went fishing for trout down at the creek on Elias Lucero's property in San Luis, he would beg me to come with him, promising to bait my hook and gut any fish I caught. He didn't have to coax me much. I liked to fish, and I liked to sit next to him on the bank, talking or just making whistles out of reed joints.

Fishing was a good escape for Peter and a happy hour or two of play for me, though it was impossible for either of us to put our stepfather out of our minds entirely. One afternoon in particular we had been at the creek for what seemed like hours, and we weren't catching anything. I finally gave up and set my willow pole on the ground, choosing to plait dandelion chains instead, but Peter refused to go home empty-handed. He kept throwing in the line and wouldn't stop even when the sky darkened and it started to rain. It fell gently at first, but then a hard rush of drops suddenly pelted us. We picked up our poles and ran, hair plastered to our heads, clothes quickly soaked. It was getting darker and darker, night swallowing what should have been late afternoon. Barely able to see our way across the pasture, we had only a glimmer of lamplight to guide us in the direction of our house on the hilltop. We ran over the squishy grass, willow poles whipping in our hands, through the increasingly cold needles of water. It might have been fun, this sprint across the meadow in a downpour, but we weren't laughing. Except for the rasp of our breath, we were running in silence. We were scared about what Wayne might do to us for not paying attention to the clouds, for not coming home before dark, for holding up our mother, who would have dinner waiting on the table. And we hadn't even caught any fish. Here we were, drenched like idiots, and nothing to show for it. What happened when we actually got home, I don't recall, but I can see the two of us clearly in my mind, my own white face as well as Peter's, outlined by a halo of surrounding darkness, running toward the light on the hill, afraid to reach it, as fast as we possibly could.

Between Morningstar and San Luis, we spent a year in Hawaii. It was 1972, and the best time in our life with Wayne. I was four; Peter six. We slept on the beach, or in our Dodge Dart when it rained. Once we drove deep into the island, passing along a cliffside and through a bamboo forest, to rent a cabin in a mango grove for a few days. We bought vegetables and milk at the local market, but mostly we lived on what we could catch. Every evening on Maui, we would make a campfire on the beach, then wade out into the surf to fish for dinner. Peter and I caught sand crabs and sunnies; Wayne hauled in a manta ray and once speared something in the tuna family called an ulua— it was so large that we roasted it on a spit and invited a crowd of people to eat it with us. Alone at our campsite after dinner, we would snuggle into sleeping bags, and I'd drift off to the murmur of voices, not always sure whether I was listening to humans or water.

Days were spent tooling around in the car, or dawdling on the beach. It's odd that later, when I went to camp for a summer in New York, I didn't know how to swim. In Hawaii, I would wade farther and farther from the shore, and then panic and shout to Wayne to come and get me. "You swam out," he would shout in reply, "you swim back." But he always kept an eye open. And though he never had to rescue me, he once saved Peter's life. Fishing from an outcropping of rock over the ocean, Peter managed to hook an electric eel. When Wayne saw what was on his line, he sprinted several yards to tackle Peter, sending him, his pole, and the flashing creature skidding across the rocks just as my brother was about to touch it. Peter was furious and screamed at Wayne for hitting him for no reason, but then quieted down when Wayne told him that the eel could have killed him.

We kept moving from beach to beach, camping in a different place each night. I'm not sure that sleeping on the sand was actually allowed. The police frequently raided Makena Beach, where large numbers of hippies tended to gather. Time after time they drove away the proliferating longhairs, though they soon drifted back.

One night two officers materialized at the edge of our campfire, but they weren't looking for campers, even hippie ones like us. They were looking for a fugitive. We were cooking dinner behind an enormous bleached-out log. They wanted to know if we had seen a thin bearded white guy. No, Wayne said. We hadn't seen anybody. But we had. Only minutes before, a man who fit this description had stepped into the firelight, just as the police had. Wayne had hidden him in the trunk of our car. After a few minutes, the men in uniform moved on. When they were far enough down the beach, their voices swallowed by the surf, Wayne told us to stay put until he got back. Then he let the thin bearded white guy out of the trunk and drove him into town.

We lived in Hawaii long enough for Peter to enroll in kindergarten on Maui. It was becoming harder and harder, though, to find places to sleep. Resort hotels had begun popping up on every crop of sand, and the beaches marked off by red surveyor's tape were now off-limits. My mother decided that it was time to leave when Wayne, infuriated by the ugly gashes where developers were pouring concrete foundations, started dropping lit cherry bombs and M-80s into the bulldozers' gas tanks.

BEQUESTS

In a blood red, leather-covered jewelry box, my mother kept the ring my father had given her for their engagement. It was a diamond solitaire on a gold band. In the years we lived with Wayne, it occupied a privileged place in my imagination. I didn't long for Lewis the way my brother did, but I was not immune to fantasies about the life we would have had with him. The ring was proof that he had actually existed. Furthermore, when they split up, Lewis had asked that my mother give the ring to me. It was my ring, I used to think. My father wanted me to have it. Along with the silver belt buckle he had made at Fort Dix, my mother was keeping it for me until I was old enough.

Whenever I asked her, my mother would let me take the ring out of her jewelry box to admire it. Slipping it onto my too little finger, I imagined I was a princess. I imagined I was a bride. I would trip around the room with it winking and flashing.

"That's enough now," my mother would say. "We don't want it to get lost." Back it would go into the blood red jewelry box.

One day, I decided that because the ring was mine, I could do with it what I wanted. We were living in San Luis and what I wanted was to show it off to my best friend, Angela, at school. My mother was gone, milking the goat or chopping firewood. It was easy to lift the jewelry box down from the raw-board shelf in the bedroom where she and Wayne piled their clothes, extract the ring, and slip it loose into my jeans pocket. Later that day, I pulled it out on the school bus. Angela was appropriately awed. When we'd admired it enough, I stuffed it back into my pocket. Then I forgot about it.

A month later, it was Easter and my mother was preparing a feast. She climbed the ladder to the attic Peter and I shared as a bedroom —our mattresses on the bare floor—to collect the apples she had cored and cut into circles, threaded with string through their centers, and hung to dry in the window over our beds. They had been hanging there all winter until Peter and I began pulling down the chewy rings and eating them; no more than a few shriveled circles remained. While she was up there, absorbing our treachery, she noticed something glinting among the dust bunnies under the window. It was the ring.

Peter and I were sitting at the kitchen table, surrounded by bowls of food coloring and tufts of green plastic grass. We had been dyeing eggs the whole day. The next morning, my mother and Wayne were planning to hide them, along with the candy we knew they had stashed somewhere. A spirit of hilarity filled the warm kitchen. Then my mother appeared in the doorway.

I don't remember what she said, if anything. The evidence of the empty sack in one hand and the ring in the other was accusation enough. We were greedy and inconsiderate. And worse yet, we were thieves. What I do remember is that she took a large bowl and, one by one, cracked and peeled each of our gorgeous eggs. Such villains did not deserve an Easter. Such piggies did not deserve an egg hunt. Once she had peeled them all, my mother cut each one of them in half. Peter and I watched in miserable, snuffling silence. She mashed the yolks, slung gobs of mustard into them, then stuffed them back into the dye-stained whites. As she dusted them with paprika, even I could see the sweet irony of what she had done: our fantastic creations had been reduced to a mound of deviled eggs.

The ring went back into the blood-colored jewelry box, and I didn't touch it again for a long, long time.

HIATUS

In the summer of 1975, we left San Luis and moved to Denver for a year. Wayne took classes in gunsmithing on the GI Bill and worked as a security guard for apartment complexes in Littleton and Aurora, small cities a few miles to the south and west of us. On weekends, he and his friend Ibra drank beer and tinkered with their motorcycles in the driveway. Every now and then, my mother would come into sums of money: gifts from her parents or a modest payout from her shares in the paper company that her grandfather Nathan had founded in the early 1930s (and which accounted for much of our family's not inconsiderable wealth). Ten thousand here, forty thousand there, the checks came sporadically in the mail. She might have renounced her former life, but she had never stopped accepting her family's money and they, even more oddly, had never stopped sending it. Peter and I also collected social security every month because our father was dead. We lived simply, for the most part, and cheaply, but never had to rely on food stamps, as many of our friends did. In Denver, she bought a used conversion van for all of us, a hot-rod black Ford pickup for herself, and a brand-new Harley for Wayne. It was white, 1000 cc, and cost three thousand dollars.

Peter and I were in fourth and second grade, respectively. In our house on Sherman Street, we had a fenced yard, our own bedrooms, and a television: I was madly in love with Captain Kirk. Every evening, I would try to fall asleep under the coffee table after our favorite shows were over so that Wayne would have to carry me to bed and tuck me in.

Wayne drank less that year. There were fewer fights. But he was a dormant volcano, we all knew. And he invited trouble. A few beers, and he would run outside to shake his fist at police helicopters flying over the neighborhood. "Pigs!" he would scream at them. "Fucking greasers!"

My mother acquired a Bible and began reading it quietly in her room.

SAN FRANCISCO DE ASÍS

The following autumn, after we moved from Denver back to Taos for good, my mother started going to church. A couple years before —

shortly after my father's death—some kind of encounter with God had led her to become a Christian; except for acquiring that Bible, however, she had done nothing about it. Then one day, when Wayne was out, she slipped off with me to San Francisco de Asís, the landmark early-nineteenth-century church in Ranchos, about a mile down the dirt road from our trailer. The memory is vague, though powerful in one respect: I still feel a chill of creepiness. It was midafternoon, I think; no one was sitting or kneeling in the pews. It was the first time I had ever been inside a church. The interior, as I recall it, was dark and cloyingly perfumed with incense. I hung in the background as my mother stood in the light of the doorway, talking earnestly to the priest. After a while, we walked back to the trailer; she, silent and bruised-looking; I, bringing her clutches of wild pea and alfalfa flowers from ditches along the road.

LEAVER AND LEFT

My mother and Wayne were fighting. He had some grievance as usual, some failure on her part that he claimed as just cause for his fury. Most likely, he was feeling condescended to. *You think your shit doesn't stink?* Anger and too many beers had made his already florid face redder still. She kept placing household objects between them as obstacles: the kitchen table, the ratty sofa, a ladder-back chair we all knew he could smash into kindling with one stroke of his meaty fist. He swept dishes off the table; the metal plates bounced on the hard-packed dirt floor, scattering rice and beans. A ceramic coffee mug broke into pieces. We'd moved out of the trailer and into the shack that Wayne had built on our new property in Talpa. It had only two rooms, with a doorway between them covered by an army blanket. Peter and I did not retreat into the second room; we cowered in the background, between the sofa and the edge of Wayne and Mom's bed, so nearly underfoot that Wayne might have stepped backward and tripped over us. Peter was eleven, I was nine. Our presence was some kind of insurance: we could step in if it got too crazy, beg him to stop, break his concentration, at least, with our pleading. But we also just needed to see what was going on. Wayne had not hit her this time; the household goods, such as they were, had taken the worst of it. In other fights, he'd blackened her eye, bloodied her lip, threatened once or twice to kill her, though he'd never broken a bone, never sent her to the hospital in need of x-rays or stitches. He went only so far, and then he caught himself. When he did, the fight ended abruptly, though the drama was far from finished. The space we lived in was too small, and his rage too large, for it simply to evaporate. Inevitably, he slammed out the door, fired up the Harley, and roared into the darkness, disappearing for a day, a week, maybe for good. For me, in every one of their fights, this moment of departure was the worst. My greatest fear was not that he would kill my mother, but that he would leave us.

This time was the same as all the others, except that when Wayne threw open the door with so much force that it smacked against the shack's outer wall and vibrated the plywood, Peter ran after him and begged to be taken along. I had asked once, too, and was refused. We were living in the trailer then; Wayne had stormed out, and I had clung to his leg, pleading to let me go with him, *please, please.* I was Wayne's sweetheart: the one who climbed onto his lap to soothe him; the one who teased and flirted to keep him from getting mad in the first place; the one who loved him enough—better than my mother —so he would not abandon us.

Wayne's rage had softened at my appeal. He knelt down and pulled me between his knees. He said he was only going to spend a few days camping on the land in Talpa. It had no well, no outhouse, no shelter but a few cottonwood trees and a plum thicket. He would sleep outside in a sleeping bag. I had to stay and go to school. I had to take care of my mother. Don't worry, he said, I'll be back. Then he'd kissed my head and left.

Now, when Peter asked if he could come, Wayne hesitated, then handed him a helmet. Wayne eased his beast of a motorcycle off its kickstand, and Peter slung his leg over the seat behind him. He locked his hands around Wayne's belly, and they roared off together on the Harley.

My mother did not attempt to stop them. *It's not fair,* I thought. *It's not fair.*

This incident became for me the "primal scene": Wayne gone with my brother on the Harley, my mother and I left behind, waiting, in a state of terror and suspense, lest they never return. We righted the chairs and swept the dirt floor free of beans and broken crockery. We washed what remained of the dishes. We went to bed. But all the while, we were listening for the roar of the Harley, watching for the headlamp cutting arcs of light across the cedar gateposts. As the days came and went, the routine of living resumed, but whatever else we seemed to be doing, we were really just doing one thing: we were waiting. We did not know where they were. We did not know if Wayne was coming back, even though Peter was with him. We did not have a phone, so they could not call us. We did not know if Wayne would call us if he could.

The threat of his violence and, worse, of his leaving kept us always off-kilter, anxious even in the quietest periods. We'd left a few times ourselves. A birthday celebration for him on a Maui beach ended abruptly when he swept the cake off the picnic table into the sand. A mouthwatering cake, store-bought, which for us was the rarest of treats, with pink sugar flowers and white icing. It landed frosting side down, and moments later was covered with black ants. My mother did not stay to fight that time. She took my brother and me by the hand, and we walked away from him down the road. Somehow, we got to the airport. My mother called her parents, and they wired money for plane tickets to New York, where we spent a week before flying back. I was sorry for Wayne then, but even as a child I recognized that it was far better to be the leaver than the left. It was the waiting that could not be tolerated, the sense that he was loose in the world—possibly gone forever, possibly dead—that could not be borne. If we left him, he remained, in my mind at least, fixed in place. We could return to the spot where we had last seen him and he would be there.

This time, with Peter, he was gone for a week. It was the first week in May: Wayne missed my mother's birthday. When they returned, we could hear the motorcycle coming from a long way off and ran outside to see them race up the driveway, the tires spitting dust and stones. They were in high spirits and full of stories. They had driven all the way to Bakersfield to visit Wayne's father. It was a warm spring evening when they left Taos, but just north of Santa Fe they had run into a freak snowstorm. Peter was wearing a windbreaker and blue jeans; by the time they got to a motel, his jeans were caked with snow and they were both frozen. Wayne thought they should spend the night and then turn back, but Peter egged him on. *Come on*, he begged. *Let's keep going.* They kept going, and now they were grinning over their adventure. We were not angry, my mother and I. We were just happy to see them. Wayne brought Mom a pair of silky black panties with golden Harley-Davidson wings emblazoned on the rear for her birthday.

WHAT MEN AND WOMEN DO

Wayne's friend Ibra was visiting us from Hawaii. Wayne knew him from Morningstar. He had come to see us on Maui, and then, after we left, moved to Molokai with his girlfriend to grow dope. It was the safest place in the world to plant marijuana, he said, leaning against the long seat of Wayne's Harley, because of the leper colony. Even cops didn't want to go there. Wayne and Ibra were drinking, of course, beer and pints of blackberry brandy, and I was standing in the door of the shack, begging for sips and listening to them talk on the cleared-dirt patch that passed for a porch. The straps of the little floral sundress that my grandmother Rose had bought me at Bloomingdale's for my eighth birthday kept falling off my shoulders; because I imagined it made me look sexy and grown-up, the dress was my favorite. Wayne, lifting a lit joint from Ibra's fingers and taking a puff before passing it back, told Ibra his own pot story: For months he'd been growing plants on the counter under the shack's main window and had nurtured a huge, bushy specimen, three feet tall and still growing. Then one afternoon, he saw a cop car pull into the driveway. Before it could roll to a stop, Wayne had grabbed the pot plant and stuffed it under the bed. Then he went out to meet the cop, his hands behind his back so the fragrance of crushed marijuana would not waft through the officer's rolled-down window.

"Shit, man!" Ibra said, his piggy, always red eyes crinkling with laughter and anxiety. He held the joint in front of him, a bad case of nerves making it quiver in his fingers. His thin face and lank brown hair reminded me of pictures of Jesus I'd seen in Sunday school, except Ibra's expression was more weasely than beatific.

"So I walk up to him, my best plant jammed under the fucking bed, the smell *all* over me, and you know what the son of a bitch says to me?" Wayne leaned toward Ibra, exhaling breath so laced with alcohol and pot that I could smell it from five feet away. "He says"— Wayne twisted his lips to imitate a heavy Hispanic accent—"'Hey, *ése*, do you know where Tommy Trujillo lives?'"

"No fucking way," Ibra groaned.

"And I say, 'No, sir, sorry,' and he backs out and drives away."

"Fuck! What a total *fuck!*" Ibra said, and they both bent over, laughing until tears ran out of their bloodshot eyes. I laughed, too, loving Wayne's stories, though I couldn't stand Ibra or his limited vocabulary.

Wayne looked over at me, as if he'd just noticed I was standing there. "Pumpkin," he said in a slurry voice, "go get me another beer."

"Okay, Pop." I skipped inside to do his bidding, and even opened his Coors at the kitchen table—though I didn't want to miss a word of the conversation—leaving a wet ring in the flour my mother had sprinkled over the table's surface in order to roll out tortillas. Hurrying back, I found Ibra and Wayne still laughing.

His face bleary, his eyes small, Wayne had a loosened, reckless look about him that I knew well: a look that said one more beer—or the empty he'd just crushed with his foot—was likely to be one too many. A sudden wariness made me raise the beer toward him and quickly step back, but not quickly enough. He grabbed the can from my hand, sloshing it on both of us, and in the same motion wrapped his free hand around the back of my neck. Then he dropped his face toward me so that his breath, shot through the gap of his four missing teeth, sprayed saliva across my cheeks.

"Now pay attention," he said, tilting my head backward, "I'm gonna teach you something important. I'm gonna teach you what men and women do." Wayne's thick, slobbery tongue, acrid with smoke and sour beer, swooped down over my mouth and probed back and forth until it pried open the tight seam I was trying to make of my lips, swirling so deeply down my throat that I choked. He laughed then and let me go, leaving a slimy trail on my chin. I glared up at him, sickened. If that was what men and women did, then it was disgusting. The thump-thump of the rolling pin marked the rhythm of my mother's movements in the kitchen. I could run inside and tell her that Wayne had French-kissed me—a concept I'd already learned about from a little boyfriend—but he was just drunk, wasn't he? He didn't mean anything by it. And what would she do if I told her?

I went and lay down on my bed under the *ojo de Dios*, wiping away the spit with a blanket. I could hear Ibra snickering outside.

END GAME

After that first visit to Saint Francis of Assisi, some of my mother's friends from Morningstar advised her to try First Methodist Church in El Prado, probably because it was one of the few churches that actually welcomed hippies. Every Sunday after that, she made me and Peter get out of bed, dress in our school clothes, and haul our grumbling selves into the black Ford pickup to drive across town in time for Sunday school. Wayne didn't seem to mind our going to church, but when she asked him to come along he refused.

Then one night in early spring, Wayne got drunk, and he started to knock my mother around again. He raged through the tiny shack, smashing whatever was in front of him, while my mother wedged herself between the rough wood cabinet in which she kept the dishes and the frame of two-by-fours that Wayne had nailed together for holding firewood. He towered over her, cursing, but he couldn't swing his fist without bashing it into the furniture. We'd witnessed this scene a dozen times, but this time my brother, eleven and big for his age, did something unprecedented. He grabbed the rifle propped under the counter that Wayne used for making bullets and pointed it at him. He yelled at Wayne to stop beating up his mother.

Peter was brave like that. His code of honor was simple: he would jump in whenever kids picked on me, and yet one day in Denver he had allowed himself to be beaten up on the way home from school because his attackers were girls. There were three of them, scratching and pulling and punching at him, but he would not defend himself. He'd said to me more than once that a boy should never, ever hit a girl.

Wayne, pivoting in slow motion on one foot, turned around, placing his wide chest in line with the barrel. Sobbing, tears and snot running down his face, Peter's arms were shaking so badly he could barely hold the gun straight.

Crouched to one side, I saw Wayne's red face and my mother's bruised one rise behind him, and then I noticed something peculiar about Peter's gun: it had a pump action against the stock. I knew guns, and I recognized it immediately. Peter didn't have my mother's .22 tucked under his arm; it was his own BB gun. Whether Wayne noticed the difference, I don't know. BB gun or no, he was incensed.

"You point a gun at someone, you little fuck, you'd better be ready to pull the trigger," he said, and then he took a step toward Peter.

The barrel wavered in the air between them, Peter's finger twitching on the trigger, but of course he couldn't do it, even knowing that his bullets were only little steel pellets, no more likely to maim or kill a man than a wasp's sting. Wayne lunged at him; Peter dropped the BB gun on the floor, dove through the army blanket over the inner door, and slammed through the outer one into the dark. Stepping over the useless air rifle, Wayne grabbed the Colt .45 that he had been issued as a security guard in Denver and ran after Peter. I followed him. There was no moon, and Wayne was fast for a short man with thick legs. I couldn't see him or Peter, who must have fled across the alfalfa field toward our neighbors' house, but I heard Wayne's heavy footfalls and then the shots. One and then another near the fence that divided our two properties. Wayne, galumphing through the frozen alfalfa stalks in the middle of the night, was shooting at my brother. There were only the two shots, and then a moment later, a yellow rectangle of light appeared and then disappeared in the direction of Celia and Deming's place. Peter was safe.

I heard someone blubbering near the fence. Remorse had hit Wayne more rapidly than usual.

My mother appeared behind me, sharp in my memory for once, shouting at me to get in the truck, *get in the truck.* She motioned toward the enormous two-ton that we'd bought for hauling vigas down from the mountains. Wayne had the keys to the Dodge in his pocket, we'd sold the van, and the Ford had stopped running, so the huge pickup was our only choice. She lifted me into the cab, then hauled herself onto the running board behind me. She'd brought a pillow to prop herself up so she'd be able to see over the steering wheel. Reversing swiftly down the driveway, paying no attention when the wide bed almost took out a gatepost, she swung onto the road and then into Celia and Deming's driveway. Peter came running out and we were on our way, heading toward the Jack Denver Motel in town.

It was not the first time Wayne had physically harmed us kids. Pretending to be a swordsman in a fencing match, he had once drawn a hot poker from the fire and caught me across the cheek with it. Another time, he had tossed me into a creek to retrieve a six-pack of beer that was floating away because I hadn't anchored it properly, causing a stick to stab through my bare foot in two places and leaving me unable to walk for a month. Still, those were "accidents," caused by exuberant thoughtlessness rather than malice. But this. Shooting at her son. This time, Wayne had gone too far. Following the counsel of the Methodist pastor, my mother made up her mind to leave him.

When we came back to the shack after a week at the Jack Denver to tell him, we found him sunken-eyed, unshaven, wearing the same clothes; he'd hardly eaten. He begged her to give him another chance. He would quit drinking and go to church. He would even, as she insisted—in order to put their relationship right in the eyes of God—marry her. True to his word, he showed up at First Methodist wearing new brown corduroys and a pressed shirt two Sundays in a row.

It's hard to say whether he would have stuck with it. On the Friday before his third visit, he and his friend Patrick drove the Dodge out to the Taos bypass, a long stretch of pavement on the south side of town. Wayne had just put in a new engine, and he wanted to show Patrick how fast it could go. It was the day before the wedding. Before they fired up the truck and then again on the road, he and Patrick drank a few celebratory beers. As they expected, there was little traffic. Wayne pushed the truck to seventy, eighty, and then, with the pedal all the way to the floor, to ninety, ninety-five. He laughed and made wisecracks while the body shimmied and the engine shrieked. Then, suddenly, Patrick saw Wayne's face go still. Up ahead a stream of cars was flashing across a bed of gray asphalt. He had misjudged the distance to the intersection with the main highway: if he ran through it, people were going to get killed, maybe a lot of them. Wayne told Patrick to get under the dashboard of the truck. Then he slammed on the brakes, rolling the Dodge four times. It landed upright on the shoulder, its cab smashed so flat that the metal frame punched a hole in the bench seat on the driver's side. Paramedics cut Patrick out of the wreckage; he emerged with a broken arm and some small cuts on his face.

Wayne was thrown through the windshield when he hit the brakes.

IMPACT

The day Wayne died was brilliantly sunny. The sky was a crisp blue, the cherry trees were in bloom, new leaves speckled the cottonwoods running down the middle of our property. Peter said later that he'd had a premonition, a tingling in his gut that told of disaster, but I had no clue. It had rained early that morning, and the dirt roads and driveways of our neighborhood were churned up and swampy. My next-door neighbor, Charlie, and I were walking his visiting grandmother's poodle on a leash, a chore we found hilarious—this ridiculous city dog, mincing around on a leather strap when all the dogs of Taos ran loose. Except that this morning it wasn't mincing: eager for home and to be free of us, it jumped forward with a ferocious tug, yanking the leash from my hand and sending me splashing into a mud puddle. One of my boots stuck fast when I tried to get out; my toe dipped into the black water before I could right myself again. We thought we'd die right there, laughing. Charlie retrieved the boot and gave me his shoulder for a crutch so I could hop home without dirtying my sock further or sticking it wet into my boot. Halfway across the beaten path through the alfalfa field, the two of us giggling like fiends, I looked up to see my brother scowling at me. His friend John Paul was standing behind him, his head hung down, his hands stuffed awkwardly into his chino pockets. I didn't stop hopping. I couldn't stop giggling.

Peter grabbed my shoulder. "Listen to me," he said. "For once."

I set my foot on the dirty ground. The color spilled out of the world.

ALIVE

The night of Wayne's accident, my mother, brother, and I slept at Patrick and his wife, Klea's, house. I lay awake on the floor for hours, listening to Peter's light snores and the occasional car on the road, afraid to let myself fall asleep. If death were so arbitrary, so sudden, then there was nothing at all protecting me, not even God. Lying on a pile of Klea's old quilts between my brother and my crumpled mother, I expected my heart just to stop. When I opened my eyes in the morning, I couldn't believe I was still there, alive.

DIRECTION HOME

After Wayne died, my mother wanted to move back to New York. She talked to her mother about it. It would have meant living in her parents' house for a while, or asking her mother to help her pay for a place of her own: The small sums she received from her shares in the paper company and from social security were enough to finance a modest life in Taos, but the money wouldn't stretch far in New York. She had nowhere else to go, and though she'd taught school a few times, basically she had no skills.

My grandmother said no. Her husband, my grandfather Juan, was just developing Alzheimer's, and Rose was unwilling to take on the additional burden of her thirty-eight-year-old daughter and two preadolescent grandchildren. So my mother stayed in Taos. Not much later, she married for the second time, and then she joined Christian Family Church, led by a charismatic Princeton graduate in architecture named Andrew Bush.

LANGUAGE GAMES

Curtis Sande was a good-for-nothing who sat at the kitchen table all day every day for almost two years, drinking beer, smoking hand-rolled Bugler cigarettes, and reading *Webster's Collegiate Dictionary* or the encyclopedia, starting with "A." My mother married him in 1980, when I was twelve, two years after Wayne's death, and a few months after he had shown up at the door of our newly built house in Talpa, wanting to know if he could stay in the shack. He was a tall, wiry man with a beaky nose, thick glasses, and large forearms. He had been a taxi driver in Paterson, New Jersey, where he had come from originally, but by the time he came into our lives he was just a drifter. My mother had known him at Morningstar.

Peter, always a good judge of character, hated Curtis from the beginning. He thought the man was only after my mother's money and muttered about not going to the wedding. The two of them were immediate adversaries. On the other hand, Curtis seemed to like the idea of having a daughter. I was cute and quick and ever willing, in exchange for love, to tickle and roughhouse and tease. From the time I was three feet high, I had known how to use a sharp wit and a cocked eyebrow to get what I wanted from men. Or at least, not to get what I didn't want: anger and violence directed at me.

Curtis was a highly intelligent person; with different opportunities, he might have been a scholar or a professor of literature. He introduced me to Tintin, George Bernard Shaw, and Ian Fleming. Like Wayne, Curtis took special note of my love of language. He used to glean esoteric words from the dictionary, then type one of them in the center of a clean sheet of paper on the typewriter in my room. When I came home, I had to look up the word and memorize its definition: YASHMAK. TINNITUS. BONZER. "Bonzer" is Australian slang for "excellent" and became my nickname for years. It was a game I liked, except that I couldn't choose not to play.

Curtis, also like Wayne, was an authoritarian, fond of having other people jump to do his often capricious bidding. He would create unstated lists of possible infractions, from forgetting to turn off the bathroom light to doing a half-assed job of cleaning out the chicken cages, and then give Peter and me a mountain of household chores, watching us closely to see that we did them the way he wanted us to. While he sat at the kitchen table, memorizing obscure words, we took care of the animals, including the chickens, but also rabbits, turkeys, dogs, cats, and goats. In addition, we planted, weeded, hoed, watered, and picked the garden; helped with cooking and housecleaning; and did any number of odd jobs, such as digging postholes, stringing wire, irrigating the two alfalfa fields, and burning the ditches on our three-acre property. We spent his entire first summer with us plastering the exterior of our new house with mud.

I will not forget to turn out the light in the bathroom. I will not mutter under my breath when I am told to do the dishes. I will not leave dirty milk glasses in my room. Subconsciously I added Curtis's rules to the long, erratic set formulated by Wayne, each new example scratched onto a mental tablet of Big Chief. Every infraction equaled a day of grounding. Sometimes Curtis would casually add another day to an already weeks-long incarceration and just laugh when I'd run across the house to my room, screaming, "I hate you!"

Being grounded, unless I had to go to school or do chores, meant sitting in the middle of my bed all day, doing nothing. I could not take phone calls, watch TV, read novels. Meals, minus dessert, were brought to me. If I wanted something to do, Curtis said, I could read my Bible, a particularly ironic twist considering my mother had married Curtis only after he convinced her that he was a good, churchgoing Christian—a pretense he dropped about two weeks after the wedding.

No matter how closely I monitored myself, it was impossible not to make a mistake. I spent an entire year grounded. My brother, who always got the worst of it, had to spend an entire day standing in a field with his arms folded, facing the hot sun.

FIRE AND BRIMSTONE

Although I was never particularly eager to go to church, I liked First Methodist well enough. The pastor was soft-spoken and gentle, we sang majestic hymns accompanied by the pastor's wife on the piano, the sermons were boring but brief, and there were lots of fun activities for kids. It gave me a sense of security after Wayne's death to be among such sane, stable people every week.

My mother married Curtis Sande in the Methodist Church, but by that time, she was already becoming disenchanted with it. The pastor was *too* gentle. He lacked the one thing my mother seemed to want most: authority. When she left Florida and then my father, she thought freedom from him and from the stultifying bourgeois life she had lived until then would make her happy, but freedom had proved deadly. The fallout from her own choices frightened her; she wanted, it is clear to me now, someone to tell her what to do.

People began telling my mother about a new church that was starting up in a former dentist's office on Salazar Road, a town bypass. The church's fiery young pastor advocated singing and dancing before the Lord. He thundered in the pulpit, a voice hollering in the wilderness. The Methodist Church was too staid and traditional. My mother wanted fire. She wanted brimstone. Perhaps, in some way, she wanted to be punished, for my father's death, and then Wayne's.

My mother, alone in the west, with few job skills and no support system, was floundering—just as, a few years earlier, my father had. Traumatized by my father's suicide, she had fallen into a profound depression for three years after his death, and when she began to come out of it, Wayne was killed. She had grown dependent on him, thought he had a good heart despite his violence, and had never been on her own before. Now her marriage to Curtis was proving to be a disaster. Taos was a spiritually feverish place; many of my mother's hippie friends, entranced by visions of pure love, had become Christians, often as a prelude to embracing something else: Buddhism, Taoism, transcendental meditation. My mother was swept along with the currents around her, but she was looking for something more than the grace of God. One of the things for which she blamed her parents— and her mother in particular—was failing to set any boundaries for her. She had no rules to live by.

My mother left Curtis at home, drinking beer and rolling Bugler cigarettes all morning at the kitchen table, and we went to Christian Family Church. She stood by the front door of the tiny corrugated box of a building, talking to the women of the church, and I dawdled in the parking lot with my brother and the other kids on Sunday morning, dreading the moment when we would be called inside for the service. As a hippie kid, I'd known plenty of eccentric characters, but these people took strangeness to a whole new level. They called my mother "Sister Terry" and kept bursting out with "Praise the Lord!" and "Hallelujah!" in the midst of the most ordinary conversations: "What a beautiful day. *Praise God! Hallelujah!*"

If I'd been any younger, I would have sidled close and hidden behind my mother's skirt. But what strikes me most is how I can see my mother clearly that day, suddenly solid, flesh and blood; from then on, she is rarely absent from my memory.

Unlike the Methodist Church, where many members had been Christians since birth, Christian Family was made up entirely of recent converts, most of whom were former hippies. One elder was an ex-con, another was a founder of the New Buffalo commune. Some were recovering alcoholics and drug addicts. Most had been divorced. The pastor, Andrew Bush, came from a well-to-do family, but his parents had cut him off when he refused to pursue architecture after graduating from Princeton; he was "saved" while drifting through the counterculture and had decided to become a Pentecostal minister instead. Everyone in his congregation, including my mother, was broken down for one reason or another. Fervent and extreme in the way that only people who feel they've been rescued from death and destruction can be, they were eager to dedicate every aspect of their lives to God.

BAPTISM

I was in trouble with my mother. Looking back, I'm unable to recall what I did wrong, but I can see myself, sulking in the flower garden next to the shack. Whatever started it, I must have said something really snotty because during the fight that followed my mother ordered me to get out and I didn't know whether she meant for good or just until she calmed down. It was a sunny day in summer. I was standing barefoot among the gladiolas and a riot of purple cosmos, wondering where to go, when I heard the shack door open. My mother approached me, a solemn expression on her face. Her hair was pulled back in a severe bun, and she was wearing an embroidered Mexican blouse and denim cut-offs. In her hands, she held a white basin, its enamel chipped away from the metal in places. We'd had this basin for years, since San Luis, maybe even Morningstar, and usually used it for washing dishes. I looked at her suspiciously through the flowers, still angry, a little afraid, but didn't move away. As she came closer, I saw that there was water in the basin. My mother tucked the bowl under one arm, then dipped her free hand in the water. She tapped my forehead and then each of my shoulders with her wet fingers, startling me. Locking her eyes to mine, as if to sear some deep truth into my being, she said, "I forgive you." Then she turned around and walked away, dashing the water into the garden as she went.

COCONSPIRATOR

The second year with Curtis was better than the first, at least for me. Peter and I still had to do all the regular chores on our property, but for some reason, our new stepfather had lost interest in policing us so closely and stopped creating extra work to keep us busy after school. I was able to join the ski club and play soccer and hang out with my friends without worrying about getting grounded every other minute. Peter still despised Curtis and spent as much time away from home as he could manage, but I was a forgiving kid, and happy for the change. My acquiescence is eerily plain in the photographs I have of that period (at least one of which, strangely, must have been taken by my brother): there's me, lying cozily in bed between my mom and Curtis, reading while they napped, Curtis's beaky nose propped against his left  arm, the right flung around my neck; me on the floor of our living room leaning into Curtis's lap, a big goofy grin on my face; and me again, having a gleeful water fight with Curtis in a ditch on irrigation day. There was no point that I could see in holding grudges.

It was only détente, however. One day I came home from school to find my mother and brother standing in the packed-dirt yard in front of our house. Peter was about fifteen then. My mother was holding onto his arm, and Peter was saying over and over that Curtis was going to kill him. I didn't know what he had done, but learned later that Curtis was insisting Peter drop out of a play in which he was performing at school, ostensibly because it took him away from home or his schoolwork or his chores, but really, my brother thought, because Curtis couldn't stand for anyone to have any fun. Following Curtis's instructions, my mother told Peter that he had to stop going to rehearsals, but Peter refused. The play, *The Diary of Anne Frank*, was set to open at the Taos Community Auditorium in two weeks, and he would not let his classmates and his director down like that. Besides, enough was enough. He had a backpack over his shoulder and was begging her to let go of him so he could get out of there before Curtis came home. She let him go. He ran past me to his motorcycle.

When Curtis demanded to know where Peter was, my mother, who knew that he had gone to stay at his friend Todd's house a half mile away, wouldn't tell him. She had stood by while Curtis spanked Peter and me with knotted shanks of piñon, let him hound us with his arbitrary rules and relentless punishments, had said nothing when he sent my brother to stand in a field with his arms folded, facing the sun. She had been prepared to force Peter out of the play at Curtis's command. No doubt, she thought her children needed discipline, even though we were good kids already and generally obedient ones. But more particularly, she had obeyed Curtis because as a Christian, devoted to following her faith to the letter, she was trying to fulfill the Apostle Paul's injunction to wives to be submissive to their husbands. It didn't matter that Curtis was a son of a bitch. The Bible made it clear: it was not her place to challenge him. But finally, as it had with Wayne after the shooting, an alarm bell had gone off in her head. She would not tell Curtis where her son had gone. When Peter was ready, she said, he would come home.

CHRISTIAN FAMILY CHURCH

My third stepfather was Jesus Christ. He assumed that role after Andrew, to his credit and against the general principles of the Assemblies of God, the denomination of which Christian Family was a member, counseled my mother to divorce Curtis because he was tearing our family apart. Jesus was a good man, but the rules in his system of discipline were somewhat vague. He said things like "Your body is the temple of the Holy Spirit." Jesus left it up to other people to clarify what He meant. Because they weren't a hundred percent sure, the pastor, the church elders, and my mother cast a wide net.

I will not watch M-TV, Monty Python, Saturday Night Live, The Rocky Horror Picture Show.

I will not go to Woody Allen movies. Woody Allen is a sex-obsessed liberal humanist.

I will not watch The Big Chill, Kiss of the Spider Woman, sex, lies, and videotape.

I will not dance to "The Mutz" at the Saint Barnard on Saturday nights, or roller-skate at the local rink, which plays secular music and where the boys pick up girls.

I will not drink.

I will not smoke.

I will not let my boyfriend put his hands under my clothes.

I will not read Love in the Time of Cholera, Lady Chatterley's Lover, Ulysses, Lolita.

I will not read Foucault.

NEW ORDERS

Not long after she joined Christian Family, my mother, with Christ and the leaders of the church as the actual heads of our household, set about the project of turning me, my brother, and herself into the perfect Christian family, the kind of family she imagined we would have been if we had all been born into the faith—freshly scrubbed inside and out, always eager to sing the praises of the Lord and to go to church. But because she came late to the religion, she was always in the process of figuring out its rules: I would be allowed, for instance, to go to a Saturday-night dance with my high school friends, and on the following Monday she would realize that dancing was not pleasing in the eyes of God and would bar me from doing it ever again.

This effort to remake us in God's image reached its apogee when I was sixteen, on the morning my mother told me not to dream. I don't mean daydream; nor do I mean that she cautioned me to be realistic, not to set my sights too high. I mean that she told me, literally, not to dream.

"Dreams are not something we want to dwell on," she said. I had bounced into her bedroom, still wearing my pajamas, the antic scenes of a particularly vivid, humorous dream bubbling in my mind. My dreams have always been like movies: complex narratives, usually logical, always elaborately detailed. I wanted to recount this one before it skittered away from me. My mother was already up, making her bed. She stopped tugging at the faded top sheet and cut me off. "If you don't focus on them, they won't have a chance to imprint themselves on your mind. I find that the more I pray before I go to bed, the less my dreams trouble me. In fact, I hardly dream at all anymore."

It took me a moment to register what she was saying; when it sank in, I was dumbfounded. A hot trail of blood rushed away from my heart, leaving me numb from the center outward. Something I was doing—who could say what it would be next?—was always wrong. I was already on guard in my waking life against the influence of books, music, movies, and relationships with non-Christians (which meant "non-fundamentalists"). Now the klieg light of God's scrutiny was to be turned on my unconscious mind.

There was a swift compression in my chest like an elevator going down. As it sank, my voice sank with it. More startling was the mass of fury the elevator seemed to be pushing under it: a fury so large and brutal that if I lifted my hands it would be only to strangle someone. Here I had danced into my mother's room, eager to share something with her, and the moment I opened my mouth, she disappeared behind the wall of God. It was her best trick. Just once I wanted to come looking for my mother and find her.

She continued making her bed. I stood in the doorway, immobilized, arms hanging heavily at my sides. I knew there was no arguing with her. There was no point in arguing with God. I could roll my eyes in disgust and often did, but it made no difference. "Yeah, Mom," I could say, as Peter and I said to whatever we thought the craziest of her pronouncements, "whatever you say." But I was too susceptible to her, too needy, too desirous of having her shining eyes upon me. My brother rebelled, paying lip service to my mother and the church, and then doing exactly as he wished. In me, there was something underneath it all that said, ever and always, "Be good." Perhaps I was simply too fearful to be otherwise. From then on, I would be unable to dream without the fear of damnation hanging over me. I had wanted to strangle someone, but the only throat I could find to put those heavy hands around was my own.

SUBURBAN SYMPHONY

The mower has stopped. I glance at the vacuum, the welter of rags on the kitchen table. I don't want Stuart to find me standing here like this. But the silence lasts only a moment, replaced almost instantaneously by the whine of the weed whacker. And then, strangely, from behind the house, the mower starts up again, a deep sound running under the shrill reed of the weed whacker—not our mower, I realize, but the neighbor's. As I listen to the sounds weave in and out, whine and growl, flute and bass, I imagine the sound of another mower starting up, and then another, each an instrument in an orchestra of lawn equipment, joining the arrangement from squares of grass all over America.

The Bible college, the early marriage to a Christian man, the lavish homemaking: these were overly determined choices. The church and my mother had channeled me toward this life. I can't deny, however, that I wanted it, at least at first. I hungered for a gentle man and a stable existence. As a kid, I longed to live in the suburbs, to have wall-to-wall carpeting and a powder blue Ford Fairlane. But serenity, it seems, was the one thing for which my early life never prepared me. My childhood was traumatic, yes, but never boring. The moment it became routine, some tragedy would come along to shift it out of its orbit. Is that what I'm waiting for now? Some crisis to release me?

My eyes drift back to the copse at the edge of the property. I can't hear the low voices of the trees now, drowned out by the machines, including my husband's, busily shredding the tasseled grass around the flower beds, but I can see the branches move. As I watch them, I recite the end of Frost's poem under my breath:

My feet tug at the floor
And my head sways to my shoulder
Sometimes when I watch trees sway,
From the window or the door.
I shall set forth for somewhere,
I shall make the reckless choice
Some day when they are in voice
And tossing so as to scare
The white clouds over them on.
I shall have less to say,
But I shall be gone.

MISSING

In the middle of the night, almost two years after my visit to Lama and a few days after that Saturday in front of the living room window, I wake up thinking about my father's chest, the one I gave to Gersh because he wanted it. It takes me this long to realize the mistake I've made. At the time, I didn't stop to consider that I had a right to say no. Now I want that chest. Lewis's things—my father's things—suddenly matter to me. Lying in bed next to my sleeping husband, I am overwhelmed by the sense that my father is missing. He has been missing all my life, and except for the man sleeping beside me, I have felt alone in the world. I have deliberately chosen to be an orphan.

My mother created a new family for herself and for me, a new history and new memories. "Old things are passed away," the New Testament says, speaking of the transformative power of salvation, "behold, all things are become new." But having lost the faith she embraced for both of us, I have lost the history and the substitute family that went with it. I'm like a house with no address, alone in a field somewhere, unconnected to streets, avenues, parkways, highways, and superhighways. I want to place myself inside my own history, draw the map of its roads so I can travel far and find my way back again. I want to reenter memory at the place where my mother veered off. More than that, I want to trace the man whose features bore such a resemblance to my own that I am instantly recognized as his daughter. As a Christian, I could not identify with my father; I could not find myself in what he was. He embodied all that my mother had come to despise: intellectualism, preoccupation with art and aesthetics, the emptiness and vanity of a worldly life. Under the old rules—the mindwash of terror my mother's system of belief favored—curiosity was dangerous. To be curious, one had to be open—to language, to the leap of association, to influence, to experience, to unsanctioned discovery. Above all, one had to suspend judgment. Anything I discovered about my father would only confirm that he was a sinner and a lost soul: he was Jewish and probably an atheist; he took drugs; he killed himself. To go in search of him, I first had to take the *ojo de Dios* down from the wall.

I call Gersh, in my mind, and say, "I'm sorry, but I want you to send me my father's chest. I can't let you keep it. I understand that it connects you to your friend, that you feel his presence through it, but you have to understand: it connects me to *my father.*"

But I don't have the nerve to pick up the phone. Instead, I get out of bed and start taking notes: *My father has been missing and I have to find him.*

In the beginning, I do not think in terms of stories, of a life embedded in other lives. That is somehow too threatening: the people I would have to deal with, the questions I would have to ask. Every query would be a departure, however minute, from the life I have lived until now. I think instead of artifacts, the evidence of hands on wood. My father is in the perfectly fitted lid of the box he made for his camera. He is in the photographs I have abandoned in the attic. He is in the chest in Gersh's workshop. He is in the sound of his name spoken out loud. When I sit down to write, I find that I do not want to bring Wayne back to life. I do not want to conjure Curtis Sande in words. I want my father, his heart fluttering on the path in front of me, to speak. I finally know what I need from him. I need a better father than those men had been.

REMAINS: AN UPDATED INVENTORY OF MY FATHER

1. A handful of photographs of him, including his high school graduation portrait and some taken in Florida by my mother.

2. A silver belt buckle.

3. Photographs taken by my father of my mother in her twenties, and of my brother and me when we were children.

4. *Architectural Record*, Vol. 145, No. 6: "Record Houses of 1969."

5. *Miami Herald*, "Dwelling Is Designed for Family Living," May 25, 1969.

6. One handmade wooden case with a 4x5 Graflex camera in it.

7. An exposed, undeveloped roll of film, over twenty years old and by now ruined.

8. A piece of soft white cloth embroidered with red thread in an exploding-star pattern wrapped around a spare lens.

9. A forty-year-old Leica.

10. A red metal army trunk full of my father's photographs, including many of my brother and me and my mother right up to the time she left him.

11. Transaction receipts from a photo shop and two construction suppliers in Florida.

12. A divorce decree.

13. A postcard to my father from a woman named Lynn.

The Aim of His Calling

The architect can become so interested in forming all the structural parts of a building that he loses sight of the fact that construction is, after all, only a means and not an end in itself. . . . But it is understandable that the architect can come to the conclusion that the aim of his calling is to give form to the materials he works with. According to his conception, building material is the medium of architecture.

— STEEN EILER RASMUSSEN, *Experiencing Architecture*

FAMILY PHOTOS

The winter before I went to visit Gersh, I spent several evenings pasting photographs into an album. It begins with my maternal great-grandparents and ends with my naked self, age two, on a horse at Lama.

Photographs of my father or his side of the family are few. Of those that exist, most are from my parents' wedding at my maternal grandparents' house in January 1960 and then their life together in Florida. My father, the picture taker, is rarely in the frame.

On my father's side, there are two photographs of my stocky, gray-haired, white-T-shirted grandfather Morris. In one snapshot, he sits with his arm around the neck of my laughing mother. In another, he stands in front of a construction site wearing a hardhat. My father's brother and sister appear only once, in a group shot of my father as a baby. It is the only photograph I have of my father as a child.

QUEST I: PHONE CALLS

I call my aunt Miriam, my father's sister, and ask if Lewis had left behind any documents. She doesn't know, she doesn't have anything. Then she thinks for a moment, and says, "Oh, you know what I have? I have a lithograph that belonged to your father. It's made out of tin or aluminum, something like that. It must be from his college days. It says LIBERALS FOR NIXON over a caricature of Richard Nixon with LEWIS WEINBERGER, CHAIRMAN across the bottom in black letters. I never thought to give it to you."

Miriam always says *your father* with a kind of emphasis, drawing it out. Hers is the accent I think of when I think of New York: lengthened vowels, dips and rises in the voice.

"*Your father*," she says, "was very political. Your great-grandfather, your mother's grandfather, took him to a dinner where Kennedy was the keynote speaker, and he loved it. He was so pleased. The next time you come, you can have it."

This is news: my father was political. Even this much I did not know. I want the lithograph, kitschy-sounding and unusual. I want to put it up, and say, "My father did that" when people stand in front of it.

Miriam promises to talk to my uncle Joe and see if he has anything.

"He cleared out your father's effects," she says. She is happy, I can tell, at my sudden interest, and she gives me my uncle's phone number in case I want to call him myself.

But I don't. The phone number is there in my datebook, and there it sits, like the photographs down the road all those years. Something inside me resists. Except for Miriam and my mother, whom I've started to call with questions—reluctantly, afraid that she won't want to answer, though she does not refuse—I'm still just looking at artifacts and photographs. A little at a time is all I can do. Occasionally, my aunt asks me if I've called Joe.

"No," I say. "I don't know him. I don't feel comfortable."

I've seen my aunt Miriam and her family once a year since I was a child, but I've met my uncle Joe only once that I can remember, at my cousin's wedding when I was sixteen. All I know about him is that he spends years at a time in places like China and Taiwan, building skyscrapers or apartment complexes.

The dread of dealing with a near stranger on the phone, it turns out, is deeper than the desire to find out what my uncle knows.

GRAVESITES

When I first began asking questions about my father, one of the things I wanted to know was where he was buried. It disturbed me that I didn't know. No one had ever mentioned a gravesite. We had certainly never visited one. My mother told me that his body had been cremated, though she wasn't absolutely certain; it didn't sound quite right to her, perhaps because cremation is a violation of Jewish custom and law. His ashes were probably scattered on Lama Mountain.

I don't know how or with whom he would have left instructions for his cremation. Did he leave a will, a note, write a letter to his brother or sister sometime before he died? People who expect to die young often talk about funeral arrangements. Like Wayne, who told us repeatedly that he wanted to have his ashes sprinkled over the Pacific Ocean. After he died, we chartered a Cessna in L.A. so that we could fulfill his wish, tossing his remains from the open door of the low-flying plane into the waves below us.

I would go to see my father if he had a gravesite, but there is none. And there was no funeral either, no ritual that might have helped me feel more fully what his death meant. My mother and Wayne drove to Taos as soon as they heard the news, leaving my brother and me with Dick and Pam, safely away from the shock and the mess. I don't remember her ever explaining to Peter and me exactly what had happened to our father.

POETIC LICENSE

In college, I took a poetry workshop. My poetry professor said, "Write a poem in which you tell five lies," and without hesitation, I wrote a poem filled with lies about my father:

WHAT YOU SAY TO PEOPLE WHO DON'T KNOW

My father never died when I was young.
He lived and grew, felt my changings,
held me when I ached inside.
Scraped knees, fevered foreheads, bedtime
prayers, through all those things he
was there. He helped me with arithmetic,

smiled disapprovingly when boys
drove me home from school. He clapped hard
and hoorayed when the curtain fell

on school plays; maybe even took me
to art museums or baseball games.
He stood proudly on graduation day, loaded
up the car when I went to college and cried
when he gave my hand away last June.

My father never spent long mornings alone,
smoking over breakfast, or passed

evenings filled by doses of white powder.
My father didn't use that gun.

My father never died when I was young.

Miriam eventually calls my uncle Joe for me. "He has a box somewhere, he thinks, of your father's papers. It's mostly letters, he says,
and poems. I bet you didn't know your father wrote poetry."

"No," I say, "I didn't know." Hearing this, oddly, I don't feel a
surge of connection. I don't think, *My father wrote poems, too.* In fact,
I'm worried that the poetry won't be any good; that it will be all
rhymed and jingly.

"You should call him," she says, meaning my uncle. "He'd like to
hear from you."

I had set the trunk against the wall and forgotten about it for a while,
but I didn't forget Gersh's story. The story of my father's fluttering
heart. I related it to a number of people afterward—not because it
was kooky but because it had a hold on me. I couldn't laugh it off.

"It sounds like *The Tibetan Book of the Dead*," a writer-friend, Mark,
told me. "It takes three days for the spirit to disincarnate."

Did this tidbit give Gersh, I wondered, more credibility or less?

I told my mother. I saw the distress in her face. She believed in
spirits, but not of the individual dead: demons roam the world, evil
spirits can inhabit things. I was not prepared for this interpretation.
If it was going to be a spirit, why not his spirit? But I felt grateful
that she didn't dismiss the story. It remained at the center of me, as
tender as a bruise.

It turns out that the papers in my uncle's possession include a journal. It isn't clear to me whether there are letters, too, although I gather that Lewis wrote poems in the journal. It's hard to tell because I'm getting the information secondhand. I feel let down somehow that the journal contains poems instead of straight-out thoughts, as if the language or the form might distort the message. I'm worried that the words won't represent Lewis's true self. I also wonder, though I don't ask, why no one has ever mentioned the journal's existence before.

Joe is reluctant to send it to me.

"He's afraid it might be too hard for you to take," Miriam says. "'She's a grown woman,' I told him. 'He's her father. She has a right to it.' You should call him."

She gives me the number again.

"And you know who else you should call?"

Oh, great, I think. "Who?"

"Irwin Sollinger. He knew your father when they were kids. He could tell you a lot about him. I'll give you his number, too."

"Okay," I say. My throat tightens. I feel panic rising. Miriam wants me to know about my father. It bothers her, I think, that I so clearly think of my mother's family as My Family. I've never asked about my paternal grandparents. I know nothing, except for my contact with Miriam and my cousins, about my father's relations.

I write Sollinger's number down but know even as I do that I'm not likely to call him any time soon.

When I phone my uncle, finally, another month later, he is leaving for Brazil the next day. He doesn't know where the journal is, he says. He isn't sure he even has it anymore. Yeah, right, I think. My uncle has a reputation in my mother's family for being a difficult character.

"I can understand your reluctance," I say. "But it would mean a lot to me."

"There are boxes of stuff in the attic," he says. "I'll have to look for it."

"If you could," I say, "I'd really appreciate it."

The next time I'm on the phone with Miriam, she asks, "Did you speak to your uncle?"

"He's in Brazil," I say. "He doesn't know where it is."

I drop it for the time being. But this time, whether because the attraction of words is too great, or because I think there might be a message for me in those pages, my attention is caught. I have the same feeling I had when I called Gersh and said, "This is Lewis Weinberger's daughter." It's a sense of my father's reality, of his being in the world. My father, to use a friend's phrase, suddenly "bodies up" on me.

THE RUSSIAN PRINCESS

In the center of my photo album is a thin slab of pictures taken in the late 1960s in Florida. I sit on the couch in the den with the album, its heavy black pages like a blanket over my knees, studying the pictures of me and Peter, of my lovely mother, the rare few of my father. Stuart tends the fire in our fieldstone fireplace and watches *Law and Order* on television. The blare of the commercials—"*Please hurry, while time is on your side!*"—makes a jangling counterpoint to the frozen serenity of the images:

Peter, a solemn round-faced boy in a handknit sweater, shorts, little blue tennis shoes, standing by himself against a background of greenery. Peter, three, with a white cloth tied Superman-style around his neck. Me with the Superman cape.

My father, his eyes focused directly on the camera, smoking a cigarette. Freckled cheeks. A dark mustache over his lip. I can't tell from the black-and-white photograph what color his eyes were. Brown, I would guess, like my brother's—who, though adopted, resembled us as much as we resembled each other—rather than green like mine.

My mother, long hair pulled forward in a brown swirl over one shoulder, in the grainy color photograph we later referred to as her "Russian Princess Picture." She kept that portrait tacked to her bedroom wall in our house in Talpa. I tried to imitate her once when I was sixteen and had a boyfriend who thought me worth photographing. Her eyes, their bright blue muted into gray-green by the softness of the image, gaze straight into the camera; I, inexplicably, stare down and to the right:

FUNDAMENTALS

"Blue," my mother says when I call to ask. "His eyes were light blue. Like his father's."

QUEST 4: POSSESSION

The next time I speak to Miriam, she has my father's journal. My uncle sent it to her directly. I hardly know what to feel—relief, mostly, that it has materialized, that I'll actually get my hands on it.

"I'll keep it until the next time you come to New York," Miriam says.

I don't argue. She also promises to send me some photographs she has of my father as a child and teenager.

"Did you call Irwin Sollinger?" Miriam asks before I get off the phone.

"No," I say. "Not yet."

"You should," she says. "He knew your father from grade school. They were in Boy Scouts together. There's a lot he could tell you."

QUEST HITCH

One day I call my mother and she tells me that she's been thinking it over and she's not going to tell me any more about her past. "You know the story of Noah and his sons, don't you?" she asks.

"Yes, Mom," I say. "I know the story."

"Noah got drunk," she tells me anyway, "and passed out naked in his tent. His son, Ham, denounced his drunkenness. But his other sons, Shem and Japheth, took a robe, walked backward into the tent with their eyes averted, and covered their father's nakedness. Ham was cursed by his father and by God."

"Oh, Mom," I say. "Give me a break."

Fortunately, I have pages of notes from our previous conversations. The only surprise is that it took her this long to cut me off.

QUEST 5: LONGING

It is the Fourth of July, 1995. Stuart and I are spending a week with my grandmother Rose in Manhattan. The next day, we are supposed to take the Long Island Railroad to my aunt Miriam's house in New Hyde Park for the day. Her three children, my cousins, are going to be there, with their children. Miriam has promised to give me my father's journal. But that isn't all. I'll also be meeting Irwin Sollinger and Stephan Klein, my father's best friends, for the first time.

Miriam arranged it. Irwin and his wife are spending the weekend in Amagansett with Stephan and his wife, who own a vacation house there. According to Miriam, the two couples have spent nearly every Fourth of July together for the past twenty-five years. Miriam hadn't originally mentioned Stephan, but she tells me that both men had known my father since grade school. She invited them to stop by on their way home.

The force of my desire to meet them startles me. Here I couldn't get myself to call Irwin, and now he is all I can think about. I'm amazed that these two men, connected to each other and to Lewis for so many years, actually exist. Two men with firsthand accounts of my father, people who, unlike my mother, preserve their memories. Meeting them suddenly means more to me than even reading the journal.

And there is something else, too.

I don't know where Amagansett is, beyond a vague notion that it's in the Hamptons, a place where rich New Yorkers go on weekends. But when I hear that Irwin and Stephan will be coming from there, envy overwhelms me. I long for the milieu I imagine these men to inhabit: a world of theater- and museum-going and the *New York Times* over breakfast, debates about the situation in the Middle East, Jerome Robbins versus Balanchine. Not the stripped-bare, dirt-floor life of my childhood. Not the bland routine I have created with my husband in the suburbs of Minneapolis. Not as a visitor once a year to my grandmother's Manhattan apartment, but as a *life*, the life my father should have given me.

DREAM BEFORE MEETING IRWIN AND STEPHAN

I go from room to room in a house I don't recognize. The walls and floor are smeared with blood. I am hunting for someone or someone is hunting for me, I'm not sure which. We follow each other in a circle through the house. Each time I enter a room, I know that this person has just left it. I realize after a while that I am holding a butcher knife covered with blood.

ARTIFACTS

My aunt Miriam and uncle Bob's house is always chaotic. Three married children, their spouses, and seven grandchildren, ranging in age from one to fifteen, drop in and out of their suburban split-level at any given time. There is always more food than anyone can eat; always two or more conversations going at once. Each time I visit, it takes me awhile to adjust.

Miriam, a small, trim woman with a narrow face and olive skin, has an apron around the waist of her knee-length shorts and is making lunch in the kitchen. I sit down at the table at the end of the room. With an hour to go before Irwin and Stephan arrive, I ask her for the first time about her parents, Morris and Kate, both of whom died shortly after I was born, and the rest of my relatives on my father's side.

Morris, she tells me, started out as a chemist in a company that made cosmetics and imported exotic skin creams from the Orient. He went into his own business in the 1920s, selling nail polish, a hot new commodity, but his partner cheated him and the business went under. "The story," Miriam says, "of his life." After several other failures, Morris borrowed money from his mother and went into business for himself as a developer of suburban tract housing, another hot new commodity. On Long Island in the late forties, the demand for inexpensive, mass-produced homes was huge, especially from returning veterans. Morris saw his chance and took it. Kate, meanwhile, learned insurance practices so that she could act as an insurance agent in her husband's business, eventually taking on other clients as well. "They were partners," Miriam says. "They really had a partnership there."

Their youngest child, my father, nine years younger than Joe and six years younger than Miriam, was the greatest beneficiary of their success.

She tells me how fond her own kids were of my father. "They were more upset than we were when he and your mother got divorced," she says, "because to them they were the ideal couple. They were sophisticated and modern, more glamorous than me and Bob. And your mother was very pretty. I mean, not that I was ugly, but she was . . . different."

She tells me, too, about the last time she saw Lewis. He was involved with drugs by then and wild with paranoia. I already know about his cocaine habit, though I can't remember where I heard it. Probably from my grandmother, maybe from my mother years ago.

"You know what he said to me once?" Miriam asks. Concentrating on the precise words, she lifts the wooden spoon out of the potato salad she is tossing and holds it suspended in front of her: "'Life is a movie and I want to be in the movie, not part of the audience.'"

I'm not sure how to fit this statement into the image I have of my father, the man who wanted stability and a nice house in Florida. But then the drugs don't really fit with that image, either.

Miriam opens the closet in the entryway and pulls out the lithograph of Richard Nixon. The thin aluminum crackles in my hands. The poster is large, unwieldy, a little bent at the edges. The black crayonlike caricature is surprisingly good—so good, in fact, that later, when I show it to my grandmother, she looks at it skeptically and says that she didn't know Lewis could draw so well. Naturally, neither did I, but I'm pleased at the discovery. I've always loved to sketch, a skill I thought I got from my grandfather Juan. I set the poster against the low chest in Miriam's linoleum-tiled foyer and step back to get a better look. Miriam stands a few feet away, too, arms folded against her blue T-shirt, watching me. Of everyone in the family, she is the least reconciled to my father's loss; mention of him nearly always brings tears to her eyes. Her interest fills me with anxiety, as if some matching emotion—an emotion I am somehow unable to produce—is required of me.

"Oh," she says, "before I forget." She leaves and emerges a moment later from her upstairs bedroom, a book wrapped in white and blue plastic balanced on her palm. She offers it to me casually, but her expression suggests that she is barely holding herself together. "Your father's journal," she says.

It has taken me two years to get it. Or twenty, depending on how you look at it. Twenty years of nothing, and then a flood. I flip through it quickly. I look at the drawings—furniture, houses, flowers, a spindly tree like the trees my mother draws—and then skim the rest, so that the unfamiliar handwriting won't be able to resolve itself into words. I want to read it slowly, later, when I am alone.

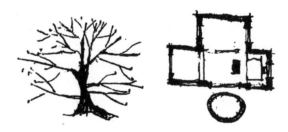

"My god," Irwin says, the moment he and Stephan jump out of the
car. I get up from the concrete front step, where Stuart and I have
been sitting, waiting for the two men. "You look just like Lewis."

"It's amazing," Stephan says.

Stuart keeps a protective hand on the small of my back as we all
shake hands in the driveway. I wonder if he can feel how damp my
skin is under my floral print jumper.

"It's like seeing my old friend again," Irwin says. His voice vi-
brates with feeling.

I smile awkwardly, involuntarily shrinking a little from his ex-
uberance. After the excessive emotionalism of fundamentalism, suspicion of overt enthusiasm has become instinctive.

"We're your father's oldest friends, Stephan and I," Irwin says.
"Stephan met Lewis in the eighth grade. I met him in sixth. We introduced him to your mother." He grins at me. "So we're responsible."

My father's oldest friends. It astounds me to realize this. I expected them to be old, although my father, born in February 1939,
would be only fifty-six now. Stephan is tall and thin, with an edgy intensity to his voice, his movements. He has curly gray-black hair, a
long face and hawk nose. Irwin is of medium height, medium build,
with jutting eyebrows and a black and gray beard. His eyes are calm
and gentle. Both are tan and fit, young-looking, wearing shorts and
T-shirts as if they've just come from bike riding or playing tennis. Both
have doctorates: Irwin in clinical psychology, Stephan in environmental psychology (the study of the effect of places on people, he tells
me). Stephan, like my father, is a licensed architect, but he now teaches
interior and museum exhibition design. They both strike me distinc-
tively as Jewish New Yorkers. I am instantly drawn to them. Except
for family visits one week a year, almost none of my life has been
spent in the company of other Jews.

Miriam shepherds us into the living room. Stuart goes out to play
chess with my uncle Bob on the patio. A girl cousin drifts in and settles into a chair across from us. Her bright-eyed interest makes me
nervous, but before long she finds us boring and slips away.

Irwin tells me that he met my father because their older brothers were friends. "Our brothers took us to the Jamaica Theater. We saw a movie and eight acts of vaudeville and got home at three o'clock in the morning," he says.

Stephan met him in 1951 at P.S. 178, a new school in Queens; all three of them were in the first graduating eighth-grade class. "Your father was vice president of the class," Irwin says. "I have a picture. I'll send it to you." They were friends into their early thirties, and even visited my parents in Florida. My father and mother, along with me and my brother, spent their last two nights in New York with Irwin and then Stephan before heading off to New Mexico in 1970. That was the last they ever saw of him.

I try to act natural as they talk. I try to relax. My response to this meeting is so intense that I have to brace my arms against my chest to keep spasms from shaking my body. All week, I have experienced an anxiety so deep that I have not slept properly. I am overwhelmed by the feeling that I am not only meeting them, I am meeting my father, if only by proxy, from the grave.

I want to impress them, to sound intelligent, thoughtful, sensitive, to ask the right questions, although I realize that I should have thought more beforehand about what I wanted to find out, that I should have come better prepared. I know almost nothing about Lewis, and yet the questions are slow to come: what kind of music did he like, did he have a sense of humor, was he a nice person? I'm relieved when Irwin asks if they should just ramble.

"Yes," I say. "Please."

With their permission, I place a tape recorder on the coffee table. I don't want to miss a word. I want to be able to savor the details in private and to give my brother a copy of the tape if he wants it, because he couldn't be here himself.

Irwin starts to speak and then stops. "Are you very smart?" he asks, taking me aback.

I laugh. What does one say to that? "I think so," I say. I think so.

"I'm sure you are," Irwin says. "I'm sure you are, because both your mother and your father were very smart. Your father was smarter than all of us. I mean, hands down."

"Everything I always think about as being intellectually interesting," Stephan says, "in high school, I connect with him. Learning about old movies—"

"Right," Irwin says.

"Jazz. Any—"

"The arts."

"Any body of knowledge that Lewis found interesting, he passed on to us. And I still remember his room in that house was filled with books. He was always reading."

Movies. Jazz. Art. Liberals for Nixon.

"Lewis," Stephan says, "from the time I knew him in eighth grade was a true intellectual. He was a person who—"

"Loved the life of the mind," Irwin says.

I feel a jolt. "He loved learning," Stephan says. "He had a way of synthesizing and pulling information together, to both make meaning and make the meaning exciting. He had an incredible mind."

"And he was an amazing storyteller," Irwin says. "In the eighth grade, we were school crossing guards, Lewis and me, and because we were not in the jock group who controlled the guard assignments, we were sent to some obscure street corner to watch for children who never came. We were reading Eric Ambler spy novels, and Lewis concocted some unbelievable fantasy about being spies on an African border patrol. He was always like that. He used to wear his Boy Scout uniform as if he were some eleven-year-old soldier of fortune."

"Was he very intense?" I'm not sure why I ask, except that I have seen it in his face in photographs, a fierce concentration.

"Intense, yeah," Stephan says. "His humor was very intense, too. He had this way of laughing and frowning at the same time. And he had a laugh that was sort of like a burst. You remember that?"

"Exploded out." Irwin laughs himself, a delighted chuckle like a cartoon character's. "I remember he had a job, when he was fourteen, working in an interior decorator shop in the city. And he thought it was a great job and someone told him, in the vernacular, 'Don't shit where you eat,' because he thought a girl there was very attractive. He didn't know what it meant, but he nodded. Then he called me up, and says, 'What do you think it means?' And I said, 'I have no idea.'"

I laugh.

"You sound just like him," Stephan says. "That's his laugh."

"And you look just like him, too," Irwin says.

"It's uncanny," Stephan says.

I smile uncomfortably as they stare at me.

"Anyway," Stephan says finally, "it was a humor we all shared. It sort of turned life upside down and looked at its perversity."

"But to give you an example of what we were like," Irwin says. "Between sophomore and junior year in high school, Lewis and I went on a youth hostel trip through New England and Quebec. He was very popular on the trip. People liked him. The leader was kind of this debutante person—it was Polly Bergen, actually—and she invited us to her house for a party. We were maybe fifteen or sixteen is all, taking the bus and the subway an hour and a half into the city, and we were both wondering, What do you say at a cocktail party? We'd never been to a cocktail party before. So Lewis decided that any time anybody said anything, we would go, 'Oh, Picasso, oh!'" Irwin makes a dismissive, offhand gesture. "And we were practicing this on the subway. 'Oh, Beethoven, oh!' You know. We'd come up with a topic and then have this kind of toss-off response. I remember being hysterical on the train. But, of course," Irwin says, laughing again, "no one talked to us so we had nothing to say to anybody. We left in half an hour."

Irwin's face is animated and vivid, energized by the force of memory. My father is as present to him as I am, sitting with him forty years later in my aunt Miriam's living room.

"We were practicing at being sophisticated," Irwin says. "This was big. This was important."

"That's actually a pretty good description of Lewis, I think," Stephan says. "He was a truly sophisticated person."

"Or practicing to be?"

"No, no, not practicing to be. He was, he was."

"Did he get that from his family?"

"No," Irwin says, drawing out the word.

"Maybe from his brother," Stephan says.

"I think he worked at it," Irwin says. "When I would be watching the Dodgers or the New York Giants, he would be reading *The New Yorker*. Stephan and I used to talk about sports all the time. Lewis would always move on to more cerebral topics."

"And quote from the books he read," Stephan adds. "Or songs. I remember this one song that he used to sing all the time. It was Paul Robeson, I think." Stephan starts to sing in a low voice, *"You Jack o' Diamonds, now you Jack o' Diamonds."* Irwin, to my delight, joins in, and the two of them croon together: *"From here to the jail, boys, yes, back to the jail."*

They both laugh. I can feel myself grinning. Who *are* these men?

"Lewis, you have to understand," Stephan says, "couldn't sing. He had a terrible voice, but that didn't stop him. He would sing this song over and over and over. *Jack o' Diamonds, you Jack o' Diamonds.* That fucking song. He drove everyone crazy with it."

Stephan and Irwin's description of my father makes him sound almost improbably intelligent and complex. ("He was bright," my mother's mother says in her lay-it-on-the-line style, "but no genius.") They speak of him with awe, a moving reverence.

They want me to know that the person who killed himself at thirty-five was not the person they knew.

"He had a deep soul," Stephan says.

"We loved him," Irwin says simply. "We loved him."

Sitting across from Irwin and Stephan as they feed each other lines or complete each other's sentences, I can't help thinking how like them he must have been.

And how, damn him, he should be sitting here with us.

"FLUTTERING HEART" 3

Stephan and Irwin ask me to tell them what I know about what happened to my father after Florida. I describe the cabin on Lama, how my mother took us away and left him there. And then, on an impulse,

I tell them Gersh's fluttering-heart story. It has been several years since I've told it. It is not as potent now, and the details are less vivid. My voice falters. Again I feel shaken. But not, this time, because of the story's hold on my imagination: I realize that the whole thing sounds pretty silly. Still, I tell it to the end: my father's spirit crawling into the bed, my fear that he understood after the fact what he had done.

"Fuck Gersh!" Irwin exclaims, almost before I've stopped talking. "That's his trip. He shouldn't have told you that. Fuck him!"

I feel sheepish, as if I've been gullible, exposing my youth and vulnerability. The spell is broken. The secular response is more palatable than the spiritual, though not necessarily more true.

"FLUTTERING HEART" 4

"Should I tell her my fantasy?" Irwin asks. His wife, Liz, has just poked her head around the screen door to let him and Stephan know that she's returned with the car. We are standing, the three of us, in my aunt Miriam's foyer, not quite sure how to say good-bye. We've exchanged phone numbers and addresses. We've promised to keep in touch. I hope they mean it as much as I do. I want to know these men. I want to maintain the electrical current of connection between me and them and my father's history and my father's world.

"For twenty years," Irwin says, "I've had this fantasy that Steph and I would have lunch with you and your brother, to tell you about your father. I knew from Miriam that you came to New York every year, but my wife said, 'You can't just call her up. You can't intrude.'" He chuckles. "Twenty years. And here we are."

"I'm sorry it took so long," I say, and then flush from chest to hairline, as I tend to do, even when I am not moved or embarrassed. To think that these men have been eager to tell me their stories, yet until Miriam mentioned them I had never even heard their names. I had only to ask the right questions to make them appear.

After they leave, I kiss Miriam and each of my cousins good-bye. Miriam asks me and Stuart to stay to dinner, but I tell her that my grandmother is expecting us. This is true, but only part of the reason I can't accept her invitation. In one afternoon, I've been given my father's journal and have spoken for the first time to my father's best friends. An aftershock of adrenaline is jarring my limbs. I can hardly stand to be inside my own skin, much less find the equanimity to join in the banter and chitchat of a large family dinner.

But the afternoon, as it turns out, is not over. When we get to the train station at Manhasset, Stephan is there, leaning on the rail above the track. He turns his head toward us, slowly, as we get out of my uncle's car.

I feel a strange lurch. Whether of excitement or dread, I'm not sure.

Irwin and Liz were not going through Manhattan on their way home to Connecticut, so they dropped off Stephan, whose wife had already driven back to their apartment in the city, to catch the train. We select a row of seats together. I sit next to the window, the tin lithograph upright at my feet. Stephan takes the middle. Stuart is on the aisle. When the train starts, Stephan curls up his long legs on the red vinyl seat to talk to me, a mile a minute, about my father. I press backward slightly into the joint between my seat and the window. Stephan's back is turned to Stuart. I can see that he does not mean to be rude: his mind, like mine, is not focused on pleasantries.

He tells me that if every kid on the block was interested in something, my father wanted nothing to do with it; but he was instantly attracted to anything esoteric. When Stephan asked him to go skiing in Stowe during the spring of their junior year, he avidly took to the sport. He was not particularly graceful, but it didn't matter. Not many people skied then, especially high school kids from Jamaica, Queens. When they started, there was only one single-seat chairlift and a T-bar at Stowe. The safety binding hadn't yet been introduced—a wire cage called a "bear trap" clamped their low, soft boots in place—and skis could be bought for $10 at the army-navy supply store. There were no slick ski suits or Gortex parkas. Stephan and Lewis wore baggy wool pants and nylon shells over layers and layers of sweaters. This ruggedness is what my father loved about it. The sport appealed to his sense of adventure.

"Your father was a romantic," Stephan says. "Not in his relations with women necessarily. I don't mean that."

"In the nineteenth-century sense," I say, to show I understand.

Stephan alarms me: I've never met anyone who talks with such jittery, single-minded ferocity. I struggle against the urge to retreat into myself. At the same time, I wish I had the nerve to pull out the tape recorder, now stuffed at the bottom of my tote bag along with my father's journal. But he might feel put on the spot. I concentrate instead on remembering his sentences as precisely as I can. When he leaves us at Penn Station, I'll write them down.

"Yeah," Stephan says. "His fantasies involved events on a grand scale: wars, politics, economic booms, busts, robber barons. He had this sense of himself as a hero in some nineteenth-century novel. Horatio Hornblower. Or Ahab. When Lewis was involved with his operations off the coast—you know about that, right?"

"The drugs?" I ask. He was not only using cocaine, he was smuggling it from Central America into the United States, via the Gulf of Mexico. I had learned this just recently, from my grandmother Rose.

"When I heard about the drug running, I thought of that heroic sense he had of himself," Stephan says. "He was acting out the novel that was his life."

My first instinct, when Stephan says this, is to dismiss it. The idea of my father, indeed of anyone, "acting out the novel that was his life" sounds corny, melodramatic. But then I think of the declaration my father made to Miriam. "Life is a movie . . ." I repeat the line, word for word and just as carefully as she did, to Stephan.

"Right," Stephan says. "That's him exactly."

To think of someone—my father—constructing a vision of himself and then setting off with such urgency to realize it. The idea amazes me, as does this man beside me, my father's friend. This frighteningly animated man. The lesson of fundamentalism is that people should conform to the same set of rules and opinions, not pursue individual impulses. "'I did it my way,'" fundamentalist preachers like to say of Frank Sinatra's trademark anthem, "is the theme song of hell."

On the other hand, I'd encountered so much wild, erratic behavior in my early life that even the revelation of my father's drug running had seemed just par for the course.

"One of your father's roommates at RPI," Stephan is saying, "David Levine, his ambition was to be the first Jewish astronaut, but he joined the Marines and became a fighter pilot instead. He was a daredevil, a risk taker, someone who raced sports cars, rode a motorcycle. He told everyone that he'd cut the pockets out of his pants in order to be in constant touch with his gonads. I think he flew in Vietnam. Anyway, Irwin heard that he was killed in Africa, flying as a mercenary. Your father was very impressed by him. He found David's life romantic."

Listening to Stephan, perhaps what I feel most powerfully is that my own life—from the moment my mother became a Christian until this day with Stephan sitting between my husband and me in a railroad car—has been a deliberate effort to narrow possibility to its finest point. I was molded into a right-wing Christian. Now I'm molding myself to be the perfect suburban housewife. Not that I want to be killed in Africa, flying as a mercenary. Or in New Mexico, either, at the bitter end of a cocaine high. Those are not the scripts I would write.

I want the train ride to end. I want Stephan to stop talking. My heart is beating too hard; my limbs are watery. In the space of an hour, my father has gone from a near blank to a man who learned the cha-cha in the basement of Stephan's house so that he could dance with Bobby Blender, his date for the senior prom. I've discovered that I have his voice and that he, too, used to blush all the time. He's gone from a man who committed suicide while on drugs to a sophisticated man of intellect who was a hero to his friends.

He's like a figure that springs forward when you turn the page of a pop-up book: still paper, but seemingly alive.

MY FATHER'S DAUGHTER

Cavities

Instead of letting his imagination work with structural forms, with the *solids* of a building, the architect can work with the empty space —the cavity—between the solids, and consider the forming of that space as the real meaning of architecture.

—STEEN EILER RASMUSSEN, *Experiencing Architecture*

A THEORY ABOUT FATHERS

"We're all searching for our fathers," my friend, the writer Sheila O'Connor, says, "even when we have them. You're searching for your father, I'm searching for my father, my husband is searching for his. The absent father, the distant father, the angry father. And it's all because of God. Constructing God as this perfect, benevolent, all-knowing male. What a thing to live up to. That's what we're all searching for. God, our father. Or Santa Claus, our father. People never talk about their mothers that way. It's one of the worst thing religion ever did. Don't you think?"

SCENE FROM A MOVIE SHOWN IN CHURCH

A little girl comes home from school. As she walks up the driveway to her house, she sees a peculiar sight: the lawn mower is on the lawn, idling. Only half of the grass has been cut. She hears the chug-chug of the motor. The little girl's father is nowhere to be seen. Maybe he has gone inside for a drink.

The little girl goes through the back door into the kitchen. Usually her mother is there, preparing dinner. They eat dinner every night at 6:00. But her mother is not there. The house is eerily quiet.

Fifteen and almost painfully impressionable, I gripped my seat with anxiety, my stomach so tightly clenched that it ached. I hated this movie. I hated the pastor and elders of my church (and my mother, though I didn't know this yet, or wouldn't admit it) for making me watch it. They thought of it as an evangelical tool: most of the kids around me were not Christians. I had even invited some of them. My next-door neighbors, Liz and Charlie, were sitting beside me in the row; Charlie was so transfixed that his mouth hung open. They'd come for the show, for the same good scare they'd get from watching *Nightmare on Elm Street*. But that wasn't why the film was being shown. The church had rented the screen and the film and sent out posters inviting all the teens in Taos to come in order, quite literally, to scare the hell out of them.

The little girl's mother is not there, but she has been there. There is a pot on the stove. The flame is on underneath it. In the pot is a stick of melted butter. The butter snaps and spits onto the stove. The little girl panics. She calls out for her mother. She calls out for her father. Then, suddenly, she knows what has happened.

The little girl's parents were Christians. They had asked Jesus to come into their hearts as their personal savior. The little girl was stubborn. She refused to pay attention in Sunday school. I tried to pay attention in Sunday school. *She would not ask Jesus into her heart.* I had asked Jesus into my heart. *But now she is sorry. She hears her Sunday school teacher's voice scolding in her head, "Jesus will come back for those who believe in him. His children will be brought into heaven to reign with him. And do you know what will happen to those who remain on earth? The Beast will get them. If they take his mark — '666' — on their foreheads, they will be his forever. And when God destroys the Beast, they will be thrown into the Lake of Fire with him."*

The little girl's mother is gone. Her father is gone. Jesus has come back for them. They have been "raptured." The little girl has been left behind.

After the lights came on, there was an altar call. I went up and dedicated myself to Christ all over again, just to be sure.

When I met Stephan and Irwin, the first thing that struck me was how Jewish they seemed. If asked to articulate just what "seeming Jewish" means, I would have to say a quick wit, certain mannerisms, ironic phrasings that seem so typical of Jewish humor—New York Jewish humor in particular. My idea of Judaism is not religious. Except for a version of Passover that primarily involves eating matzoh and hard-boiled eggs dipped in salt water with my mother's family on Long Island, it has little to do with rituals. How could it? Almost all my relatives are atheists. The Jews I know are highly literate, liberal-minded people who feel linked to other Jews through a common culture and a common history, especially the Holocaust and anti-Semitism. That is Judaism to me.

The second thing that struck me was how much Christianity had separated me from my family. My mother had devoted years of ferocious and vengeful energy to trying to convert her mother, and though her behavior toward the rest of the family was more restrained, it was still defiant. Once, at a Passover celebration my mother's family held at the Waldorf-Astoria, some fool asked my mother to say a blessing. She did. She stood up and, in the sighing, sensual voice she uses for prayer, thanked Jesus for the seder meal, which her secular Jewish relatives were about to eat—and for which they, as my grandmother Rose later pointed out, not Jesus, would pay the bill. Years later and even after she and my mother had made some kind of peace with each other, mere mention of this incident could provoke my grandmother to rant for twenty minutes.

Nevertheless, despite the sometimes crackling hostility between them or other members of the family, there had never been a complete break. My mother's family, for one thing, would never have severed the relationship with Peter and me. We belonged to them—no matter what beliefs my mother espoused—and they embraced us without reserve, no matter that we espoused the same beliefs as she.

I embraced them, too, but not unreservedly. I viewed them with suspicion. I had to: they were not saved. Their influence had to be distrusted. Their view of the world was not our view. I felt deeply conflicted about the religion my mother forced me to promote so ardently

—ever since joining Christian Family Church, she had mortified me by giving tracts to waiters and stewardesses, telling store clerks that Jesus loved them, turning every passing conversation with a stranger into a polemic on the need for salvation. Once a year when we came to visit my grandparents, we would take a taxi from La Guardia Airport to their house in Queens and, as Peter and I tried to melt into the upholstery, my mother would press her face to the plastic partition between the seats and talk to the driver for the whole forty-minute ride in a soft, concerned voice about his life and the need to accept Jesus into his heart—but no matter how embarrassed I was by my mother's excesses, I went home from our visits and prayed for the souls of my grandparents, aunts, uncles, and cousins.

It's easy to wonder how my mother could have transformed herself so completely—people who knew her before found the change flabbergasting—but perhaps she was more her old self than anyone realized. My grandmother Rose recalls that even as a small child my mother was attracted to religion (an attraction, Rose feels now, that she should have found some way to indulge); friends from my mother's high school years remember her as having "intense passions"; friends from my mother's hippie days remember her as being aloof and often disapproving of other people's behavior. In becoming a hippie she had, perhaps, adopted the trappings of bohemianism without absorbing its essence—like her mother before her, who had dabbled in the Greenwich Village art scene of the 1930s and was a passionate leftist without ever really being less than middle class in spirit. In fact, though Rose could never comprehend what drove her daughter to make such extreme choices, in some ways she was only carrying her family's professed ideology to its logical and perfect conclusion: my mother was the one who renounced capitalism and adopted a communal style of living, both as a hippie and as a Christian.

She was following family precedent in other ways: her father, Juan, had left his religion (Catholicism) and his country (Chile) as a young man and never looked back; he wrote to his mother, sent her money, and visited her once, but he never spoke of her to his children, never talked to them of his homeland or his past. He adopted my grandmother's family as his own. My mother did the same, choosing a group of people with whom she had no prior affiliation, no blood and therefore no bad blood, to replace the ties forced on her by biological fiat.

Bitterness toward her mother was clearly at the heart of many of her choices. My mother, quiet and artistic, like her father, rather than vociferously opinionated and cerebral, like her mother, often felt either browbeaten or invisible around Rose. What better way to command her attention and to get under her skin than to take up with brutish men like Wayne and then to become a Christian, a resounding repudiation of a Jewish parent, no matter how secular? The name of Jesus, she quickly found, was a more effective weapon than any other. Indeed, my grandmother eventually became so incensed by the years of relentless, hectoring criticism of her politics and morality, not to mention the religious pamphlets left on bedside tables after our visits, that she told my mother to quit proselytizing or stop coming to Queens. Furious and weeping, my mother almost packed us up and left for good, but her brother, John, advised her to reconsider. Someday, he said, you're going to need each other. My mother, bolstered by his reasonable voice and the Lord's insistence that she honor her father and her mother, agreed to keep her religion to herself. From then on, the relationship improved, though it meant avoiding all but the most innocuous topics of conversation.

Yet my mother's conversion was not entirely motivated by spite. My mother would attribute it to a supernatural encounter with God, neither more nor less. I think the trauma of Lewis's and Wayne's violent deaths made her seize Christ as a lifeline, but that her need of faith went back further. Aunts and cousins remember her as the darling of the family, having everything—beauty, poise, adoring parents —but she never talks of her past self with any confidence. She was prized for her loveliness, she felt, but not for what was underneath. She was, in part, challenging her mother to accept her, no matter what she was, did, or professed. It was as if before becoming a Christian, she did not exist; belief gave her substance.

Still, for all her denunciations of the past, my mother wanted to hold onto some sense of a Jewish identity—not that there was much left once she abandoned the culture of her New York family. My mother thinks you can be both Jewish and Christian: Jewish in heritage, Christian in faith. She doesn't think "Jews for Jesus" is an oxymoron. Occasionally, she would celebrate Passover with the family, but even more often with her non-Jewish church friends, who liked Jewish holidays, too. When we were in high school, she used to light the Chanukah candles with my brother and me, reciting *Boruch Atoh Adonoi Eloheinu Melech Ho-olom*, as the candles representing day one and day two took flame. The rest were lit in silence because that was all she knew of the prayer.

Her certainty that converting to Christianity did not negate one's Jewish identity made me think that *I* could be both, too—until I was eighteen and took a trip to Israel with my grandmother and a busload of American Jewish Congress members who considered me to be, unequivocally, a Christian. I'm not sure how they knew this. I probably bowed my head over each meal to say grace. Or maybe I told them I was attending North Central Bible College, or that I was engaged to be married, young as I was. There was no hostility from the rest of the group, but I realized that I had to choose. I did not consider for a moment that I could choose *not* to be a Christian. With the savage conviction of a girl who had lost not one father but two, I believed Christ when he said, "Whoever denies Me before men, I will also deny him before My Father who is in heaven." But more than that, I believed in hell. Fear of hell had been seared into my soul by my pastor and those vicious rapture movies.

If anything can be said to have broken that fear, at least enough for me to slip sideways through its clutching fingers, it was reading *Portrait of the Artist as a Young Man*. It was assigned to me, for the third time since high school, in a literature course when I was a college senior. By then, I had stopped going to church regularly. I still believed in God, but only because I was too afraid to stop. When the class came to the hellfire-and-brimstone sermon halfway through the book—nearly twenty pages of vivid torment—the other students laughed, astonished that what they saw as mystical humbug could have power over anyone:

> Every word for him! . . . His flesh shrank together as it felt the approach of the ravenous tongues of flames, dried up as it felt about it the swirl of stifling air. He had died. Yes. He was judged. A wave of fire swept through his body: the first. Again a wave. His brain began to glow. Another. His brain was simmering and bub-

bling within the cracking tenement of the skull. Flames burst
forth from his skull like a corolla, shrieking like voices:
—Hell! Hell! Hell! Hell! Hell!

I didn't laugh. I sweated as I read it. I wanted to rush home and
repent. But I resisted the urge, stuffing the fear back into the dark
cellar inside me.

That sermon marks the turning point of *Portrait*. After the sermon
and an ecstasy of contrition, capped off by a period of extreme devotion and a momentary consideration of the priesthood, Stephen Dedalus
loses his religion. He opts for the sensual confusion of this earth rather
than the "chill and order" of the Church. Like Lucifer when he fell
from heaven, Stephen commits the sin of pride, "rebellion of the intellect," when he decides that he "will not serve." After reading those
terrifying pages for the third time, I determined that I would not
serve, either, not until I could claim that my motive was love for God
rather than fear of hell.

For several years afterward, I chose nothing. Then I met Irwin
and Stephan, and hearing them talk about my father, I knew what I
wanted to be: Jewish. What this meant, exactly, wasn't entirely clear
to me given that I knew I did not want to be religious. A cousin once
asked my formerly Catholic grandfather why he didn't convert to Judaism, and he replied that he couldn't exchange one dogma for another. Neither could I. But I wanted my heritage: the customs and
jokes; the emphasis on education, intellect, and social conscience; the
shared history and even anxiety; the bond of an identifiable if not co-
hesive community. I am Jewish by birth. And my mother's conversion
had separated me from this identity. By reclaiming my Jewishness—
embodied for me in many ways by my father—I could finally embrace
my family as fully as they had always embraced me.

MUSTERING

Once when I was sixteen, sprawled on the grass of an empty soccer field
with my next-door neighbor Charlie, I decided that I was furious at Lewis.

"The selfish bastard killed himself," I said. It was late fall. At the edges of my vision, the bare-branched cottonwoods of Lower Ranchitos touched the sky. I pulled tufts of dry grass out of the ground in violent jerks. "He made his choice, didn't he? So that's it."

But my fury wasn't genuine. It was an idea of grief rather than grief itself, the assumption that this is what a person ought to feel when someone she loved killed himself. Charlie was two years younger than I, and easily awed. Attracted to the drama of my own outburst, I tried on fury like a costume in some theater production. In truth, I didn't feel any particular thing. Not even indifference.

A THEORY ABOUT FATHERS 2

In high school, I wrote a paper about Odysseus's return to Ithaka for Mrs. Jenkins's humanities class, senior year, 1985. One line in *The Odyssey* jumped out at me as I lay on a blanket with my friend Susan at the Junction bridge, absorbing the last rays of summer into our soon-to-fade tans. ("O, rosy-fingered Dawn," we chanted to each other. "O, gray-eyed Athene." And then we turned over to roast the other side.) Odysseus, biding his time, holes up in the hut of the swineherd Eumaios. Along comes his son, Telemachos, who is unable to believe that either the beggar he first meets or the godlike man revealed under the beggar's rags is his father.

"Telemachos," Odysseus says in Richard Lattimore's translation, "it does not become you to wonder too much / at your own father when he is here, nor doubt him." And then the line that has stayed with me ever since: "*No other Odysseus than I will ever come back to you.*"

No other Odysseus than I.

Telemachos must accept both the beggar and the prince in his father, I wrote, before he can accept the beggar and prince in himself. I wrote, too, about the child's original perception of his father as an infallible god, followed by the adolescent's disgust with the all-too-apparent failings of the actual man, and the ultimate integration of the two in the adult child's understanding and acceptance of his father as both wise man and fool, strong man and weak, moral and immoral.

Mrs. Jenkins loved that paper.

"No, I am not a god," Odysseus says. "Why liken me to the immortals? / But I am your father, for whose sake you are always grieving / as you look for violence from others, and endure hardships."

"I put him into your hands now," Eumaios says to Telemachos, before Odysseus's true identity has been revealed. "Do with him as you will. He names himself your suppliant."

Beggar and prince. Do with him as you will.

YOUR QUIET MOMENT IN NEW MEXICO
For Lewis, my father (April 1992).

The smell of lilacs must have hung
like draperies
over the open windows, clinging
to the drenched evening.
The dust on the turquoise sill
must have been spattered
into mud by drops dashed
through the screen.

It must have been very quiet.

Even the tourists, wandering
from their shops and museums,
must have been silent
as they passed your garden wall,
hushed by the rain,
or the coming night.

Perhaps they could not speak
through the scent of lilacs.

The room must have been dusty, thick
with the caliche that covers
everything. Even the pictures

of your children
must have hung under caliche
thick as a clay mantle.

The quiet, the scent of rain
and lilacs
must have filled that room,
pushing outward

on the earthen walls,
the skinned beams, until
with one sharp, dark noise
that made the tourists turn
and look, one startle
of wings in the lilacs, that room

must have fallen in on you.

STREETWISE

On the platform at Penn Station, Stephan stands with Stuart and me
a little longer, reluctant, it seems, to let us go. At Miriam's, he said
that the last time he had been there was twenty-one years before, the
week after my father died. Miriam and Bob had held a memorial service, and Stephan, profoundly shaken by the death of his friend, had
sat with them long after everyone else, talking and talking about
Lewis. He couldn't get himself to leave. I have the sense that whatever held him there then has him in the same grip now.

"Wow," Stuart says, when we finally find ourselves alone on the
long escalator that rises from the belly of Penn Station to Thirty-fourth
Street. "He's intense, isn't he?" Stuart is a quiet man. Of all virtues,
he admires restraint the most.

"No kidding," I say, closing the small blue notebook in which I've
been frantically scribbling. Stuart has been holding the lithograph; I
take it back from him, regretting that I didn't ask Miriam to ship it
to me, and wedge it under my arm, where it crackles and flexes. It's

a relief to get into the open air, away from the oily underground heat of trains, away from the effort to go on listening to and conversing with Stephan. The afternoon is sticky but not sweltering. It's been a cool week, often rainy. I love the city on these days: its washed grays and rare intensified greens, taillights and neon a muddled graffiti on the slick asphalt. Now there is a small refreshing breeze. We should take a cab uptown to my grandmother's. The clock hanging above the station exit reads 6:10. My grandmother will have the table set. She will want to eat by 6:30 or 7:00. But I'm not ready to go back. I can't sit down to dinner. There is such a clatter in my body that I think if I put it in a chair it would start to flop and lurch like a fish in a bucket. I have to walk.

I know I should stop at a pay phone first and call my grandmother. She worries when Stuart and I are alone in the city. But for some reason I don't want to report my whereabouts. I don't want to explain myself or argue for the time I need. This small assertion, of which I am not often capable, is important to me. Though I have no desire to upset her, something is stirring inside me, and I can't cut it short because dinner is on the table. This is about me, I think. This is not about being a good girl.

We stop at the lip of the station exit, confused for a moment about where we are, which way is up or down, east or west. Turning onto Seventh Avenue, we have to speed up to avoid being run down by the crush of walkers. A bombardment of people—delivery men carrying bags of takeout, a woman in pink pedal pushers and pink platform shoes with pink hair, a man in a Bolshevik worker's cap who looks like Jason Robards—comes at me, but I don't tense, or duck my head with fear. I have the lithograph in front of me now, Nixon's face to my chest, so that no one will bang into it or get cut on its edges, but I'm not using it as a shield. I want to be swept along with the crowd, to be one with it, lost in it, tossed loose on its swell. Even the heat rising in thick waves from the subway grates is oddly pleasant, steamily sensual. Everything excites me. The pneumatic brakes of buses wheeze air. There is a sudden smell of sawdust. JUDGMENT IS COMING! a sign declares. Someone pushes a leaflet announcing a sample sale into my hand. We surge forward against the light, just clearing the intersection as a silver Mercedes charges across as if it means to mow down everyone in its path. A man in an enormous puffed leather hat pushes past me. "You ain't got no money," he says, playfully, to his friend, "don't say another motherfucking thing to me. Leave me the fuck *alone!*" His voice is so rich, so resonant, I want to laugh.

Stuart is quiet, but he seems as delighted by the spectacle as I am. Ordinarily, he hates crowds and cities and heat. At the moment, to my relief, he just seems glad for the opportunity to use his camera, stopping to photograph a pizza man in a paper toque and blue smock leaning out of his shop window, electric signs pulsing above him. I am grateful for my husband's presence, for his solid, comforting silence. He won't ask me how I feel or what this day has been like for me. He won't make me force words up out of myself before they want to come. Lured by stacks of golden cookies and the smell of sugar, I run into a bakery to buy chocolate-dipped madeleines as an offering to my grandmother. Stuart smiles at me, sweetly, indulgently, as I come out with the fragrant white bag. Maybe it is my pleasure that he is enjoying. He is happy for me, for having regained a small piece of what has been missing in my life for so long: my father. He wants this for me. He believes I should recover as much of him as I can.

I am inspired by the realization that the city itself can connect me to Lewis, and later that same week we take a bus (not the subway, we're afraid to ride the subway) downtown to Greenwich Village—the first time I have ever been there. We both stand gaping at the red stone clock turret of Jefferson Market Library, the hectically arranged tree-lined streets and charming shops. It seems so warm, vibrant, so lavish in texture and color and culture. We eat at a table on the sidewalk of a little French café on the corner of Sheridan Square, where the waiters actually seem to be French.

"I want to live here. Let's move here, Stuart, if only for six months, a year. That would be enough."

He laughingly agrees, bowled over himself. He is a good man, Stuart.

Neither of us knows yet that being a good man is not necessarily enough.

My father was not a jock but a brain. With the exception of skiing, he hated sports; like me, he was clumsy and uncoordinated and had almost no athletic ability. Still, if the "most sophisticated" Bobby Blender dated him, his awkwardness couldn't have made him completely unpopular. Maybe his intellect was the attraction. He read voraciously, passionately, about history, the arts, architecture. While his friends were playing stickball in the schoolyard, he would be in his room, reading about the Crimea. Even the Dodgers, folk heroes to nearly everyone else in the neighborhood, held no interest for him. The Museum of Modern Art turned him on instead. In his crabbed print, he would copy out poems by Vachel Lindsay and e. e. cummings, whose iconoclasm he and his friends adored, and carry them in his wallet. Kids across the country shrieked when Elvis Presley came on the radio; my father went around singing left-wing songs like "The Peat Bog Soldiers." At the instigation of his brother, he read Frank Lloyd Wright and proclaimed his deep admiration for the Bauhaus and Ludwig Mies van der Rohe, whom his friends had never heard of. For a bar mitzvah present, his brother-in-law, my uncle Bob, gave him *The Military History of the Revolutionary War*, a two-volume set that he says my father was up to reading even then.

Maybe he had the allure of the moody, brooding man, the kind who makes a woman feel that she and only she can get through to him. He thrust his head and torso forward in conversation; only the lower half of his face lit up when he smiled: his forehead remained furrowed, his dark bushy eyebrows bundled over his nose. He became so intent when he talked that in high school he once dropped a cigarette into the cushions of his chair—one of a matched set in Stephan's parents' living room—and was too absorbed in conversation to notice the smell of burning nylon curling up around him.

"You're on fire," Irwin finally said to him. "Better get up."
He got up, put out the fire, and kept on talking.

VOCABULARY GAMES

"Did I say that?" my grandmother Rose asks me. "That he was 'no genius'?"

I nod. It's a little unnerving, I know, to be quoted back to oneself.

"Well, a genius to me is an Einstein. He wasn't an Einstein. But he was very bright."

ARE YOU VERY SMART?

In high school I devoured *The Odyssey*, Dostoyevsky, James Joyce, T. S. Eliot, Joseph Conrad. I loved picking a text apart, its subtle intricacies spinning in my head long after the class had moved on. And I loved arguing a point; to keep my hand down in class, I would have had to tie it behind my back. Teachers praised my work effusively. Pride in self was, of course, a sin, yet I craved praise, validation of something other than Christian virtues, and I had a hunger to learn.

My mother had come from a family that worshipped education and achievement, their only religion. Neither an avid student nor ambitious, she bitterly resented it, yet it was in her, encoded despite her efforts to wipe it out. She could see that it was in me, too. My mother followed my progress closely: she read my papers, went to teacher conferences, listened to my ideas. When I made the honor roll, she took me and my friends out to dinner. At the same time, she harped on what she saw as my arrogance. I was not to put too much stock in my own worldly intellect. Humility, goodness, self-sacrifice, these were the virtues I should cultivate. I knew chapter and verse well enough: "For what is a man profited, if he shall gain the whole world, and lose his own soul?"

I wanted to please her. My mother, I thought, had suffered so much grief in her life, I didn't want to cause her any more. I also worked at being the kind of person she would value. Everyone in my school knew I was a Christian. I argued vehemently against abortion:

"It's murder!" I shouted once in a crowded restaurant, banging my fist on the table so hard that the silverware and my companions jumped. Homosexuality: "With the help of the Lord," I spouted, "any sin can be overcome." I was known to have walked out of *The Life of Brian* because it struck me as heretical and *The Rocky Horror Picture Show* because it was perverse. I didn't drink or smoke or allow my boyfriend to do more than let his hand roam under my clothes. When my friends lost their virginity, they avoided telling me, for fear I would disapprove.

And yet my mother never seemed to appreciate my devotion or my sacrifice. Understandably, I suppose. No matter how much I abstained or acted as Christ's witness, my body betrayed me in church: it slumped when it should have sat attentively straight; it refused to sway or wave its hands in prayer along with everyone else. I was often in trouble for being sullen. On weekend outings with the youth group, I'd drag behind all the other eager kids, unable to bring myself to speak to anyone; on Friday nights, in glum silence I'd slap sandwiches together for the derelicts at the church soup kitchen. I wanted to be a good Christian, I really did; still, I never managed to cooperate as fully as I always intended. My resistance to prayer sessions at the kitchen table left me so numb that sometimes I couldn't force my tongue to form words. But my mother wouldn't budge until I did.

WHAT MIRIAM REMEMBERS

"Your father was a mischievous child. One day, he took your grandfather Morris's pocket watch and buried it in the backyard. When Morris found out, he was very upset and demanded that Lewis return it. But Lewis couldn't remember where he'd buried it—a beautiful gold pocket watch that my mother gave my father when they got engaged. He dug up the whole lawn looking for it. He was just a little boy."

ARTIFACTS 2

Irwin sends me a photograph of the eighth-grade graduating class at P.S. 178. It is made up of tiny individual oval portraits, including Irwin, my father, and Stephan:

IRWIN SOLLINGER

LEWIS WEINBERGER

STEPHAN KLEIN

He also sends me C. S. Forester's *Hornblower and the Hotspur*, which he says was the first book my father suggested he read. It seems to be about ships and sea battles in the early nineteenth century—a boy's book, which, I must admit, I don't expect to enjoy reading.

BOY SCOUT

From the time my father was a child, he loved history, and military history in particular. The Napoleonic Wars, the Spanish civil war, strategy and heroism, these things fascinated him. The more obscure the history, the better. He relished the story, for instance, of how the Finns  during the Russo-Finnish War cornered the Russians when a fire broke out in the forest where they were fighting, and the Russians' riderless horses plunged into a lake to escape the flames. The water froze at night, and in the morning the Finns found the horses dead. The lake was a sheet of ice with the horses' heads, hundreds of them, their eyes open in terror, scattered across the surface. He got the story from *Kaputt* by Curzio Malaparte, and he told his friends they must read the book.

When they were children, everything was war. There were movies, of course, a tidal wave of them beginning in the early 1940s. Every boy wanted to be Humphrey Bogart's wily tank commander holding off an entire German battalion in *Sahara*, or Hugh Williams, the foreign correspondent in *The Day Will Dawn* who, along with Deborah Kerr and Ralph Richardson, sabotaged a U-boat base off the coast of occupied Norway. And before every movie, the Movietone News would broadcast war bulletins and short films exhorting the audience to buy Victory bonds. Recruitment posters were plastered everywhere (I WANT YOU FOR THE U.S. ARMY), and the streets, especially in Manhattan, were thick with men in uniform. At six, Stephan sang "This Is the Army, Mr. Jones" onstage at the New Yorker Hotel, and he and his friends would march around their neighborhood bellowing, "*Whistle while you work / Hitler is a jerk / Mussolini is a meanie / and the Japs are worse!*" At home, conversations revolved around the war, and everyone listened to Roosevelt's Fireside Chats—Stephan and Irwin both remember the rainy April day on which Roosevelt died, and how people wandered the streets like zombies, crying. War themes dominated radio shows, comic books, even cartoons. Disney put Donald Duck and Mickey Mouse in uniform, and brave Lassie had to trot behind enemy lines to save a stranded American paratrooper.

The war permeated the imaginations of children. They played war games day and night, often using real army materiel in place of toys. Stephan had a German pith helmet, a bayonet, Nazi medals, and a standard-issue Russian rifle that were given to him by his uncle. The kid next door had a Luger.

There were guns in my father's house, too. Joe was too young to serve, although at fifteen in 1944, the possibility must have loomed. Even so, he owned rifles, which he would take apart and refinish, letting his little brother help him sand the stocks. The firearms fascinated Lewis—in fact, almost everything Joe did fascinated him.

"It gave me the creeps," Irwin says. "He liked guns. It wasn't something we shared."

The things my father was good at, the things he loved, often had an air of militarism about them; they required strategy and a survival instinct. He couldn't compete on the playing field; instead, at thirteen, he blossomed in the Boy Scouts.

It was in the Boy Scouts that Irwin and my father's friendship really began. Before finding himself in the same troop at Hillcrest Jewish

Center, Irwin had not seen Lewis since the first time they met, when their brothers took them to the Jamaica Theater for a movie and eight acts of vaudeville. The next year, 1951, they would go to the same grade school, P.S. 178. When my uncle Bob married Miriam, he was Irwin's brother's best friend, which made Irwin and Lewis practically family.

Lewis matured sooner than the other boys. He grew facial hair and developed muscles by the time he was twelve and would roll up his sleeves to look tough. He slicked his dark hair to the side of his forehead and began wearing Clark's "desert boots," soft suede lace-ups with crepe soles, which he said had been developed by Field Marshal Montgomery for his troops in North Africa during World War II. (Later on, in high school, he would go around in an English trench coat because it was "official British officers' issue" and had D rings on the belt, originally designed, it pleased him to know, for hanging hand grenades in front and ceremonial swords in back. In college, he would affect English tweed sport coats with leather elbow patches.) The onset of puberty gave him a physical advantage, an aura of machismo that awed the other boys. Every summer for three years—before Lewis, at age fourteen, found a summer job working in a decorator's shop in Manhattan—the boys would spend two weeks at Ten Mile River Boy Scout Camp in the Catskill Mountains, near Monticello, New York, the center of the Borscht Belt. It was so rustic that the campers used straw ticks instead of mattresses. "He was seen as a star in that kind of setting," Irwin says. "He was always a rank ahead of me." He thrived at Boy Scout camp because many of the activities emphasized mental agility rather than sports. They hiked, tied knots, learned to survive in the woods. There was no football, no baseball, no jock culture that would mark him for exclusion.

Of all the boys in the troop, Lewis was the only one elected to the Order of the Arrow, the Scouts' national honor society, whose members were elected by their peers. A prospective inductee had to spend at least fifteen days camping in the woods, including one six-day-long experience, then undergo "the Ordeal," which involved keeping silent for a set time, eating only minimal amounts, working on projects around the camp, and sleeping alone, away from the other Scouts. After that, he was taken to a secret place, inducted into "the Brotherhood," and given—or so Irwin imagines—the secret password and handshake.

"He never talked about it. He was thirteen, and this was very prestigious. He was the only one in it. Alan Hundert wasn't, I wasn't, nobody was. He never told me what the secret words were, even though I pressed him."

"It was the paramilitary," Stephan says.

Irwin chuckles. "He loved it."

ITEMS MISSING FROM THE INVENTORY OF MY FATHER

1. A cigar box containing writings, photographs, memorabilia from my father's elementary school P.S. 134, an Order of the Arrow Boy Scout badge, and several thousand dollars in cash. The box, Irwin tells me, was found beside his body.

2. His father's pocket watch, which Lewis wanted when his father died. At first, his sister refused to give it to him. Their mother was still alive, she says now, sighing. She wanted to keep everything together. The watch had sentimental meaning for everyone. But then Joe told her that he thought she should let Lewis have it, and she did. It was not found among his things when he died.

TOUGH JEW-BOY

My father's father, Morris, was a formidable man.

"Thick," Irwin says.

"Thick in body, thick in personality," Stephan says.

Morris once took a shovel away from a group of workmen on a job and showed them how to dig a hole. Lewis was with him. He dug it deeper, wider, better than anyone else. My father admired him for that. He admired his father's toughness, his strength. In high school, he'd read a novel about Israel whose main character was a "tough

Jew-boy." He quoted that description back to Irwin. This was the sort of boy, Lewis seemed to think, whom his father would respect. A tough Jew-boy, not an introverted kid like himself.

"I think Lewis was torn," Stephan says. "His family's values were not always his."

Morris could not have been entirely unsympathetic. Miriam says they were all readers. Morris read all the current novels, and he used to stay up all night, devouring books about Jewish history and Zionism. As a girl, Lewis's mother, Kate, would pick out books at the library every Friday, working her way around the stacks. And yet, according to Stephan and Irwin, Morris's values were completely material: he advocated hard work and practical action; his son was much more contemplative, though he longed for some connection with his father. When his parents joined a country club near Jamaica Estates, Lewis took some golf lessons. His father was on the course with him one day when Lewis happened to be playing well. "You should be a golfer," his father said. Lewis glowed. He reported his father's comment to Irwin. *You should be a golfer.* It was a rare compliment. He loved golf after that.

If Morris was hard to please, Kate was no easier. She used to complain that Lewis's bed-wetting—which continued well into sixth grade —had caused her varicose veins because she kept having to get up in the middle of the night to change his sheets. At the time, my father did not talk to his friends about what was going on at home. The language of self-help and pop psychology had not yet entered the culture; they did not discuss their family lives then, but years later, as an adult, musing about what had gone wrong for him, my father spoke of the bed-wetting episodes to Irwin (and again, around the same time, to a therapist and to Miriam). Even as a teenager, Irwin noticed that Lewis often seemed anxious around his parents. His voice changed when he spoke to them, dropping deep into his throat. It was defensive and labored, as if he found it difficult to get out the words. The difference was so marked that it seemed as if he had one voice for his friends and another for his parents. The atmosphere in his house was somber, at least to Irwin. No one seemed to laugh or smile much.

"I was a reasonable kid," Irwin says, "but I always felt like I was doing something wrong just by being there."

Irwin spent a lot of time with Lewis, but in all the years he knew him, Irwin was never invited to dinner, not once. He had eaten several times at Stephan's, and Stephan had often eaten at Irwin's house. But as soon as the dishes were laid on the Weinberger table, it was understood that any visitors had to leave. Most difficult of all for my father was the fact that his parents spent his entire last semester of high school in Florida, staying there for the whole winter without him. He lived alone in their house, his friends say, with a freezer full of frozen dinners.

DREAM-CATCHER

In high school, Stephan, Irwin, and my father were, each in his own way, lonely boys. Stephan's mother had died of cancer when he was thirteen; since then, his father had become increasingly remote, often silent at dinner or, until he remarried when Stephan was seventeen, out on dates. Irwin's parents were divorced and, in the reshuffling of their lives, they paid little attention to what he was doing. Lewis was a late child; he seemed to be an afterthought, maybe not planned, maybe—did he think so himself or was it only the impression of his friends?—not wanted. His parents' extended stay in Florida halfway through his senior year apparently left him feeling abandoned. "Orphaned," the three boys became family to one another.

They spent much of their time together roaming the city. Manhattan was a magnet for them, a touchstone, a dream-catcher. On Saturdays they would go to folk concerts, foreign movies, jazz performances, plays at Circle in the Square or the Cherry Lane Theatre. It was the mid-1950s, and the age of the auteur film director: Antonioni, Godard, Fellini, Truffaut. The film *Rashomon*, which Lewis and Irwin saw together, boggled their minds. Truth, they discovered, was fractured and unreliable. Sometimes they took dates to night court and watched the prostitutes being arraigned.

For them, New York City was more than a physical place. It was a symbol. "We used it," Stephan says, "to define ourselves as urban and arty and intellectual, and yet we didn't live in the city. We lived in a tree-shaded suburb of detached houses. In some ways we were very conventional: we belonged to high school fraternities and went to the prom in powder blue rented tuxedos. But we were also adventurous. We would have been very different kids if not for the city."

They hung out at the Museum of Modern Art, wandering the permanent collection so frequently that Rousseau, Léger, Dada, the elongated walkers of Giacometti's *City Square*, became as familiar to them as the Dodgers lineup was to other boys (though Stephan and Irwin knew the lineup, too). And the changing exhibitions gave them a glimpse of the landscape of new American art: de Kooning, Rothko, Jackson Pollock. They weren't avant-garde in their tastes, they weren't trailblazers; they took direction from *The New Yorker*. Still, they were eager for revelation. They rarely went to the Metropolitan: old masters didn't have the appeal of cutting-edge modernism. It was modern art and modern buildings and the bohemianism of Greenwich Village that attracted them. Everybody in the world was familiar with Rembrandt, but how many of them had embraced Franz Kline or Mies van der Rohe? How many had heard of Brother Theodore, a downtown club performer who dressed like a vampire and delighted his audience by insulting everyone in it?

Brother Theodore was a discovery of my father's. He loved him. He also loved W. C. Fields, on whose curmudgeonly persona he modeled himself. The Museum of Modern Art often included Fields in its screenings of revival films. Lewis even looked a little like him, or maybe a cross between Fields and H. L. Mencken, another figure in his pantheon:

Lewis went around quoting Mencken while speaking in a W. C. Fields accent.

When they weren't in museums or at the movies, the boys would browse the bins of used bookstores on Fourth Avenue or hang out at Caffé Reggio on Bleecker Street, hoping for a glimpse of the writers and painters who made the Village so alluring. Emerging from the subway, fresh from the hinterlands, nothing could have been more dazzling. It was a new world, bursting with vitality, a kind of commitment to *living* that the boys had never encountered before. They would walk the twisty, cobbled streets, wondering at the lives behind the many-paned windows, imagining those lives as their own. Poets scribbling in shadowy bars, radicals plotting revolution in their sixth-floor walkups, onetime speakeasies behind hidden doors. They soaked up its magical aura, feeling as if this, not Jamaica Estates, was where they really belonged, their true home. The folk music magazine *Sing Out!* had its headquarters on Sixth, next to the Waverly Twin. A few blocks away was the great Eighth Street Bookstore. Eighth Street was the city's version of Main Street: the heart of the community, wide in its range of offerings, yet modest enough in scale to have a small-town feel. It wasn't lined, as it is now, with cut-rate shoe stores and paraphernalia shops whose mannequins have spiky dog collars around their necks. The Whitney Museum's original home was on Eighth, as well as a branch of Brentano's bookstore. An art theater in the middle of the block showed foreign films, and close to that was the jewelry store where, in college, they all bought wedding bands for their girlfriends so they could check into motels without getting arrested. Stephan and Irwin bought tights at the dance store, on the pretext that they were going to take ballet lessons to improve their skiing, but mostly because the girl behind the counter was very beautiful. At the Marlboro Bookstore, which sold remainders, they picked up cheap reproductions of the paintings they had seen at the Modern: except for Lewis, whose father, Irwin thinks, did not allow him to put up whatever he wanted on his walls. Irwin and Stephan plastered their rooms with them.

On the south side of Eighth was the Village Smoke Shop, where they bought Egyptian cigarettes and Gauloises. They had started smoking when they were thirteen or fourteen, with Camels and Lucky Strikes, in imitation of World War II bomber pilots. It was Lewis who introduced Irwin, and later Stephan, to cigarettes. "Bogart went to his death," my father would say with a smile, tamping a fresh, unfiltered cigarette on his palm, "smoking two packs a day." By the time they were in high school, at his instigation, they had enhanced their personas with pipes made to order by the Wilke Pipe Shop on Madison Avenue. They had their own blends mixed from the glass jars that Wilke's daughters, who ran the shop, kept on the counter; each of the boys had a card on file with his special recipe recorded on it.

On Saturdays, they hung out in Washington Square Park, where folksingers would come to showcase their talents. They gathered with the rest of the crowd around the concrete fountain and sang along, accompanied by strummed guitars. At midnight they attended Pete Seeger concerts at the Knights of Pythias Concert Hall. My father loved jazz and Kurt Weill, but music was the one area in which his friends pioneered more than he did. Stephan had been raised with folk music and, like my mother, had spent many summers at a left-wing camp in Massachusetts where evening sing-alongs featured Woody Guthrie union tunes and usually ended with multiple choruses of "Irene" and "Wimoweh." He was fascinated by folk, but also by the new music, "rock and roll" and "rhythm and blues," which Alan Freed played on the radio. Irwin, for his part, was hooked on Symphony Sid, the jazz disk jockey and MC at Birdland, where the boys frequently went to sip wine and worship the virtuoso musicians. Irwin would secretly stay up late at night, listening to Sid on a small radio in his bedroom.

If he lagged behind in music, my father made up for it by introducing his friends to new places in the city. Luchow's, for instance, was one of his discoveries. Located on Fourteenth Street, Luchow's was an enormous German brauhaus that had been in existence since the 1880s. It was noisy, dark, rich with the smell of beer and sausages. Dressed in lederhosen, the waiters sailed back and forth through the restaurant's long string of rooms, carrying big slopping steins to their high-spirited customers. They had music festivals and, at Christmas, a goose festival. In the uproar of German songs and good cheer, my father and his friends would imagine being transported to the heart of old-world Europe. They loved Luchow's and its seeming authenticity, just as they loved Café Geiger on East Eighty-sixth Street, which evoked 1930s Vienna. A miniature ski lift, mountain, and cable car dominated the front window, the glass counter inside oozed German cakes and huge tortes, and a string trio played schmaltzy Strauss waltzes while they ate, for $2.95 a plate, *jaeger schnitzel* in a heavy brown mushroom sauce. On days when they went to the Museum of Modern Art, they dined at Larré's or the Champlain, little French restaurants in midtown where they would order what Irwin laughingly calls "the blue-plate special," *coq au vin*, and were always served wine even though they were underage. After each excursion, they would get on the subway and schlep back to Queens.

EXODUS

All of Irwin and Stephan's Manhattan stories end the same way—with the long trip home—just as they all begin with getting on the bus, then the subway, spending an hour and a half in transit to the city. None of them had cars, no one drove. For the rest of America, this was the era of teenage cruising, but in New York the minimum driving age within the city limits, which included Jamaica, was eighteen, so none of them had even learner's permits. The suburbs, which their own fathers were helping to build, were a world away. Each trip into the city was like an exodus, Irwin says. They had to go.

But weekdays were a different story for my father. He did not attend Jamaica High School with my mother, Irwin, and Stephan. He went to Stuyvesant in Manhattan, one of the city's three special high schools for gifted students, devoted at the time to math, science, and engineering. Founded in 1904 as a manual trade school, Stuyvesant was located on East Fifteenth Street in those days, though it has since moved farther downtown to a pink stone and glass building overlooking the Hudson River. A recent article in the *New York Times* called it an "educational Valhalla on the Hudson, a free public school . . . [that] has been seen for nearly a century as an Ivy League dream-ticket for the poor, the rich and especially the immigrant." My father's father had gone there before him.

Stuyvesant, his friends think, was one of the first great disappointments of my father's life. It's true that it gave Lewis unprecedented access to the city, and he did have a few friends there. But it could not have suited him less. When he found out that he had gotten in, Irwin asked him how he felt about it.

"My father wants me to go there," he said.

It was a long commute by bus and subway each day; the school, at the time, was all male; his friends had to set him up with dates, and, except for Stephan and Irwin, he lost access to the social life of Jamaica Estates.

Most significant, however, was that my father loved history, literature, and art, not engineering. Though the caption under his photograph in the yearbook says that he planned to study architecture at the Illinois Institute of Technology, the only teacher he ever mentioned was Nat Werner, a distinguished German-Jewish sculptor of some reputation. Lewis loved Werner's classes and hung out in the shop classroom with him as much as possible.

I think of him alone on the train every morning and afternoon, traveling over an hour each way. Maybe to pass the time and glamorize the dull, gritty commute, he imagined himself as Holden Caulfield, riding the night train from Pencey Prep to freedom in New York. My father loved *The Catcher in the Rye*; he quoted from it and got his friends to read it, too. Holden was the ideal to which they aspired, world-weary, citywise, meeting girls for dates under the Biltmore clock. It spoke to them: disaffected teenagers, half abandoned, longing to be free of all the phonies and bullshitters. They loved Holden and they also loved Salinger's Glass stories. Seymour Glass was the antihero they were really waiting for—Jewish this time, brilliant, and doomed, too sensitive to endure the bourgeois banality of the world.

Or perhaps my father imagined he was the young man in John Dos Passos's *U.S.A.*—another series of books he loved—who *"walks by himself, fast but not fast enough, far but not far enough,"* the young man who *"must catch the last subway, the streetcar, the bus, run up the gangplanks of all the steamboats, register at all the hotels, work in the cities, answer the wantads, learn the trades, take up the jobs, live in all the boardinghouses, sleep in all the beds. One bed is not enough, one job is not enough, one life is not enough. At night, head swimming with wants, he walks by himself alone."* He thought it was one of the all-time great novels, with its combination of fiction, reportage, essays, its "Newsreels" and "Camera Eyes." It was the beginning of the American century, wide-ranging, tumultuous, sprawling out before him. Did he read *U.S.A.* on the subway, an intent boy, serious and fierce-looking, a flap of dark hair falling into his eyes? Did he hunch against the train wall and move his lips, memorizing? He quoted passages from *U.S.A.* incessantly. To this day, his voice, repeating pieces of "The House of Morgan," remains lodged in the minds of his friends. They quote it for him: *"Wars and panics on the stock exchange, / machine-gunfire and arson, / bankruptcies, warloans, / starvation, lice, cholera and typhus: / good growing weather for the House of Morgan."*

QUEST 7: RECONSTRUCTION

My discoveries of my father come in excruciating little bursts that leave me weary and overwhelmed. I spend weeks transcribing the tapes of my interview with Stephan and Irwin, rewinding every few words, struggling to decipher language from bangs and crackles and interruptions, and then more and more weeks organizing their anecdotes and stray memories into a coherent narrative. I relish the way my father is taking shape in my hands. I feel as if I'm putting Humpty Dumpty back together again. And yet the effort exhausts me. It's as if I'm going through a growth spurt, my bones stretching and grinding in their joints. I haven't even read my father's journal yet: weeks after my visit to Miriam's, it is still sitting in its blue and white plastic bag on a shelf by my desk. I don't know what I'm waiting for: something keeps me from opening it, though it hovers in my thoughts. In the meantime, I'm preparing for my MFA exam and plan to teach creative writing to undergraduates in the fall, while Stuart, who still works at the same grocery store in South Minneapolis that provided his income through college, tries to start a business as a freelance photographer's assistant. Except for an occasional mower in another yard and the distant voices of children, the house is very quiet. Sometimes I just sit at the computer in the upstairs office and stare out the window. Centered in the peaked roof, it looks out on a gnarled crab apple tree in the backyard. I've never felt that Minnesota was my home, but I do love how green it is. A view of leaves, especially in sunlight, calms me as nothing else. In the late afternoon when he's at home, Stuart usually comes upstairs with a cup of tea for me, hot and sweet with honey.

In late July, Stephan sends me a long letter, two books my father gave him, some slides of him and Lewis on a bike trip in Europe when they were seventeen, a black-and-white snapshot of my father on the trip, and the beginning of a short story and a screenplay he wrote about my father in November 1979. One of the books is Louis Kronenberger's *Company Manners: A Cultural Inquiry into American Life*, which the cover bills as "A Lively Appraisal of American Attitudes toward Art, Theater, Radio & TV, Humor, Business, Morals, Manners, Books" and is essentially a diatribe against American vulgarity and soulless materialism; the other is *The Vintage Mencken*. The former actually belonged to my father; the latter did not, but it looks exactly like a copy he did own: it has an orange, black, and yellow cover, with a picture in one corner of Mencken smoking a cigar. From the slides, I see that my father did not take up photography in Florida. He had a camera slung around his neck during the bicycle trip through Europe. A Voigtlander, or an Exacta, definitely German. "Those were the quality cameras back then," Stephan writes, "and he would have known about cameras."

The short story—more of a journal, really, handwritten, a little chaotic, an outpouring—is interesting mostly for the impact it shows my father's death to have had on Stephan. Five years later, it is still an intense preoccupation. It also reveals some of Stephan's ambivalence about my father's role as hero-adventurer, leader of their little pack. At one point, he interrupts himself to ask why he keeps calling his friend "Lewis": "I don't know why I'm using that name. I always call him Louie. Lewis is what Irwin calls him, some sign of respect which I rebelled against at a time when all our friends were known by their nicknames. Maybe it's a newfound respect for the dead."

In the letter, Stephan writes that he was quite touched by our meeting, he and Irwin both. "It not only brought up memories," he says, "but it's uncanny how much you resemble your father, in looks, in mannerisms, in voice-timbre, and as Irwin says, you didn't even know him. For us, it was as if Lewis had come back."

In August, Stephan sends another, longer letter. This one includes more slides, as well as newspaper clippings and letters from people he's contacted at Rensselaer, my father's college. He also gives me the phone numbers of other people who might know something, leads I can follow up on if I care to. He tells me that my father nicknamed him "Toad," after the character in *The Wind in the Willows*, because he was always getting carried away by his latest enthusiasms. And I'm inclined to say, Well, you are being a little obsessive, aren't you? Irwin had sent the photograph of their graduating class and a book, and that was it. I want to stay in touch with both of them, but somehow Stephan's actual desire to do so is more than I can handle. I respond to his long letters with a short note in which I try to express appreciation that sounds sincere. Instead, I sound terse and chilly. I feel, without recognizing it immediately, resentful and even a little angry. I don't want to tell Stephan to stop sending me things. But his joyful discoveries are making me feel inadequate. I do not, I think, have a suitable sense of excitement. I am not, I think, capable of it.

Why haven't I read the journal? Why didn't I tear it open the moment I came home?

Obviously, the search has inflamed Stephan: tracking down people to call, this leading to that, the puzzle pieces fitting together. But it is not *his* dead father we're talking about. I want to know, but then again, I don't. I imagine adopted children experience a similar contradiction of desires when they find their birth parents: the sense of loss at the moment of discovery is so great. For days after meeting Stephan and Irwin, I was repeatedly waylaid by an urge to call my father on the telephone. He was that real. But my father is not out there in the actual world to find. He is here, in the center of me, between surges of interest and a numbness as dense and substantial as a block of wood.

THE HOUSE ON TUDOR ROAD

The Weinbergers' two-story Tudor house had a brick front porch and half-timbered white stucco exterior. Lewis was eight when he and his family moved there from a little bungalow in Queens Village, a neighborhood they were glad to leave because, as Miriam says, it wasn't a place that welcomed Jews. Father Coughlin, the virulently anti-Semitic Roman Catholic priest, used to preach on Hillside Avenue. And once, while Morris was out of town, building defense housing in Ohio, someone stuck a hose through a basement window and flooded their new oil burner. Most people still had coal furnaces then, but Morris had been able to add this improvement to their house because he was in the construction business. It was apparently more distinction than the neighbors could bear.

Jamaica Estates, on the other hand, was a Jewish neighborhood. The older section, along Midland and Utopia Parkways, was hilly, graced by big trees and terraced gardens. It had an air of Beverly Hills about it: large Tudors and Colonials built in the 1920s. That's where the money was. Stephan, whose father was a builder, too, but an even more successful one than Morris, lived in a large house on the last, northernmost hill of this affluent area. The Weinbergers' neighborhood was appealing, but the houses were somewhat more modest, built on smaller lots. Theirs had three bedrooms, a band of shrubs framing the yard, and a landscaped garden in the back that Lewis's brother, Joe, had planted when he was living at home. It was a well-kept house, beautifully maintained. Kate was very proud of it and always stayed "*au courant*," Miriam says. Whenever a new appliance came on the market, Kate had to have one: a Sunbeam waffle iron, an electric knife, a top-of-the-line KitchenAid mixer. Miriam still uses her mother's collection in her own kitchen. The interior, as Stephan remembers it, was dark, heavily curtained, full of brown upholstered furniture and polished wood. Kate and Morris would come back from Florida once in a while, but most of that last semester of high school, spring 1956, Lewis was on his own. The house became "party central" for him and his friends on weekends.

Lewis was dating Bobby Blender, a pixyish, blue-eyed blonde who was, Stephan says, "the first master of the putdown I ever met." Lewis, clumsy and in her presence often tongue-tied, was a perfect target for her barbs. She could make him blush with a look. After escorting her home at the end of a date, he would return to Tudor Road, cold, disgruntled by the long wait for the Q44 (the only bus from her house on the Nassau County line to his in Jamaica Estates, over eighty blocks and an hour's ride away), seething with sexual desire because she refused even to kiss him, and often furious over the latest in an endless string of fights.

His friends would be waiting for him, frustrated themselves and well into his father's liquor, marking the decanters with a line so they could fill them back up with water. The girls would have all been taken home by then. Nobody was actually having sex, just doing a lot of heavy petting, and it always left everyone riled up and a little crazed. As soon as they were alone, the boys cut loose. A guy named Steve threw up in the bushes, someone pissed in the flower beds, and once, on a dare, Stephan and another boy ran around the block naked. When Irwin passed out in the bathtub, Lewis and Stephan put a portable record player on his chest and turned it on high to wake him up.

They were all tremendous drinkers. It was cool, they thought. It was sophisticated—even if it inspired them to run around the block naked. My father, true to character, had romantic notions about alcohol connecting him to history and literature: the Lost Generation sipping their way through Paris, Hemingway and his grappa, Dylan Thomas drinking himself to death in the White Horse Tavern. And who was W. C. Fields, he of the bulbous red nose, if not a witty drunk?

"I remember one time we were in Af-a-ghanistan," my father would go around repeating in Fields's whiskey drawl. "We lost our corkscrew, had to live on food and water for three weeks. Terrrrible, terrrrible . . ."

They felt on top of the world. Seventeen, about to go off to college, hot tickets who thought they were Noel Cowards or Cole Porters. During one of their late-night drinking sessions, the three boys declared themselves a triumvirate, bound together by their estrangement from their families and a sense of their own specialness. To make the triumvirate official, they gave each other nicknames, half-affectionate, half-hostile: Stephan, tall and reed-thin, became "The Gawk"; Irwin was "The Goopy Kid," which had something to do with his wanting things his two friends could afford but he could not; and my father, because of his burly presence, was dubbed "Godzilla."

They drank to one another and to themselves, then fell into various beds to sleep it off.

On the first step of the first dance of the senior prom, my father tram-
pled Bobby Blender's foot and she refused to dance with him again.
It didn't matter, though: by then he was already in love with my
mother. It's impossible to say what impression he'd made on her because my mother doesn't remember when she met him or where, but
his friends think they got together during a freak snowstorm at the
end of March or the beginning of April 1956. Lewis had just turned
seventeen and was about to graduate from Stuyvesant; my mother
would be sixteen in another month. She had been dating a cute, all-
American—"except for being Jewish"—guy named Eddie who lettered
in sports and cheerleading. He could croon Broadway show tunes and,
with my mother as his partner, dance the Lindy, overhand kicks and
all. Irwin tried this move once and ended up kicking his date in the
chest. My father, of course, could hardly hop, much less sweep a date
across the dance floor like a bebop Fred Astaire.

It was the end of their senior year, college applications had been
filed, classes were almost over. The boys, waiting for the next phase
of their lives to begin, were feeling all the power of their seniority.
On a weekday evening in March, Stephan dragged Alan Ross, another
friend from the neighborhood, into Manhattan to see Shirley Jones
in *Carousel*, which had just opened at Radio City. Stephan had a huge
crush on the blond, bright-eyed actress and didn't want to wait for
the movie to open in Queens.

"In my opinion," Stephan says to me, "you owe your life to Shirley
Jones."

When he and Alan emerged from the theater, they were met by
huge fat flakes of falling snow. It was strange and magical. Instead
of going home, they came up with the idea of riding the bus out to
my mother's house on Peck Avenue to see her and another girl who
they knew was spending the night. My mother was a good friend of
Irwin's; Stephan knew her through him. By the time they arrived
at the 210th Street and Union Turnpike bus stop, the steadily falling
snow was three or four inches deep. They shuffled through it in their
street shoes. My grandmother Rose was not particularly happy to
see them, but because they were wet through, she invited them in.

The snow kept falling on and on, and they had to spend the night. That was a Wednesday. The snow continued till Friday, dropping a record twenty-one inches. The entire New York City school system shut down for two days. Packs of kids roamed the streets, having snowball fights and sled rides. Irwin came over to my mother's to join Stephan and Alan: my grandmother remembers Irwin as the boy who wouldn't call his parents for two days to tell them where he was and finally had to be forced to go home. Sometime during the four days of this impromptu carnival, Lewis entered the picture and Irwin introduced him to my mother. She was altogether different from Bobby Blender: sophisticated, like her, but quiet, with all her intelligence showing in her eyes. (She says she was probably flirting with Irwin and that he introduced her to Lewis to put her off. Irwin laughs when I tell him this. Later, he describes her to me, almost reverently, as "stunning.") The sun came out late on Friday, dazzling and warm, and everything started to melt, creating a heady mixture of blizzard and spring.

Eddie the crooner lost out.

BEAUTY

My mother was one of the popular girls in high school, a cheerleader, a beauty, or very nearly so. She was small, only five two, and fine-boned. Her fair skin tanned easily. She had her mother's thick brown hair, bleached blond by the sun, and her father's deep-set blue eyes, a straight nose, and an oval jaw. A European face. From babyhood on, my great-aunt Anna tells me, she was so adorable, so radiant, that people gasped when she walked into a room. In high school, her friends would come around at all hours, my grandmother says. "Téresa Olíver's secretary," my grandfather, in his heaviest Spanish accent, liked to quip when he answered the phone. I have trouble imagining her as vivacious, but I'm told she was.

"Sophisticated" my father's friends say, although not Most Sophisticated. That honor went to Bobby Blender. But if Bobby Blender was Most Sophisticated, my mother was Most Bohemian, a better word for her still. She wore South American belts and exotic-looking jewelry, and had an aura of worldliness about her that she got from her parents. And yet my mother didn't look bohemian in the photographs of her in high school: she looked like the girl who learned to sew in home ec and turned herself out for family gatherings in fashionable faux Chanel suits.

EXERCISE I: TESSIE

Her beauty amazed him, how small she was and lithe, how perfect her legs were, how lovely her face, but not only that: the way she dressed, with that artistic flare, the way she held her head, so effortlessly poised on her neck, the way she ate, each bite traveling an exact path from plate to mouth—mesmerizing. She could take his breath away just by the way she cut a veal chop. She was so quiet, and yet so smart. Tessie had these sculptural eyes, like a Modigliani. (Everyone at school called her Terry, but her mother and aunts called her Tessie, and he liked that better.) Her eyes shone when he talked, and she never interrupted, even though she probably knew more about art and politics than he did. She was like a Siamese cat: he was never exactly sure what she was thinking, but he imagined it being profound. There'd never been a classier girl. Obviously, she got that from her parents—he wished his own family could be as dashing. His father knew how to manage the Republican ward bosses so he could build houses on Long Island. But her father knew artists like Moses Soyer and Rufino Tamayo, and her grandfather was such a big philanthropist that he was invited to museum openings and major political events all the time.

And then there was her mother. His own mother was a smart woman whom he respected, but to her, being modern meant buying the latest home appliance. Tessie's mother couldn't care less about that stuff. The women in her household had raging arguments over cocktails about Khrushchev or the Montgomery bus boycott or what would happen between Israel and Egypt now that Nasser had been elected president. He was impressed by her mother's passion, by her ability to shred any argument to pieces.

She's a bit of all right, Tess is, he thought. He knew no higher accolade than that.

FIRST DATE

On their first date, my father took my mother to see *The Last Days of Hitler*. She remembers that they got in free because it was the second show and no one was in the box office.

"It seemed auspicious," my mother says.

JEWISH 2

I wonder if, meeting my father for the first time, I would notice how Jewish he seemed. I wonder how he carried that identity, inside himself and out. When his friends talk about my father, they refer to his youthful fascination with all things English and German. They talk about how his favorite expression, his highest praise for a meal, a movie, or a fine piece of art, was the peculiar Briticism "a bit of all right." And yet his mother came from an Orthodox family and was observant herself. My father was sent to Hebrew school and, like most Jewish boys, religious or not, he was bar mitzvahed. His family kept the dietary laws, including separate plates, separate pots, and separate dishtowels. In fact, it wasn't until he was nearly ten that his parents broke kosher for the first time, and then only outside the home, after Morris and Kate moved into the house that Morris had built in Jamaica Estates. (Once a week, four or five other couples from the neighborhood used to meet at Periwinkles, a seafood restaurant on Hillside Avenue. This was new for my grandparents, who rarely went out because it was hard to keep kosher in restaurants. Week after week, they would order broiled fish, a neutral dish, while everyone else ate lobster — strictly forbidden. At the end of the meal, they all would split the bill. After a few weeks, my grandfather decided that he wasn't paying for everyone else's lobster while he ate plain fish: he and my grandmother would have lobster, too. I don't know if she protested, but she ate the lobster — and loved it. "She discovered," Miriam says, "a whole new world.") It's hard, however, to fit this information about the Weinbergers into any image I've formed of my father. Miriam says that he was probably indifferent to religion—just like his brother, Joe. But Judaism is not based on the fiery rhetoric of damnation. Secular Jews don't seem to carry the vestiges of their religious childhoods with the soul-seared unease of apostate Catholics and fundamentalists.

I doubt my father thought of his identity in terms of the Holocaust, either, though that history is usually integral to contemporary Jewish self-conception. His brother's wife, who was Belgian, had survived the war in hiding, but Lewis knew no one personally who had been killed. When he and Stephan made plans to take a youth hostel trip together the summer after high school graduation, they didn't have any qualms about including Germany on their itinerary. Nor, apparently, did their parents object to their plans, though both of their fathers were avid supporters of the new state of Israel, and Stephan's father refused, then and for the next thirty years, to buy any German-made products. But the linkage between the Holocaust and the Jewish self had not yet been formulated (wouldn't begin to be formulated until after the Eichmann trial in 1961), and, like many assimilated Jews, the boys thought of themselves first and foremost as Americans.

For Stephan and Irwin, Jewishness, at least on a casual day-to-day basis, is a way of speaking, a way of telling jokes, a way of sighing or arguing or complaining ("utzing"); it is also a consciousness of certain exclusions and pretensions—like Eddie the crooner who was an athletic all-American type "except for being Jewish." Jewishness permeates everything. Even my mother, I realize, falls unconsciously into this way of viewing the world when she talks about that period in her life. Describing David Levine, my father's daredevil friend from college whom Irwin heard had died flying as a mercenary in Africa, she says that he looked Waspy, like a movie star, a prince of the world, and even though he was Jewish, there "was nothing Jewish about this guy."

MEDIUMS OF EXCHANGE

I'm afraid that if I don't respond to Stephan's overtures, he might give up and go away. I spend a week writing a long letter to him, similar in length and breadth to those he has sent me. I tell him a little about my life with my mother. I tell him about my life now: my husband and my dog, my house in the suburbs, my graduate program. I send him a little piece of the book I am writing about my father. And then we start to send e-mails back and forth.

Subject: Orson Welles
From: Stephan Klein
To: Anna Cypra Oliver-Skoven
Date: 30 Jan 96 9:29 p.m.

In some way that I can't exactly express Lewis reminds me of Orson Welles. In a way they looked alike with the same expressions and posture. Not the fat Orson Welles of later life, but the brilliant young director and actor who never made a film before he made maybe the best film ever directed.

EXERCISE 2: EUROPE, SUMMER 1956

Eighteen hours to London, a stop in Gander, Newfoundland, and another in Shannon, Ireland: Stephan and my father imagined their journey as a creeping white line like in the movies, the background buzz of the propellers a reminder to the audience that the characters were traveling vast distances. They crossed the ocean on a Flying Tiger Line DC-6 used (during the war, they imagined) for hauling cargo. Seventeen, just graduated from high school, and on their way to college, neither of them had ever been to Europe. In fact, it was so unusual for American high school students to go abroad that when they applied American Youth Hostels didn't know what to do with them. They were proud to be anomalies, of course, even if it meant that they were tossed among an oddball collection of travelers, most of whom were college age or older.

Europe! At last, the real thing after years of rehearsing at Luchow's and Café Geiger. Europe seemed more real to them than America, more substantial. America was plastics and tail fins and television. Europe was tweeds and round spectacles, discoursing on Kant at outdoor cafés.

Europe was also the war. As children, they'd experienced it vicariously through movies, games, war toys, and comic books; now they were on the actual streets where it had been fought. Evidence of the devastation was everywhere. In London, the buildings around Saint Paul's Cathedral were bombed flat. Rubble was still being carted away. Every side of the massive edifice, miraculously spared, was a construction site. Germany, of course, was much worse. On some streets in Munich, only the facades of the nineteenth-century apartment houses were still standing—the boys could see the sky through blackened windows.

Subject: Trips Across the Surrealistic Landscape
From: Stephan Klein
To: Anna Cypra Oliver-Skoven
Date: 18 Feb 96 10:17 a.m.

It was the summer of 1956, just eleven years after WWII. Lewis and I had decided it would be fun to hitch back from Bruges. So we stood at the edge of town with a sign saying Antwerp—I think it was Antwerp—and our thumbs pointing in that direction. After two boring hours we were about to give up when a guy pulled over in one of those small cars that Renault or Fiat used to build during the war because gasoline and metal were so expensive. He spoke no English but mo-

tioned for us to get in the back which, we discovered, was piled to the roof with false limbs!
Arms, legs, ankles, hands, feet, elbows, you
name it. He was a traveling salesman for body
replacements. So we squeezed ourselves among all
the body parts and proceeded on our way embraced
by strange arms and legs. As we entered the city
and drove through residential areas, he would
screech to a stop every time he saw someone on
the sidewalk who had a missing body part. (There
were quite a few.) Then he would frantically
rummage through the pile in the back seat, pull
out a couple of legs or arms, and run out after
the person to try and sell . . . his merchan-
dise. We thought it was all very funny. Well, we
were only seventeen. . . .

If my father, who loved modern
European history more than anything, was excited to see where the
bombs had fallen, Stephan, for his
part, had just finished reading *An-
napurna* by Maurice Herzog and had
not stopped talking about it. Pic-
turing the crags and hamlets of Hem-

ingway's Alps, he announced that the bike trip would not be complete
without an assault on a mountain. The prospect of doing something
so esoteric and possibly dangerous thrilled my father, and he happily
agreed that as soon as they reached Chamonix in the French Alps,
where Herzog was mayor, they would go climbing.

Chamonix was a legendary ski town, and its mountains were
spectacular, so famous that they'd heard tales about them recounted
around lodge tables at Stowe. They couldn't wait. The Mont Blanc
massif was 15,770 feet of sheer rock and glacial ice. As kids, my father
and Irwin spent hours poring over Richard Halliburton's *Book of Marvels*, wondering if there were any adventures left in the world for
them. They loved the description of George Mallory's climb up Ever-

est in the early 1920s, and the opening salvo of Halliburton's chapter "The Top of the World": "*Do you like to climb? If you had an apple tree in your back yard, would you climb to the highest branch for the biggest apple? Or would you just stay on the ground and knock it down with a rock? And what about hills and mountains? Does a mountain, with a glorious view from the summit, offer you a challenge? Or would you rather sit on the front porch, down in the valley, and play casino?*"

When the boys reached Chamonix, they were not disappointed, either in the town, with its cobbled streets and mansard roofs, or in the mountain itself: the great blunt peak, capped in snow, was more stunning than they could have possibly imagined. As soon as they arrived, they headed for one of the gear shops to rent crampons and ice picks. A guide service promised to produce a reputable person to take them across the Vallée Blanche in the morning. Long after lights out that night, they hunkered down on their narrow beds in the youth hostel, whispering about what they should wear, how to cull just the right combination of practicality and insouciant mountain glamour from the meager collection of clothes in their saddlebags.

My father, eager as any actor to throw himself into a role, particularly as swashbuckling hero, insisted that as soon as they reached a village with some decent shops, they would outfit themselves in lederhosen, stag horn–decorated suspenders, and Alpine hats with chamois goat tails thrust through the felt—the clothes that all the European boys were wearing, as well as the peasant men in the villages. No more having to make do; besides, they wanted to look cool, to distinguish themselves from the horde of "ugly Americans" in Bermuda shorts who had flooded the Continent since the end of the war. A chamois tail was the badge of an Alpine marksman—though, of course, a marksman usually shot his own animal. Swiss and Tyrolean peasants, my father told Stephan, traditionally handed down each pair of lederhosen to the next generation, father to son. This knowledge delighted him. To complete the picture of himself in the outfit, he decided to start growing a mustache and goatee right away.

In the morning, they rushed over to the gear shop where the guide was supposed to meet them. From a long way off, they could see him coming: a wiry little man in a black sweater and black cap with ropes slung across his chest, a rucksack dangling from one shoulder. They glanced at each other, eyebrows raised. He must have been at least sixty-five or seventy, and had a face so wizened it looked like beef jerky. They curved their lips into pleasant smiles as the man, exposing teeth stained a nasty yellow-brown by tobacco, called out, "*Bonjour, messieurs,*" but they could hardly keep their cynicism from showing. They wanted a grand adventure, to climb the mountain, as Mallory so memorably declared, "because it's there," and here was a creature who looked as if he could barely walk down the street, much less lead them on a miles-long trek through ice columns and crevasses at twelve thousand feet.

"*Belle promenade, oui?*" the old man said, pointing at the red car of the téléphérique, whose path was so steep and high that they could not see the black line of the cable against the gray rock at the top. "*Belle promenade.*" They nodded back, but now they were not only disappointed, they were annoyed. What did he mean, "Lovely walk"? Their French was minimal, but that much they did understand. They didn't want a "lovely walk"; they wanted to conquer a mountain. Obviously the service hadn't taken their request seriously. The guide shuffled ahead of them in the direction of the cable car, ropes swinging, back hunched under the weight of his pack, while they hesitated. "This guy is on the edge of death," my father said, speaking softly out of one side of his mouth. "You watch," Stephan replied. "We're going to wind up carrying this old goat down the mountain."

The valley swooped out below them as the téléphérique climbed straight into the sun. The car made a last great surge over the rock face, then slowed and bumped to a halt at the top. The guide strode out even before the door had slid completely open, and they followed him down a slope onto the snow-covered Vallée Blanche. They had hoped to ascend Mont Blanc itself, but once they listed their past mountain climbing experience for the guide service (Mount Hood in Oregon for Stephan, none for my father), that didn't seem to be an option. The guide jabbed a finger toward a mountain, and, flashing his stained brown teeth, said again, "*Belle promenade, belle promenade,*" then set off at an astonishingly brisk pace. The boys had no time to take in the dazzling eruption of peaks all around them before they were rushing to catch up with him. Sweating under too many layers of clothing and breathing hard from the altitude—and perhaps because of all the cigarettes they'd smoked since the age of fourteen—they had to admit that, all right, maybe they *had* underestimated their guide a little.

They stopped for lunch at a *refugio*, where the guide ate five plates of spaghetti that they had to pay for. Finally, just when they thought he'd never finish, he wiped his chin, drained the last of the wine, and began to gather his gear. "*Belle promenade,*" he said again, "*belle promenade,*" and off they went to test their true mettle on the most awesome part of the route: the *Mer de Glace*, Sea of Ice, a long glacial floe just below the imperious face of Mont Blanc. Here was where they could get into trouble, swept into a crevasse like Whymper's party on the Matterhorn, lost forever behind a sudden cloud like Mallory and Andrew "Sandy" Irvine on the slopes of Everest in 1924. They adjusted the crampons on their shoes and took their picks in hand, psyched up for the dangerous traverse. The guide hiked out on the floe as if it were asphalt. The boys were peeved, but they didn't have much time to think about it: they had to walk across crevasses and narrow bridges of ice with small precise steps. Even the guide took it seriously enough to rope them all together. They descended the nearly vertical face of the

ice fall, fingers and toes dug into rubbly chunks of ice, each step an exhilarating challenge and an agony. At the bottom, the guide recoiled the rope and slung it across his chest, then set off again on the long hike down the frozen sea of the glacier. The sun was brutal, pounding down on them, and their waists were thick with the clothing they had shed. Toward the bottom, the snow grew deeper and deeper and, as the end of the day neared, it began to soften. They sank at every step. If they stood still for more than a second, their calves would start to jig up and down, and, standing or moving, their thighs were burning. The guide, meanwhile, just marched ahead. Every so often, he'd stop and shout back at them, "*Belle promenade! Belle promenade!*" The boys waved feeble hands in response.

When the guide turned his back again, they flipped him the bird. "*Belle promenade* to you, buddy," my father said, and the friends both laughed and struggled onward.

Subject: Your Father's Voice
From: Stephan Klein
To: Anna Cypra Oliver-Skoven
Date: 01 Feb 96 10:13 p.m.

I can hear your father's voice so clearly in my memory. I wish I could hook a hose tap up to my head and pour some of it into yours.

MEDIUMS OF EXCHANGE 2

I love the stories he tells me. I love that he is willing to tell them, and I love the rich detail of his memory. But when Stephan begins to run out of stories and memorabilia, I write that I would like to know him, through, but beyond, my father.

RAPTURE

As a child, I was always adventurous. Tough, outspoken, a tomboy, the leader of my pack of friends: always Tom Sawyer, always Jaclyn Smith when we played "Charlie's Angels," always the director and lead when, at age ten, we staged scenes from *The Muppet Movie*. I was the first to climb trees, the first to stick the Barbies together and make them screw. We were a television generation, even there, in Taos, in Talpa, even without a television set most of those years. We were imaginative, but we gleaned fewer scenarios from books than my father and his friends did. I told the other kids how to act, what to say. I was bossy. Even with adults, I was a wiseass, a natural authority. But that was before Wayne died, before my mother married and divorced Curtis, before she committed herself to the church. As I grew older, I became quieter, more serious, more and more fearful. My fear of death, in particular, was so great that I sometimes spoke aloud of suicide. My father had given me permission.

I never made a plan or seriously considered doing it, but I could understand its appeal: you could choose the date and the hour. You could stop walking around with your shoulders hunched, waiting to be struck from behind.

The belief in an afterlife is supposed to release people from the fear of death. Mine only increased the anxiety. My church talked constantly about the imminent return of Christ. It had been drilled into me: two thousand years and only a matter of days now. The rapture. The new heaven and the new earth, which would cause the old heaven and the old earth to pass away. I was meant to long for that day. "To live is Christ, to die is gain," Saint Paul says. But I just longed to live my life. Paradoxically, I entertained the idea of killing myself only because I was so afraid to die.

Subject: "Fluttering Heart"
From: Stephan Klein
To: Anna Cypra Oliver-Skoven
Date: 19 Feb 96 7:40 p.m.

Re: the memory of Gersh about the Apparition and Irwin's comment at Miriam's house. I need to say that I don't agree with Irwin. I have had times in my life when I have sensed spiritual forces or presences or feelings that are outside conscious perception of the senses. I don't discard, a priori, parapsychological experiences. I think that modern medicine has done a lot to shut down these possibilities because they don't fit neatly into the positivist paradigm. I don't know Gersh. I wasn't there, either at his telling the tale or when it happened. I just wanted you to know that my silence when Irwin spoke was not an agreement with what he said. Although I know he spoke out of caring about you.

SCENE FROM A MOVIE SHOWN IN CHURCH 2

It was September, a beautiful autumn day. I was sixteen and had just arrived home from school. I crossed the dirt yard to our front door. The door was open, but the screen door was closed to keep out the flies. The house was quiet.

"Hello," I called.

No answer. I walked across the enclosed porch and stepped up into the living room. The house was small, even with the porch. The interior was dark, cool. The walls were thick, unpainted adobe. Particles of dust floated in the sunlight streaming through the large rear window. Through it I could see the moody peaks of Taos Mountain across the valley.

"Mom?" I called. The bedroom doors stood open. The bathroom door was open as well. The house was empty, but the oven was on. A half-rolled pie crust lay on the kitchen table. Flour dusted the surface.

And then I knew. My mother was gone. My mother had been raptured. Despite accepting Jesus into my heart, I'd been left behind.

I stood in the middle of the living room, my backpack dangling from my hand. Before I could decide what to do, my mother banged through the screen door. In her hands were several large zucchini from the garden. It took minutes for the frozen panic in my chest to thaw. Everyone who grew up in my denomination could tell a similar tale. We all called it "A Rapture Scare."

SOME THINGS I'D TELL YOU IF I HAD THE CHANCE 2

During each of our annual visits to see Grandma Rose and Grandpa Juan, we'd trek into the city to a museum of some sort. Mom liked to do that. We saw Whistler, Matisse, Monet, Rousseau. We went to the ballet, too, but Mom stopped going with us after she was reborn because the men's costumes made their genitals protrude. And some acrobatic dance group from Russia completed an otherwise cheery program at Radio City with a number set in a dark forest swirling with mist, body paint on half-naked limbs, wild cavorting, beating drums. I could feel Mom's whole body tightening, synapse by synapse. The scene was demonic; they were dancing in ecstasy, calling up spirits. She left with a violent lunge in the middle of it. I felt like crying. Should I go too? But she didn't make us walk out with her. She didn't tug at our elbows and say, Come on, we're going now. She just walked out by herself, leaving us sitting there with Grandma. I sat through to the end, but the whole evening was ruined.

Everything was like that, really. In movies, before she pretty much stopped going or I refused to go with her, she would hiss out loud sometimes. During sex scenes, usually. We'd pick some tame thing that everyone thought was going to be safe, and then suddenly the characters would be humping on the couch. The moment the action headed in that direction, I'd clench up. She would make a long, loud ss-ssss sound like a large tire going flat, and I would want to slide under my chair and curl up among the drifts of popcorn and Reese's wrappers. She'd glance over at me, a provocative little smile on her lips, to see how I was taking it. But she never made us walk out with her.

It was a relief when she finally let us go places by ourselves. She never asked me what movies I was seeing with my friends. Nor did she review, as other Christian mothers did, my class book lists to tell me what I could or could not read in school. Maybe her love of literature was too great to deny me, or maybe she thought she could rely on me to police myself. Whatever her motives, I did not take chances. I hid Hermann Hesse's Siddhartha and didn't tell her we were watching such decadent classics as The Graduate and Cabaret in Humanities. You have to understand how pervasive it was. It wasn't just sex or religion. Merlin the Magician, Gandalf the Wizard, shapeshifters, elves, trolls, witches, fairy godmothers, ghosts, leprechauns, soothsayers, genii, crystal balls, potions, magic amulets, magic curses, magic wishes, creatures of myth such as fauns, minotaurs, dryads and naiads, serpent-tailed dragons, Mickey Mouse as the sorcerer's apprentice. All the wild creatures of imagination: minions of the devil, every one.

I guess I'm being a bit of a tattletale: Mom did this. Mom did that. But then, if you hadn't killed yourself, she might never have become a Christian. Certainly not such a fanatical one. I used to say that to her, back in high school, when I was a believer. Sometimes, she'd get upset and say how sorry she was that she left you, how sorry she was that everything turned out the way it did.

And I'd tell her, "But Mom, if he hadn't died, we might never have come to the Lord."

Consulting the Orders

Realization is Realization in Form, which means a nature. You realize that something has a certain nature. A school has a certain nature, and in making a school the consultation and approval of nature are absolutely necessary. In such a consultation you can discover the Order of water, the Order of wind, the Order of light, the Order of certain materials. If you think of brick, and you're consulting the Orders, you consider the nature of brick. You say to brick, "What do you want, brick?" Brick says to you, "I like an arch." If you say to brick, "Arches are expensive, and I can use a concrete lintel over an opening. What do you think of that, brick?" Brick says, "I like an arch."

. . . . You can have the same conversation with concrete, with paper or papier-mâché, or with plastic, or marble, or any material. The beauty of what you create comes if you honor the material for what it really is. Never use it in a subsidiary way so as to make the material wait for the next person to come along and honor its character.

— Louis I. Kahn, *Between Silence and Light*

WHAT BOBBY BLENDER REMEMBERS
"He was not like other boys.
"We were a terribly boring generation, just on the verge of Vietnam. Middle-class kids. Post–World War. Post-Beat. America was a pretty dull place in the fifties. Eisenhower's America. And we were

terribly desirous of being cultured, well read. We were all so affected, with no real substance. We did quite a lot of posing, and underneath was just childishness.

"Lewis was very smart, with this quirky mind. Upper-middle-class Jewish kids wanted to be snazzily smart, and he was. There was a cult of being smart. Lewis had been to museums, to Europe. He was much more sophisticated than the rest of us—a master of sophistication. He went to MoMA every Saturday of senior year. It helped that he went to school in Manhattan. 'Our man in Manhattan,' we used to call him. He brought the news home. It's hard to say, though, how much was artifice and how much was true learnedness.

"His parents, a lot of our parents, represented an American success story. The question is, what happened to the next generation? We once wished we were in Paris, living in a garret. But ultimately, most of us became terribly conventional."

SUCCESS STORY

In 1913, when my mother's grandfather Nathan first arrived in the United States, he couldn't spare a nickel to ride the trolley to work every day, but to me, born over a half-century later, it seemed as if our family had always

Mahopac, 1943

been rich. Nathan came to America penniless, but he didn't stay penniless for long. He had more than immigrant chutzpah: he had arrogance. The only reason he couldn't be president of the United States, he used to tell his wife and children, was because he was an immigrant born in Poland. He could, however, become a millionaire. And he did, manufacturing such things as stationery and adhesive tape, though it took him ten years longer than he promised: he reached his goal at fifty instead of forty years old. An American success story.

That success enabled Nathan's adult children to pursue art and politics and seductive bohemianism instead of concentrating all their energy on making a living. Rose got a degree in zoology, then danced for a while with a modern troupe. She met her future husband, Juan, at a Greenwich Village party and, after announcing to her parents that they had gone down to city hall and gotten married, lived with him in a walkup on Bank Street. She also joined the Communist Party in the early 1930s, went to rallies, held meetings in her home.

Those were heady days, but, in the end, the compulsion to be responsible parents and wage earners, to live in the center rather than on the fringe, got the better of them. During the early years of their life together, Rose worked in a chemistry lab in New Jersey, and Juan, a talented artist, exhibited in galleries on Fifth Avenue and in Greenwich Village, as well as at the Corcoran in Washington, D.C. But then they had children, and just as his work was becoming known in New York, Juan decided to go into his father-in-law's business. Rose, despite her left-wing politics and ardent feminism, stayed home after the birth of my uncle John, her second child. Only after her children were grown did she go back to work. She completed a Ph.D. in psychology at the age of sixty-three, converted my mother's bedroom in their house in Queens into a waiting room, John's into an office, and started a therapy practice.

My mother grew up confused about class. She spent summers with her parents and grandparents on Lake Mahopac. She lived in a nice house and wore nice clothes. And yet she was asked by her mother to identify with the working class, to feel solidarity with them. She was to have working-class friends, like the super's "wild kids" in their apartment house in Brooklyn, and, she says, "pretend to be just like them." But by the time my mother was ready for college, she had become more and more aware of the discrepancy between what her mother and her mother's friends *said* they believed and the way they actually lived.

Communist politics and capitalist economics: mixed messages she eventually came to resent.

Senior Prom, Hotel Biltmore, 1956: front row, from right, Bobby Blender, my father; second row, second from right, my mother, her date, Ernie Kirschman, directly behind; second row, from left, Stephan, his date Brenda, Irwin's date Anita, and Irwin.

PHOTO COURTESY OF BOBBY BLENDER.

COLLEGE

In the fall of 1956, following their adventure in Europe, my father started school at Rensselaer Polytechnic Institute, and Stephan went to Cornell, where, believing that the point of education was to acquire a job skill, he planned to major in civil engineering but transferred almost immediately into architecture, which was still practical but appealed more to his artistic side. Irwin studied history at Columbia. The three of them spent a weekend together in Stephan's dorm room, getting drunk and writing philosophical declarations on the order of "'God is dead' — Nietzsche, 'Nietzsche is dead' — God" on butcher paper deep into the night. Stephan also remembers visiting a whorehouse on Green Street in Troy with my father and his RPI frat buddies. After their first year, however, each immersed himself in activities on his own campus. The old friends saw less and less of one another.

BACK IN BUSINESS

After Lewis went to college, his parents sold the Queens house and moved to Florida. But Morris didn't go there with the intention of continuing his work as a builder; Kate suffered from arthritis, and they thought the warmer climate would benefit her. It wasn't until after they settled in that Morris, ostensibly retired, decided to build a couple of apartment houses on Biscayne Bay off the Seventy-ninth Street Causeway in Miami. He might have been bored or just wanted to keep his hand in the business, but he did it mostly because Kate prodded him.

His older son, Joe, meanwhile, had been working on a tunnel excavation project for the Delaware River Aqueduct, and living in Roscoe, New York, a bleak little town on the edge of the Catskills that his wife was desperate to escape. He followed Morris to Florida as soon as his father broke ground for a residential development called Pickwick. Suddenly Morris, with Joe in tow, was back in business.

GUIDANCE COUNSELORS

At my aunt Miriam's house, I ask Stephan and Irwin if they found it surprising that my father had gone into architecture rather than history or even literature. I would not have asked this question if not for a conversation I'd had with Miriam earlier in the day. She said that a professor at RPI had encouraged my father to get a master's degree in history, instead of continuing in architecture, the first I'd heard that anybody thought my father might have been in the wrong field.

"I thought that architecture was a big, big mistake," Irwin says. "And he hated it."

"He should have been a professor," Stephan says, "and written books on history."

"He hated RPI."

"Really?" I ask. I have always rolled that name so proudly off my tongue: *Rensselaer Polytechnic Institute.*

He went into architecture, they tell me, because his brother had gone to the Illinois Institute of Technology to study it.

"He had been inspired," Miriam said, "to study architecture by his older brother."

"I mean, Lewis knew everything about architecture," Stephan says. "He'd even read Henry-Russell Hitchcock—not the usual thing for a high school student."

I try not to look quizzical. I have no idea who Henry-Russell Hitchcock is. I have never given any thought to architecture. Buildings are just there. Natural. Inevitable. What would a skyscraper look like if not a glass box? I had never heard of Mies van der Rohe, either, until my mother mentioned that he was one of my father's favorite architects.

"But he shouldn't have been an architect," Stephan says, "and I don't think he was ever very . . ."

Very good, he was going to say. *I don't think he was ever very good.*

"He painted this kind of picture of the romance of American architecture," Stephan continues. "In some ways I owe the fact that I'm an architect to him, because I was going to be an engineer."

The romance of American architecture: from which I gather that my father loved the notion of architecture, not architecture itself. A notion he gleaned from books, not from his hand on the drawing board, not from pacing a landscape. Though maybe that is too sweeping: Lewis did spend a lot of time walking through the city with my mother, looking at buildings.

"He loved architecture," Stephan says, "but that doesn't mean he should have been an architect. An architectural historian, yes. That would have made sense. A Lewis Mumford, a Charles Jencks."

My father had not wanted to go to RPI. He wanted to go to the Illinois Institute of Technology, partly because Mies was the dean there at the time, and partly because that was where his brother had gone. Lewis idolized Joe; at the same time, his friends think he was locked in competition with him. When Lewis was nine, his brother came home from Chicago, having flunked out after only two semesters; they shared a room in the house on Tudor Road for a while. Miriam told me that it had always been important to Morris and Kate that their children—or at least the boys—do well in school. If they came home with poor grades, there was hell to pay. Joe, who was only seventeen when he left for IIT, had never been away from home before and all his roommates turned out to be veterans of World War II: years older, much wiser, much more experienced than he. Joe wound up spending much of his time at school partying with them instead of studying.

Lewis, then, would succeed where Joe failed, thereby winning his parents' respect and approval. But my father got a New York State Regents scholarship, worth several hundred dollars, and Morris insisted he go to RPI.

"Even though they had enough money—" Irwin says.

"Yeah," Stephan says.

"To send him anywhere."

Why was it so important to have an architect in the family anyway? So my grandfather could create a Weinberger and Sons of the building trades? Was this dream, a version of which came to fruition in the Florida development, my grandfather's dream from the beginning? When Miriam told me about the professor who had suggested that my father study history, I asked her if my grandfather discouraged him. It was becoming obvious that my grandfather had a lot to say about my father's choices (and it was the fifties, after all, when parents directed their children's lives a good deal more than they do now). But she surprised me by saying that my grandfather had *wanted* Lewis to get a graduate degree of some kind, and my father refused.

"*Morris?*" Irwin exclaims, when I tell him and Stephan.

"I'd always heard it differently," Stephan says. "That Morris had no sensitivity whatsoever to your father's intellectual values."

"Lewis wasn't admitted to RPI," my grandmother Rose tells me later. "Did you know that? He was admitted to IIT, but not RPI. So Kate went up to RPI and talked to them. She said that he'd lose his Regents scholarship if he went out of state, so they finally said okay."

"Your father's parents," my mother says, violating her own moratorium on the past, "didn't want him to go to IIT because they felt he was only doing it to follow in his brother's footsteps. 'Let him be him,' his parents said, 'you be you.'" I can hear the possessiveness in her voice. She wants to claim some of my father's history back from Stephan and Irwin. Morris was her father-in-law. What do they know?

Lewis can't, however, have simply wished to emulate his older brother because Joe himself had not wanted to be an architect: he had wanted to be a scientist or a doctor and went into architecture only because his father decided he should. Morris wanted Joe to design houses for his development projects, and he was the one who wrote away for information about schools. And as Stephan points out, if the scholarship was really the issue, there were other colleges in New York.

"Lewis wanted to transfer to a liberal arts college," my grandmother says. "I know that. He felt he was in the wrong place. But Morris said, 'You started there, you finish.'"

"It was a different time," Miriam says. "You didn't do all this transferring from school to school like you do today."

I don't remind her that my mother had transferred from Barnard to Skidmore and back to Barnard again.

He could have changed his path, of course. He could have gone to graduate school, as his friends did, later on, before he had children, before he committed himself to his father's business in Florida. Or even afterward. What aspirations or exhaustions prevented him from choosing a path that everyone agrees would have made the most sense for him?

"You be you."

Easy enough, assuming you know who "you" is.

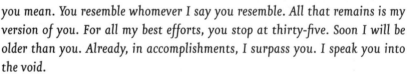

VENTRILOQUISM

"You" is an affectation. I do not think you are there. I don't converse with you in my head. I don't even dream you.

"You" is a construct. Pure Imago. Pure Word. The ideal Father. You mean what I make you mean. You resemble whomever I say you resemble. All that remains is my version of you. For all my best efforts, you stop at thirty-five. Soon I will be older than you. Already, in accomplishments, I surpass you. I speak you into the void.

But this "you" is not even my you. The images, the memories, sometimes the exact words I use to describe you, all belong to other people. You are as much Stephan's Lewis as "my father." My "you" is nothing but a plagiarism. That's all you are. A ripped-off citation. A soup of quotations.

I'm so pissed off at you, Lewis, I could spit nails.

Subject: Is There Telos in the Universe?
From: Stephan Klein
To: Anna Cypra Oliver-Skoven
Date: 26 Feb 96 6:39 a.m.

As I was thinking about you Sunday morning driving into East Hampton, lo and behold on the
radio there was an interview with Paul Robeson
so fresh that I thought he was still alive. That
Jack o' Diamonds song your father was forever
singing came from a Paul Robeson record. We
began all this with 'What music did he like?'
What a strange question to start with. What
music do you like?

Subject: John Lennon Who?
From: Anna Cypra Oliver-Skoven
To: Stephan Klein
Date: 26 Feb 96 8:02 a.m.

I've only started listening to music, other than
classical, which my husband likes, in the last
couple of years. When I was a kid, we listened
to country music mostly, so I have a soft spot
for old Waylon Jennings, Jessie Colter, Tom T.
Hall, kind of stuff (it makes me think of shooting pool in smoky redneck bars and conning
Shirley Temples off sleazy old guys). Just to
give you an idea: I was twelve when John Lennon
got shot, and this friend of mine came up to me,
crying. 'Isn't it terrible,' she said, 'John
Lennon got shot.' I looked at her, and asked,
'John Lennon who?' In high school, Peter had a
small stereo and played the Police, David Bowie,
U2, a lot. But when he left for college, the
music left with him. Now I like anything mopey.
Mopey, that's what I love.

On a gray August afternoon a month after Miriam gives it to me, when I'm feeling mopey and blue, I pull out my father's journal. The blue and white plastic bag has the words OCEANIC ARTS written across it. I sit on the couch in the family room of my house with the journal on my knees. It isn't raining, but it's dark enough to turn on a lamp. The dog slides as close to the couch as she can, shaking a little. She hates storms. I can't hear any thunder yet, but the air is humming.

I examine the journal carefully before reading the words. I want to absorb its smell, texture, the black scritch-scratch of my father's handwriting. I take notes. Cobwebs and desiccated spiders are flattened like dried flowers between the pages. Dirt hazes the yellow cover. Humidity or the dampness of age has smeared the dye from the cover across the first page. The top left corner is torn from the spiral and creased back on itself. I find a spider body in the fold.

STRATHMORE SHELBURNE SKETCH, it says. "An economical general-purpose sketch. 9 x 12, 100 sheets." I count the pages. The journal contains sixty-seven of a hundred. Where are the rest?

A sudden clap of thunder rattles the storm drains. The windows turn dark with rain.

It's easy at first. The first dozen pages are pencil sketches of furniture. New Mexico–style couches: boxy, benchlike, hard-looking, a few with blanket-striped cushions, others with ornamental carvings across the back, followed by a full page of curved-in chairs that make me think the man who drew them was longing to be cradled.

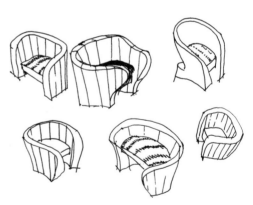

I want it to register with me, to sink in: the object I now hold, my father once held. I try to feel the pencil sketches in my bones: a sailboat, a spiral with pennant flying, a doodle of lines and arrows and circles on the yellow cover, figures totaling 1,680 and 1,200 and 11.20, all from my father's hand. (The same figures—1,680, 1,200, multiplied, subtracted—fill the last page, too. And the same numbers are found again on a page in the middle. A mantra of numbers. A subtle frenzy.)

And then I turn the page and read the first words: *If I had been wiser there might have been a house / Could it have been a calm loving house? / Could we have been more loving?*

That's the end of my writerly composure. I start to cry. I remember a conversation I had with my mother shortly after my visit to Gersh about how much anger had developed between them, how little love they expressed toward each other by the end, how much she had wanted a loving house. I want to tell her that he felt as she did, that he understood the loss, although in a way this realization makes their history seem all the more painful. But she hasn't asked me about the journal. She believes in forgive and forget, especially forget.

The rain comes down in sheets, crashing to the ground like tin torn loose. The shaking dog squeezes herself between the couch and the backs of my knees.

I read the journal through to the end. His words, every line, every phrase, the poems in which he expresses himself beautifully (*Every moment of your / descending form,* he writes of an unnamed woman, *is the love I wanted*) are loaded with immense pain. He records only one date: Saturday, March 2. He died on April 9. It is not just his journal, I discover, but the journal he kept in the months before he died, right up to the end.

I cry and cry.

Subject: All the Way to the Jail, Boys
From: Stephan Klein
To: Anna Cypra Oliver-Skoven
Date: 26 Feb 96 10:13 a.m.

I'll look for mopey music for you. What is mopey music? Are blues mopey? I think Jack o' Diamonds is mopey. It goes, you Jack o' Diamonds, now you

Jack o' Diamonds, all the way to the jail, boys,
yes back to the jail. I think it's about gambling,
lost money, lost opportunities, and lost lives.

REMAINS: AN UPDATED INVENTORY OF MY FATHER

1. A handful of photographs of him, including his high school graduation portrait and some taken in Florida by my mother.

2. A silver belt buckle.

3. Photographs taken by my father of my mother in her twenties, and of my brother and me when we were children.

4. *Architectural Record*, Vol. 145, No. 6: "Record Houses of 1969."

5. *Miami Herald*, "Dwelling Is Designed for Family Living," May 25, 1969.

6. One handmade wooden case with a 4x5 Graflex camera in it.

7. An exposed, undeveloped roll of film, over twenty years old and by now ruined.

8. A piece of soft white cloth embroidered with red thread in an exploding-star pattern wrapped around a spare lens.

9. A forty-year-old Leica.

10. A red metal army trunk full of my father's photographs, including many of my brother and me and my mother right up to the time she left him.

11. Transaction receipts from a photo shop and two construction suppliers in Florida.

12. A divorce decree.

13. A postcard to my father from a woman named Lynn.

14. A tin lithograph that says LIBERALS FOR NIXON.

15. A photograph of my father's eighth-grade graduating class at P.S. 178, class of June 1952.

16. A sleeve of slides of my father and Stephan on a youth-hostel bicycling trip to Europe the summer they were seventeen.

17. Copies of Louis Kronenberger's *Company Manners*, *The Vintage Mencken*, and *Hornblower and the Hotspur*.

18. A postcard from my father and my mother in New Mexico to Stephan.

19. A photograph of the Jamaica High School Senior Prom, Hotel Biltmore, June 6, 1956.

20. My father's journal.

LYING STILL AND ALONE
AT REST WITH MYSELF FOR A MOMENT

YOUR WEIGHT AND HAIR AND LENGTH
DESCEND ON MY

LOWERED SLOWLY AND
WITH TENDER CARE

AND MEMORIES OF EVENTS
BOTH REAL AND IMAGINED
COME FLOWING BACK
EVERY MOMENT OF YOUR
DESCENDING FORM
IS THE LOVE I WANTED

AND THEN GONE
DISSOLVED AND FLED
THE TINGLE OF MY
SKIN
REMAINS
AND I MARVEL
THAT YOU CAME TO ME
FOR A MOMENT
SO LOVING

THE RECORD PLAYER STILL SOUNDS
AND THE ROOM IS COLD
STILL
LET YOU GO
AND LIVE FOREVER
I GROW FOOLISH

QUEST II: A COLD CUSTOMER

After reading through it the first time, I put the journal away for a couple of months. I can't face it again immediately. And then, although I feel peculiar doing it, I take it to a copy place and stand in front of the pulsing machine, making a duplicate of every page—one side, then the other, then another of one that comes out too dark. I'll have to sketch in the words where the original is blurred. I feel an odd disconnect as I handle it—lift, flip, close, click, hnnn, the hungry flash of light. It seems cold.

"You're hardhearted," I hear my mother saying, the stunning accusation with which she flattened me in high school. "A cold customer."

When I ask the lady at the counter to make three more copies of the copy I've made, she looks at me distrustfully. "Is this copyrighted material?" she asks snippily. She's in a sour mood. There is no one else in the store, and I'm bothering her.

"No," I say, snippy back. "Of course not. It's from my father's notebook." I take pleasure in saying this. *My father's notebook.* I almost say, "He's dead so it belongs to me," but I know this means nothing to her. It's more than she wants to know.

I send a copy to Irwin and one to Stephan, in exchange for the information they've given me. Another is for me so I can make notes on it; the fourth is for my brother, although I don't send it to him. I expect that he will want to examine the original before getting a copy in the mail. But the truth is, I don't volunteer that either. I feel selfish about the journal. I want Peter to read it. But I don't want to give it to him. I want to keep it. He has been curious about the journal, but he doesn't ask to see it. He was always the one who talked about Lewis—the only one, really—and he had wanted the photographs, too, but now that I have them, he has not asked about them, either. He doesn't bring the subject up, and I don't offer. He is absorbed in his life: his wife, his first child, his real estate business in Boise, where he moved after college for the expanding market and the mountains.

He holds his son in his arms and says to my husband, "This is the only blood relation I've ever met," a statement that chills me to the bone.

ARTIFACTS 3

The journal is divided into two sections. It contains both poems and letters. I didn't realize at first what my uncle meant when he said he had letters belonging to Lewis. Did my father send them? Did he write them here first, then transcribe them onto stationery, or just tear them out? Is that what became of the missing pages? The first half is devoted to a woman named Mara. He seems to have lived with her for a while, or at least helped her with a building project: he says they spent four months together working on a house for some "young people." My father built the cabinets and felt good that the young people liked them. I wonder if Mara was an architect, or if she was just one of many in New Mexico trying her hand at house building. It's clear that she and my father were involved, and that she had just broken off the relationship. In the second half, the letters are addressed to Lynn, the woman who wrote the postcard from Cape Cod. She seems, from the tone of the journal, to be a friend rather than a lover. The second half is calmer, more balanced, than the first.

At first glance, the division between these two halves appears to be a child's drawing. I'm fairly certain it was drawn by my brother. My father says a few pages earlier that we are coming to spend Saturday, March 2, with him. But we aren't the reason for an evident change of mood, much as I might like to think so. Mara came to see him the same weekend. Something seems to have been resolved between them, and whatever they had as a couple is apparently over: *It was nice that she / missed me and said I love/ you again / even if it was only / a bad moment / and now I'm only a / stop on a busy weekend. / If that's the way it is / That's got to be / all right too.*

After reading through the journal a second time, I go back to the trunk upstairs. I search through the photographs until I come to one who I think is Lynn: a thin, sweet-looking blond woman with octagonal glasses. She looks as if she's in her midtwenties—about the age I am now. I don't know how I know this is her. She looks shy, a little eager to please. Suddenly, I feel grateful to her, for being in my father's life.

There are two who might be Mara. A blonde with large eyes and a skinny freckled woman with tight curly hair. The skinny woman posed naked for him as my mother had done. There are a lot of photos of both of them. I think the blonde is Mara, maybe just because she is the prettier of the two, maybe because she has the sultry mouth and eyes of a woman looking at her lover. The skinny woman seems to be just vamping for the camera, not staring through the lens at the man behind it.

QUEST 12: UNHAPPENING FUTURES

I read myself into places in the journal. Toward the beginning, he writes:

Mama!
She's gone
And you
Being sweet
    Being lost
        Being strong

But there is no need to succumb to your
Weakness
Leave off then
    I'll draw you a flower then
Instead of all the unhappening futures
    Would I have . . . I couldn't

And then he does. He draws page after page of flowers. Big, big blooms, like chrysanthemums, petals sketched around the spokes of an asterisk, always drawn from dead center. Each one takes up half a page. Of all the poems in the notebook, I like this one the most—or find it, anyway, the least distressing. I like the mildness of his voice, the sorrowful but contained quality that is missing in other entries. *I'll draw you a flower then / Instead of all the unhappening futures.*

I like it, primarily, because when I first read it, I thought the child in it might be me. He wrote the poem, I thought, and drew the flowers for me. But after a more careful reading, I realize my error— the yearning of a daughter never once named in her father's last testament. The child is not me. The child is imaginary, a device used to express his own fear of being lost and alone, his own urgent desire for someone who is gone. The challenge not to "succumb" is to himself, though perhaps to the child as well: "If I can make it, you can," or maybe the reverse: "If you can make it, I can."

And yet he also finds a way to distract both himself and the child from despair and from the "unhappening futures" represented by the mother who has left him. He tries to comfort the child through a creative act. Throughout the journal, drawing, sketching, designing, are clung to as ways of surviving emotional loss.

"Leave off then," he says to the child (my father says to me). "I'll draw you a flower then." A poor speller throughout the journal, though probably just careless in this instance, he actually writes "unhappeing." Might he have meant "unhappying"? I'll draw you a flower then, instead of all the *unhappying* futures.

I want to make sense of the journal. But I worry about my urge to ascribe intention to these poems. There are no drafts, no scratched-out phrases (unless he tore out those pages?). These are outpourings: he writes, as most people do who dabble in poetry, to express his pain and confusion. He didn't consider multiple meanings or worry about being clear. Still, these jottings constitute his only suicide note, the only explanation he offers for that final gesture.

"Things to do enough," he says in another poem, "to obliterate thought," a line that reads now, of course, with terrible irony.

"The words of a dead man," W. H. Auden says in his elegy to

William Butler Yeats, "Are modified in the guts of the living." And though there are no valid parallels between the artistry of Yeats and my father's scribblings, Auden's pronouncement expresses exactly what I feel: a wrestling in my gut with what my father meant and what I think he meant and what I want him to mean.

"Tell you more later," my father writes in his last letter to Lynn. Those are his last words.

A MESSAGE TO THE FUTURE

"To write a letter," writes the Argentinean novelist Ricardo Piglia in *Artificial Respiration*, "is to send a message to the future; to speak of the present with an addressee who is not there, knowing nothing about how that person is (in what spirits, with whom) *while* we write and, above all, *later*: while reading over what we have written. Correspondence is the utopian form of conversation because it annihilates the present and turns the future into the only possible place for dialogue."

SOME MORE THINGS I'D TELL YOU IF I HAD THE CHANCE

I used to love to design things, design and build. I built the entire set for The Muppet Movie *out of cardboard and scraps of fabric in the basement of my grandparents' house when I was ten. Any landscape described in a book, I wanted to construct: the Shire of Middle-earth, Cricketland, the Hundred Acre Wood. I built dollhouses, a doll village, a Barbie-sized motorcycle out of wire and cast-off car parts. The gas tank was the white end of a spark plug. On irrigation day, I made elaborate mud houses along the ditches of our property in Talpa. I furnished them with tiny braid rugs woven from yarn, tables and chairs of matchsticks and varnished plywood, sofas constructed from fabric remnants stuffed with cotton batting. Mom saved scraps for me when she sewed. Sometimes I pressed flat stones into the ground for flagstone floors and stretched plastic across matchstick frames for windows. The houses lasted only as long as the next hard rain, but I didn't care. It was the act of building that mattered.*

Mom still has pictures of those mud houses. They were incredible, you know? Their detail, the patience it required to deck out the rooms like that. I furnished them as if they were about to be photographed for Architectural Record. It amazes me because I don't have that kind of patience now.

I did think, though, for about two minutes in college, of majoring in architecture. A curious sort of homage: maybe I thought it would give me access to your mind, your way of seeing the world. But I'd never paid that much attention to actual buildings, and someone told me that architects had to be good at math. My math score on the SAT was laughable.

In 1960, John F. Kennedy was elected president, sit-ins were staged at lunch counters in Greensboro, North Carolina, Adolf Eichmann was seized by Israeli agents in Argentina and carried back to Jerusalem. John Updike published *Rabbit, Run*, William Shirer, *The Rise and Fall of the Third Reich*. *To Kill a Mockingbird* won the Pulitzer, and *Psycho*, *Exodus*, and *Hiroshima, Mon Amour* premiered in the movie theaters. Le Corbusier completed construction of the Monastère La Tourette at Eveux, near Lyons, France. Clark Gable died of a heart attack at age fifty-nine two weeks after wrapping *The Misfits*. Charles Van Doren, of *Twenty-One* quiz-show fame (and America's "ur-WASP," as Philip Roth's Alexander Portnoy calls him), was arrested for testifying under oath that the answers were not given to him before the show. Viewers, who liked to boast that the egghead contestants on *Twenty-One* and other hugely popular game shows proved that, *Sputnik* or no, Americans were superior to the Soviets, got their first shattering exposure to the manipulative power of television.

"You know about the *College Bowl* quiz contest?" Irwin asks me while we're sitting in Miriam's living room.

"Mmhm," I say, by which I mean, Yes, I know my father was in it. In photographs, he sports a dark suit and narrow tie, his hair slicked down and side-parted. It was a cross, I think, between a game show and the speech and debate team. My father was captain. Beyond that and the fact that it was nationally televised, I know nothing.

"Okay," Irwin says excitedly. "He was absolutely brilliant."

"RPI, this little engineering school," Stephan says, "beat Harvard and every other school on the program. They retired undefeated, which had never been done before."

"This was like the *Seinfeld* and *Murphy Brown* of New York. I mean, everybody watched it," Irwin says.

"And Lewis would proudly remind us that RPI's entire undefeated *College Bowl* team was on probation."

"He flunked out," Irwin says.

"It was great," Stephan says.

"He won. He was the captain! He answered most of the questions."

"Not in mathematics," Stephan says.

"History and English questions, he knew cold," Irwin says, "but he flunked out that semester. He went on probation, flunked out and had to go back. That was the kind of thing he would do."

"He didn't take it too seriously," Stephan says. "I remember him talking about a fancy party that was held at some muckety-muck's house, the RPI president or something, and the team members all got drunk and caused a big scene. I can still hear his exploding laughter —it was just a great big humorous adventure to him. He loved that the school began to fawn over them, wining and dining them—the aggrandizing Gatsbyish quality of it all. And here they were, getting drunk at the president's house and acting like buffoons."

After the show was over, they tell me, someone recognized my father on the street in New York. "You're the guy," someone said. "You're the guy . . ."

L.WEINBERG R BARRY

COLLEGE BOWL — Lewis Weinberger and Barry Fishkin are shown during tense moments of the final College Bowl contest.

Team Gives Personal Views Concerning Bowl Victories

By JACK TITLEY

"The final half-hour before show time was hell, about all we could do was to watch Ted Mack's Amateur Hour, which we came to hate." Those were the feelings of the College Bowl team and the sentiments of the Rensselaer student body as the last few minutes of waiting passed.

Then the full burden of weight fell on the shoulders of the "varsity scholars." How did it affect them? As Barry Fishkin put it, "All of the five weeks on the show, I had that tremendous feeling of being a part of a great team rather than the feeling of being up there alone."

Team Confidence

"I got a tremendous charge out of hearing our buzzer. If a question on music came up, I knew Melbert could handle it, on science or astronomy—Finch, or art—Weinberger."

For Roland Finch, the first week was the most nerve racking. The long rehearsals of three hours before each game helped smooth out the rough spots. It was during these rehearsals that the teams practiced with their opponents. Finch recalls that "U-Conn. came close to us in these warm-ups but they were the easiest in the real thing."

Warm-ups

After fairing rather poorly in the warm-ups with Indiana Louis Weinburger felt we would lose to them. "We had just about given up. But then the Alumni cheered us up and started us off. We were really worried for a while."

"Things tended to become some what easier as time went on. We had cooperation among us that the other teams seemed to lack." He mused

that "Maybe this was the result of writing up labs together."

Melbert

Every summer, Tom Melbert, set a goal for himself such as reading a book a day. His taste in literature varies among all types of books. Melbert considers himself an "anti-scientific" which he defines as being antagonistic toward "the attitude of excellence in one field to the point of exclusion of other interests."

In regard to the humanities at Rensselaer, Barry Fishkin does not believe that it is feasible for liberal arts to have a heavier emphasis with the present tough load of scientific subjects. This, he thinks, is a crime. In his opinion, a five year course with five or six more courses in the liberal arts would turn out better engineers and more well rounded individuals.

Admiring girls have sent love letters to some members of the team. Weinberger has received six, thus far. One, he particularly likes, is from a girl named Suzie. It seems that she loves him for his "sophisticated manner." Weinberger has also been approached by a Texan who wants to invest 'his" nine thousand dollars in the publication of a religious book.

Alumni Interest

Some of this popularity has rubbed off on to the school. Among other people who have learned of Rensselaer, it seems that the old grads have rekindled an interest. Alumni contributions have gone up since the school has been televised which measures the publicity the school obtained.

The team members agree that it *(Continued on Page 10, Column 4)*

Ice on the Hudson: black birds skimming the surface anchor themselves briefly on the silver sheets, moving comfortably downstream
before swooping up again into the electric blue air. Through the smeary
train window, I watch them. It is a beautiful sunny day, the landscape
razor-edged yet shimmering. Even the dirty snow glitters along the
banks. I'm on my way to Troy to visit RPI, but the destination has
begun to feel like an excuse: this trip through the river valley is reason
enough to travel north. The thought of my father making the same
journey gives it the tint of colorized archival footage.

When my stop is announced, I collect my backpack and wrap my
green scarf more tightly around my neck. Outside, it is freezing. Several people in business suits are waiting at the taxi stand. Ten minutes later, a battered gray Buick pulls up. We are told to get in, three
in the back, one in front. The other passengers, all on their way to
the capitol building in Albany, are dropped off first. The detour is mad-
dening. I don't have time for this. It's already 11:00, and I want to
catch the 5:20 train back to New York, where my grandmother is expecting me for dinner. I'm visiting by myself, without Stuart, who is
at home in Minneapolis.

"You a student, honey?" the driver asks once we're by ourselves.

"No," I say, annoyed by his familiar tone. "I'm older than I look."

I sink back into the seat, not wanting to talk, but then it occurs
to me that he might be helpful. "Do you know where Bordentown is?"
I ask. "Is that near here?"

"Bordentown?" He sounds perplexed. "I don't know of any Bordentown. There's a Stephentown. Stephentown Center. That's just
south of here."

Now I'm confused. At some point, my mother had told me that
she and my father lived in a rickety old house in Bordentown when
he was at RPI. I'm sure I have the name right. We ride in silence for a
while, until I see the aged brick facades of what must be Troy: an old
industrial town still carrying the soot of the nineteenth century. Above
it, on a hill, is the school. I get out at the student center. There will be
echoes of my father on this campus, I think, traces of his presence in
the hallways, the classrooms he studied in. I've come to look for ghosts.

I'm also here because I've been told that RPI has an archive of information on the 1961 *GE College Bowl*. Last July, when Stephan called on my behalf, the archivist dug up two articles, but she knew nothing more about the RPI team. In thirty-five years, no one else had apparently shown any interest in it; but Stephan's inquiry, by strange coincidence, turned out to be the first in a flurry. Not long afterward, Barry Fishkin, one of the team members, came up to visit RPI, and found that even though his team's triumph had increased donations and raised the school's profile, the Bowl had been forgotten and the silver loving cup they had won was missing. I learned this firsthand from Barry, after Stephan, by another, stranger coincidence, had met a man at a party in New York who turned out to have been Barry Fishkin's roommate at RPI, enabling me to track down his phone number. Shortly after Barry's visit, the team coach, Professor Ernest Livingstone, died at the age of eighty-two. His widow donated his papers to the library, including dozens of articles, congratulatory telegrams, letters, and a brief autobiography Livingstone had written for his family. He had kept the loving cup, which is now on display in the lobby, along with photographs from the Quiz Bowl and a range of other memorabilia.

RPI in the early 1960s was a men's college with about three thousand students. Now, it's coed and has an undergraduate population of fifty-three hundred, plus another forty-three hundred graduate students. The campus is bigger than I'd imagined it, with more grass, more trees, more ivy-covered brick buildings. Even on this cold March day, covered with old snow, it's pretty. Because I don't have a death certificate, I can't get my father's records; Phi Sigma Delta, his fraternity, which I'd hoped to visit, doesn't exist anymore. I can see halfway across the quadrangle that the architecture department, at least, hasn't been moved since the 1960s. In the trunk, I had found a picture of a brick building on campus: a white banner that said WEIN-BERGER! hung horizontally from an upper window, and below it someone had pasted a cutout of my smiling father. The building in front of me has the same wide, multipaned white windows; the same stone lintel with ARCHITECTURE cut in block letters above the glass door; the same ivy, leafless now, as when they'd beat five teams in a row that January on national television.

In the department's sun-streaked, oak-filled library, I take pictures. *He sat at these tables. He read these books.* The few students working in the cluttered drafting room look up at me, bewildered. *He used these tools.* I stare, hungrily, at the designs pinned to the wall, the coffee mugs, rulers, glue, half-finished models, swirls of thin paper on the jammed-together desks. I quickly snap two frames and leave.

I take a picture in a deserted classroom of the empty desks.

I'm trying to portray absence, embody lost hope. I know how maudlin this effort seems, how sentimental, but I don't care. I have to do it.

Before I leave, I go back to the department's library to look at the yearbooks. Those are in the main library, the boy behind the counter  tells me, but my father's thesis might be here. They have them bound and arranged by year on the shelves behind him.

His thesis! In the trunk, I'd found a pack of negatives wrapped in wax paper that turned out to be photographs of blueprints: one set of plans drawn for Bethlehem Steel by Vorhees, Walker, Smith, Smith and Haines, the architectural firm where my father worked in New York after graduation, and others for a Shakespearean theater and a complex of row houses in Florida. I thought the latter might have been drawn for my grandfather Morris, but Stephan thinks they were probably both school projects. Finding those was a gift—anything that came from his hand was a form, however muted, however oblique, of communication with him—and now I might get ahold of his thesis, too.

But it isn't there. The boy goes through all the shelves twice, with no luck.

"He might not have done one," he says. "It's not always required."

Deflated, I thank him, and with a last look at the squares of sunlight on the oak tables, head for the main library.

In a modern concrete building that didn't exist in my father's time, I fill out a slip for each page of the Quiz Bowl archive that I'd like to have copied. A stack of them is rising at my elbow. I already have Stephan's two articles, a series of five more from the *Rensselaer Polytechnic* which Barry sent me, and dozens of photographs from the trunk. Nothing in the files seems earthshattering, but I'm learning not to judge too hastily which material might prove worthwhile.

It's curiously unsettling, scanning articles from the *Polytechnic* and local papers like the *Times Record* of Albany, to read the words attributed to my father. I want to find him in them, the cadences and lilt of his speech, what is true, what his story is; I want him to speak for himself. But the words are unnaturally stiff and the stories slip sideways, falsified in some way by the need to compose a self for the public record:

"My preparation for architecture and the high school influences that led me to choose this profession lie behind any special ability of mine to help our team win," says Lewis Weinberger, captain. "Over and beyond design, architecture embraces so many fields of human interest—art, psychology, literature, history, science—that the honest students must plunge deep into all fields of human thought and action."

Brought up at Jamaica, L.I., Lewis attended Stuyvesant High School in Manhattan and found it staffed with writers and artists who were teaching for a livelihood. They led him into wide reading of history, the works of Hemingway, Faulkner, Steinbeck, Koestler and others, the study of sculpture and painting.

The vast resources of the N.Y. Public Library were just a few blocks away and a little further uptown was the Metropolitan Museum, so there was no problem for Lewis in filling the free hours.

One summer he bicycled through Europe, visiting libraries and museums as he jumped from hostel to hostel.

"One big thing I learned," Lewis says, "was not to be scornful or surprised at new ideas and expressions in art, literature, and architecture."

He bicycled through Europe, *visiting libraries?* And why mention the Metropolitan when his friends specifically said they didn't go there much? Did the Met have more cachet than the Modern? Was it at

Stuyvesant and not from Joe or the bookstalls on Fourth Avenue that he discovered the authors he loved?

Why these details matter, I don't know. I don't expect my father to be anything other than elusive. "Identity," as the Uruguayan author Eduardo Galeano writes in *The Book of Embraces*, "is no museum piece sitting stock-still in a display case, but rather the endlessly astonishing synthesis of the contradictions of everyday life." This is the grandest refusal that I know, and the most hopeful: even my mother could not make her whole self conform to the system that she chose. Even so, I sometimes want a fact I can heft in my hand like a stone without it turning to dust the next moment, one pebble I can mortar to another, and say, "There."

Still, I'm grateful that my father was a man who had entered the public record at all. I wish I knew what his voice sounded like. I understand that he had narrated a short film about the school which was broadcast during the *College Bowl*, but it has since been lost. Nor does CBS have any footage of the program. During his flurry of research after we met at Miriam's, Stephan called the studio; an archivist told him that the reels had not been properly stored, and all of them had disintegrated.

It disturbs me to want him so much.

Flipping through each of five possible years of *Transit*, the school yearbook, I'm unable to find his name or picture under "Architecture," but there is one candid photo in the upper right-hand corner of 1961 that leaps out at me: a student is seated, face tilted down so I can't be sure if it's him, hunched over a set of plans on a drafting board, pen in hand. A dark-haired boy with a side part, thick eyebrows, ears that stick out a little. I can't understand why I feel so excited. On other pages of the yearbook, I find photographs of Nixon and Kennedy campaigning on campus: there's Nixon, surrounded by suits,

absorbing a hard handshake with good humor; there's smiling Jack reading the *Polytechnic*. *Liberals for Nixon* must have been made for those events. I'm building my father, one anecdote, one image, one scrap of evidence at a time.

If he missed getting his photograph in with the other architecture students, he had better luck with Phi Sigma Delta. Among the small headshots of each member, I find my father and his three roommates: Ken Schatz, David Levine, and Alan Hundert. By eerie coincidence, three of the four are now dead. Irwin says that Alan, an executive at Colt, was rushing to get off a commuter train, slipped, and died under the wheels. David was the "mercenary pilot" who Irwin heard had been killed in Africa, though someone else later told me that he died in the Israeli Air Force, demonstrating a plane Israel wanted to sell to South Africa. He apparently attempted a maneuver that hadn't been cleared by his superiors and crashed.

While I'm studying these faces, a middle-aged woman, petite and well groomed, walks into the library. Tammy, the archivist, introduces her to me as Mrs. Livingstone, Coach Ernest Livingstone's widow. Another coincidence. She was in town for the afternoon and decided to stop in and see the lobby display before going home to Rochester.

"I was so sorry to hear about your father," she says. Barry Fishkin had told her. "It's such a shame."

I offer my condolences in return, then ask about a passage in her husband's autobiography in which he describes his concern about "the most brilliant and fragile of my team" who was having a hard time adjusting to the end of RPI's giddy five-week run. Livingstone and his wife had invited him over for dinner and "tried to paint his future life in the rosiest colors."

She shakes her head, almost apologetically. No, Dr. Livingstone didn't mean my father. "Your father, as I remember, was a very mature, stable person."

I feel mildly, if somewhat nonsensically, disappointed. I want him to be the most brilliant and also the most fragile. It sounds romantic, like suffering from melancholia or consumption, but I knew before I put the question to her that it couldn't have been Lewis: he had married my mother after his sophomore year and would have been with her, not alone at the Livingstones' having supper. Mrs. Livingstone doesn't remember much else about him, and when she says she has to go, I feel relieved. It's nearly 4:30. I had hoped to wander through downtown Troy when I finished up in the library, but I am suddenly exhausted.

Bordentown, I now recall, is in New Jersey. They lived in that house when my father was in the army, stationed at Fort Dix.

CORRECTIONS

When I tell her I've gone to visit RPI, my mother mentions the "Liberals for Nixon" poster of her own accord, telling me that her brother, my uncle John, has a copy of it hanging in his house, too. She has been less adamant lately in her refusal to discuss the past, and if I catch her off-guard or in a good mood, sometimes I can get her to talk to me. It wasn't drawn by my father, she says, but by a professor named Donald Mochon, an artist and *éminence grise* in the architecture department who was a great favorite of my father's. He had a lovely modernist house in the woods, she remembers; they used to go there and have dinner with him and his wife fairly often. They were devastated when they later discovered that the couple had gotten divorced.

QUEST 14: THE ENGINEERS

Barry Fishkin, who knew my father only from the *GE College Bowl*, tried out with him and thirty-four other students. After a written test, the thirty-four were narrowed to twelve, and then, after a series of mock games conducted over several weeks, to the final four and an alternate.

"It was not unlike *Jeopardy!*" Barry tells me. It required "exquisite timing" and the ability to anticipate a question before it was completely out of Allen Ludden's mouth.

Ernest Livingstone, an assistant professor of language and literature, had been at RPI for only three months before he was asked to coach the team. He accepted reluctantly. Convinced that "RPI would lose against any major university," he feared a defeat might hurt his standing at the school. Roland Finch, a member of the team, characterizes him as a "sophisticated, mild-mannered, European guy" — a description that makes me think of the Stuyvesant art teacher Nat Werner and my grandfather Juan, the men to whom my father was most drawn.

After weeks of preparation, the team scrimmaged against Skidmore, which was scheduled to compete on the program two weeks before RPI. The scrimmage was held at Skidmore and the school's whole student body turned out to watch, apparently, Barry surmised, because they "thought it would be like shooting fish in a barrel." When RPI beat them so soundly that Skidmore hardly had any points on the board, my father and his teammates were as surprised as anyone. Maybe an engineering institute had a chance against a liberal arts college, after all.

My father's team put RPI on the national map: they might be scientists, their victory declared, but they were men of letters, too.

VARSITY SCHOLARS

Undefeated Champions of the College Bowl, Rensselaer's team of varsity scholars scored an impressive series of victories over other colleges.

The four personable young men who took their places under the bright glare of studio lights might have been new television personalities, and indeed so they became, but they were a good deal more. They were the Rensselaer team of varsity scholars preparing to compete with other colleges and universities on the College Bowl program. But where were the bright uniforms, bulky padding and cleated shoes typical of intercollegiate teams? Such trappings were unnecessary for the Rensselaer men, for they were concerned with mental rather than physical activity. In a question and answer contest that depended on the ability to quickly recall specific facts they had no need for the paraphernalia of the athlete. Without the pageantry and color of the "big game" the College Bowl team stirred the enthusiasm of students, faculty and alumni.

Coached by Ernest F. Livingstone, assistant professor of language and literature, the team was captained by fifth year architecture student Lewis Weinberger and included Thomas Melbert, a junior in language and literature, Barry Fishkin who will graduate this June in Aeronautical engineering and Roland Finch, a sophomore chemical engineer. The alternate team member was Steven Manson, a physics major.

Defying the predictions that they wouldn't have a chance against strong liberal arts colleges, the Rensselaer team compiled an impressive series of victories. They defeated Indiana, Fisk, and Fordham Universities then Grinnell College and the University of Connecticut. Their undefeated record earned them a silver trophy and brought $9,000 in scholarship funds to the Institute from the program's sponsor, the General Electric Company.

Rensselaer Alumni News, "Varsity Scholars," March 1961

A few days after our first conversation, Barry Fishkin calls me back. He's come up with the phone numbers of another member of the *College Bowl* team, Jay Finch, and my father's remaining Phi Sigma Delta fraternity brother, Ken Schatz.

Ken knew my father and mother before RPI: he grew up in the same neighborhood in Queens, Jamaica Estates. Besides Jay and Ken and Bobby Blender, whose number Stephan had, an ad I placed in the Stuyvesant alumni bulletin leads me to Jerome Yavarkovsky, a man who knew my father at RPI and Fort Dix. Stephan also finds, by sheer strange coincidence, a number for one of my father's architecture buddies, Jeremy Grainger. His name turned up as a contributor in the table of contents of a book of essays on urban planning.

WHAT JAY FINCH REMEMBERS

"You had to have a dust-catcher's brain. Lew was the oldest at twenty-two—architecture is a five-year program. I was only nineteen, a sophomore. Barry was a junior. We spent five intensive weeks preparing and five more competing on the show. Your father and I almost flunked out because we were putting so much time into it." Jay laughs. "We didn't graduate, we just survived.

"Lew had a way about him. He was married and living off campus then. He was a senior, doing studio work, odd hours. He got the most fan mail. He was proud that women were writing to him.

"He looked like an English professor. Tweed jacket, leather elbow patches. He combed his hair straight across. Your mom, she was a real bon vivant. She looked in 1961 the way women would look in 1968. Short skirts, straight blond hair. A precursor of the sixties upheaval. She was more independent than most women. Ahead of her time.

"RPI had a kind of inferiority complex. The same year we won, the school took the NCAA hockey title. There was tremendous publicity. Walking through Troy, we'd be mobbed by girls. They'd ask us for our autographs." Jay chuckles with pleasure. "I remember when I came home, my parents had strung used-car-lot pennants all over the front of the house and they were standing outside with a shaker of cocktails. There was a sign over the door: THIS IS THE HOME OF JAY FINCH, TV STAR." He laughs dryly.

"Lew handled the situation best. It was not a big deal to him. He had a high degree of perspective on what was important." Jay is quiet for a moment. "He was very bright. But it's possible to peak too soon. Everything can be downhill from there."

LEWIS J. WEINBERGER, 22, Captain of Team, fifth year student 'n architecture, to be graduated this coming June. Married, no children. Lives at 179 Second Street, Troy, New York. Son of Mr. and Mrs. Morris W. Weinberger, 150 N. E. 169th Terrace, Miami, Florida. Member of Phi Sigma Delta fraternity, assistant manager Cross Country Team. Hobbies: skiing and painting and sailing. Career goal, private practice in architecture.

GE College Bowl Biographical Data, 1961

WHAT JEREMY GRAINGER REMEMBERS

"I remember your father as a standout. You know, I grew up in Pittsburgh and I would go to New York and see some exhibit at MoMA, and your father had already been there. He struck me as urbane, a sophisticate. He smoked a pipe. Whoa, that was cool! And he always used to draw with a particular kind of pen that was very hard to use—they taught that sort of thing in New York high schools. He was very interested in modernism, high modernism. He had an intellectual orientation that a lot of people at RPI didn't have: painting, literature. I always looked upon him as artistic, artsy in an engineering school where people wear plastic pocket protectors in their shirts all day.

"We had this other friend, Arthur Spector. He and Lewis were good friends. When we were freshman, Lewis introduced Arthur and me to Bennington, the avant-garde girls' college. He came up with the idea of buying some Italian sandwiches, wrapping them in plastic, and putting them in a violin case. Then we carried the violin case out into the middle of the Bennington lawn, opened it, and took out the sandwiches. The idea was to meet girls, but of course, no one paid any attention to us."

IDEAL COUPLE

My mother wears a cocktail dress. Black, sleeveless, simple: black straps and the elegant, straight line of the bodice emphasizes firm arms, delicate collarbones. Around her throat hangs a strand of pearls. Her neck is long, sinewy. Her face is tilted sideways and down. A glossy sweep of hair ends in a crown of braid on her head. From her ear dangles a gold and pearl earring. Her parents gave her the pair as a wedding present.

My father in a dark suit, dark tie, and white shirt sits beside her. On a table in front of them is a half-eaten plate of food. A full wine goblet. His arm is either around her or rests on the back of her chair. Light falls on her cheek, her shoulder. His face, the arc of white teeth, recedes into shadow.

They are so beautiful, glamorous, perfect. Golden girl and captain of the *College Bowl* team.

WHAT KEN SCHATZ REMEMBERS

"Your mom was a real live wire. An avant-garde thinker, vivacious, the life of the party. I met her when I was a junior in high school: she fixed me up with Judy, my date for the prom, and the four of us went together. Your parents were a tremendous couple. She could have chosen anyone. Your dad was quiet, not a cheerleader guy, introverted. He was serious, but he also had a sense of humor.

"I never heard anybody say a word against him. He was a guy with guts to him. Very empathetic, other-centered. A great listener. I had the impression that his dad was very controlling, but he never talked about it. He wasn't the type to reveal his problems to people. And no matter what he did, he kept his humanity. Not like me. I was very raw, intolerant sometimes. Lew, he was a mensh. When I think about your dad, I always think about that line from *Deliverance*. You know that story? One of the characters says of the guy who gets shot, 'He was the best of us.' That was your dad. 'He was the best of us.'"

Barely visible behind the arrayed might of network television the Rensselaer team take their places.

EXERCISE 3: GE COLLEGE BOWL

It was hot under the lights. You would never have known it was March and slightly raw outside. My father swept a hand the length of his narrow dark tie, smoothing it flat against his shirt, then buttoned his sport coat over it. Five minutes to airtime. He looked for my mother, seated somewhere in the tiers at the back of the studio, but he couldn't see her because the lights were in his eyes. They bristled from the ceiling like riled porcupines.

It was their third time on the *GE College Bowl*, this time against Fordham University. No one could quite believe they had made it this far. Everyone they knew thought they would be massacred in their first match, against Indiana University. They'd proven, with Skidmore, that they could compete against a liberal arts college, but Indiana was a much bigger school and had just defeated Fairleigh Dickinson, the four-time defending champion. Besides, during the three-hour rehearsal at the studio, Indiana *had* massacred them. Warmed up from their win the previous week, the Indiana team was faster on the buzzer, shutting them out time after time. My father was convinced that RPI was going to lose. Barry, afraid of looking like an idiot on national television, had called everyone he knew and told them not to watch. But everything turned around on the actual program: Livingstone had advised them to press the button first and worry about the answer afterward, even if they had to take a five-point penalty for getting it wrong. They ended up beating Indiana 200 to 155. The Indiana coach was so pissed off that when the match was over, he refused to shake Livingstone's hand.

The players seated themselves at the two long booths in front of the cameras. They'd all been in the studio since 11:00 that morning, sizing one another up. In warm-ups at least, Fordham was much better than Fisk, their previous adversary: RPI had beaten Fisk by an almost embarrassingly wide margin. They had been smart, but not aggressive enough. To win required fast, risk-taking reflexes: whoever sounded the buzzer first got first crack at answering.

The assistant director raised his hand in warning. Four minutes to air. Waiting for the final countdown, my father's shoulders were as taut as strung wire. The first time on the program had been the worst. They'd practiced for weeks, going so far as to design a mock set complete with buzzers and lights, and as Jay Finch says, "war-gaming it," but nothing could replicate the clutching tension of waiting for the cameras to roll, knowing that their faces were about to be beamed into millions of homes. At least now, they were pros.

The whistle sounded, signaling the start of the program. Allen Ludden introduced each of the players, then briefly explained the rules to the audience: tossup questions were worth ten points and could be answered by any of the eight players; a correct answer earned that player's team a bonus question, but if he answered incorrectly the other team would be given a chance at the question.

"All right, teams, for ten points and a twenty-point bonus question, here's your first tossup. Deduce the identity of the world-famous statesman who spoke these words: 'We have not journeyed all this way across the centuries, across the oceans, across the mountains, across the prairies, because we are made of sugar candy.'"

My father's buzzer sounded.

"Rensselaer! Weinberger?"

"Winston Churchill."

"Winston Churchill is right! Now for the bonus question and twenty points, subtract the Roman numerals X-X-X-I-X from C-I-V."

"Sixty-five," Barry shouted out.

"Yes! Sixty-five it is. All right, I have a thirty-pointer. Eli Whitney invented the cotton gin, James Hargreaves the spinning jenny. Tell me, who invented the sewing machine? Fordham!"

"Elias Howe."

"That's right, Howe."

Fordham got twenty of its thirty bonus points, but the next tossup, a quotation from Aeschylus, stumped both teams. They were neck and neck.

"All right, you're playing for a forty-point bonus question. For ten points, name the action by which the surface of a liquid, where it is in contact with—"

A buzzer. It was my father's teammate Melbert. "The capillarity principle," he answered. He was the king when it came to anticipating questions.

"The capillarity principle, that's right. Now, Rensselaer, I'm going to show you a series of paintings. For five points each, identify the painter and, if you can, the saint whose image the painting depicts. . . ."

The pace was fast, no amiable chat from the host or pause for breath between questions. The players' attention couldn't lag for a moment. Livingstone had made each of his players study a set of subjects, instructing them to attempt questions in other areas only if they were one hundred percent sure of the answer. My father was a "specialist" in politics, art, and literature, though his interests included history and psychology, and he answered a lot of those questions, too.

They slumped back in their chairs while an ad ran for the GE

Toast-R-Oven. Livingstone, who had been pacing back and forth along one side of the studio, gave them a thumbs-up. My father, the captain, leaned toward his teammates to offer a ten-second pep talk—everyone was a little tense, worried about the narrowness of the team's lead—and then the whistle blew again, announcing the start of the second half.

"I'm going to show you a diagram of three chemical formulas," Allen Ludden said, and the RPI team pressed forward, fingers tensed over buzzers. "Of these three, identify the one that could safely be drunk in a glass of water."

There was a seconds-long lull, a seeming eternity, the clock ticking menacingly in the silence. Then a buzzer sounded: Fordham. RPI sat back. So much for being scientists. Fordham had it, and now the bonus question as well. They were nearly tied. My father correctly identified Leibniz's "principle of sufficient reason"; a question on arthropods went to Fordham. Maybe they were going to lose this round after all. But then, Fordham conferred on a tossup, incurring a penalty, and RPI answered the question correctly. They had the bonus question now, and only seconds on the clock.

"All right, Rensselaer. If an 'aesthete' is one who cultivates an unusually high sensitivity to beauty and an 'aesthetician' is one versed in the theory of beauty and artistic expression, for twenty points, explain the difference between 'gourmet' and 'gourmand.'"

That was easy. My father had the answer. "A gourmet is a connoisseur of food and drink. A gourmand is a glutton, someone who loves food indiscriminately."

"That's right! And there's the final whistle, ladies and gentlemen. And the score is: Rensselaer 210, Fordham 165! Rensselaer is our winner for the third straight time."

My father heard clapping from the tiers, the sound, he thought, of his name being called. They'd won! he realized. They'd won! Only two more times and they would retire undefeated, only the fourth school to do so in the Quiz Bowl's history! He was elated, though he sat calmly, kept his cool. No one jumped up and down: no backslapping or cavorting. It was a little anticlimactic, but this was national television, after all, and they'd been instructed to sit quietly, sportsmanlike and poised, through Allen Ludden's spiel for education and General Electric at the end. It wasn't in his nature, anyway, to hop around, to be more than nonchalant about the whole business. But he was pleased, he couldn't have been more pleased about it. They'd won!

And he searched for my mother once again through the light's burning glare.

WEINBERGER!

SOME THINGS I'D TELL YOU
IF I HAD THE CHANCE 4
We didn't watch the news when I was growing up or read the newspaper. I didn't know who Martin Luther King, Jr., was until I was a junior in college. I had thought that he and Martin Luther were somehow related, though who Martin Luther was, I wasn't sure either. That was partly the Taos school system: we learned about Vasco de Gama and the Treaty of Guadalupe Hildalgo instead of the civil rights movement. But I'm not talking about just the ordinary ignorance of the young. It's a measure of how far away Mom had drifted from her upbringing and her life with you. She never talked about history or current events. I had heard of John Kennedy, but not Bobby, certainly not Malcolm X. "Vietnam" was just a word rattling around inside my head. Most of my childhood, we'd had nothing but AM radio. When we finally wired electricity into the shack, Wayne put a TV on a high shelf above the cookstove's wood stack, mostly so that he could watch World Wide Wrestling and Muhammad Ali. We got only two channels anyway, and those not very clearly. My mother did tune in to Holocaust, the miniseries. It was the first I'd heard of the event, though I didn't fully realize the story wasn't fiction. In high school, Peter watched football. After he left for college, the television remained dark most of the time. Mom and I supported Reagan because he was antiabortion. That was politics enough for both of us.

After college, Irwin and Stephan, as they'd both dreamed of doing, rented an apartment together in Greenwich Village, and my parents moved to a third-floor walkup on Second Avenue and Ninetieth Street in Germantown, the Yorkville section on the Upper East Side.

"One room," my mother says, "one window, and a door. A nothing of a kitchen. We wanted to live in the Village, but everything was so expensive in Manhattan, even then."

Irwin went to graduate school, and Stephan into the army. Later Stephan worked on a community park project in Harlem. He moved to St. Mark's Place, a funky, bohemian area in what was fast becoming known as the East Village instead of the Lower East Side, and considered so marginal that his father claims to have cried when he walked down his street for the first time. They saw little of Lewis, though they both visited my parents a couple of times in the Yorkville apartment, where a gigantic wooden drafting board dominated the tiny living room.

My mother had nearly flunked out of Skidmore. She had transferred there from Barnard to be closer to RPI after she and my father married. When they moved back to the city, Barnard reluctantly readmitted her. She was twenty-one, beginning her senior year. Lewis got a job with a midtown architectural firm.

My mother and father had a lot in common: a love of art, books, architecture, history. They were both Anglophiles and would entertain themselves by charting a chronology of English kings and queens, trying to map out the twists and turns in royal lineage from William the Conqueror to Elizabeth II. "Hash history," my mother calls it—a mishmash of dates and events, maybe in the right order with the right details, maybe not. A humorous history of England called *1066 and All That* was the source of their information, as well as their favorite private joke. Whenever one of them was frustrated or irritated, the other would elicit a smile by declaiming in a sonorous tone: "Into this maelstrom grimly strode Philip IV of Spain."

They shared a passion for avant-garde films, too. "We used to go to the movies a lot," she says. "Marcello Mastroianni, Fellini. We were really influenced by Fellini. That's when movies were changing, starting to comment more directly on people's lives. We had grown up on Doris Day, movies in which nothing bad ever happened—well, maybe John Wayne blew people away. Many of Fellini's movies are obscure, mysterious, sort of 'what's the meaning of life?' They had a big influence on us—on a lot of people."

They loved the city. On weekends and evenings when the light began to fade, they would wander the streets, visiting churches, the Frick Collection, the Pierpont Morgan Library. They'd look at paintings, remark on the merits and faults of buildings. Cornices. Arches. The sweep of a doorway. They'd stare dumbstruck at the Guggenheim. My mother preferred anything nineteenth-century, but Lewis went for clean lines. Philip Johnson, Mies van der Rohe, and the designer Charles Eames were his idols. In comparison, the Frick was a mausoleum. He could understand it, enjoy it even—the slippery green of the central fountain and pool, the craft in carving all that marble and wood—but it didn't move him. When he stood across the street from the Guggenheim, the breath caught in his throat.

I have few photographs of them then. Even in the trunk, I found only one snapshot, from a little earlier, in Troy: a casual but posed picture, perhaps taken with a timer or by a visitor. Both look strangely stiff, their expressions vacant. Still, though she does not say so explicitly, from the way she talks, they seem to have been happy.

MOVING PICTURES

The movies are in color, but there is no sound: Weinberger home movies, whose existence I discovered only recently, reels of them, which Miriam had transferred from 8 mm to video not long ago.

I am sitting cross-legged on a bed in one of the upstairs bedrooms in Miriam's house, straining forward to concentrate on the screen. What if I don't recognize my father when I see him?

But there he is, appearing so suddenly and briefly that I have to rewind the tape. He's wearing the black, thick-framed glasses from the *College Bowl* photos, a pipe dangling from his mouth: the combination gives him a slightly comical, Groucho Marx quality. His expression is flat, serious, and then he lifts his eyebrows and lips, flashing his teeth in a fake, clownish smile, before his face settles again, going somber.

I'm transfixed.

Kate comes up behind him and gives his neck an affectionate pat. I assume that my grandfather Morris was the cameraman. He cuts away to one of Miriam's children, and does so over and over again. There is a sense of total preoccupation with the babies, which I suppose is the way of home movies, and perhaps the point: to capture those ephemeral little faces. Other family members are caught only incidentally. Each time my father appears, he startles me. Glimpses of him take the form of sightings: a dark-suited figure climbing after the children in a city park, airlifting a child down a slope; his arms and torso, holding something—a camera case—the movie camera following his body as it walks away, until it is just a blur of moving shirt filling the screen. Dream-like, ghostly, he's there for the briefest moment and then dissolves. Often all the screen offers is a fragment: a bit of face, a hand on a steering wheel that might be his. Most of the time, it seems as if he's trying to avoid the camera's eye, and then, resigned or unable to resist, he looks directly at it from under his eyebrows and offers a quirky, fake smile. The moment he produces it, the camera cuts away.

The movies aren't in sequence. The camera pans over a building made of lacy white concrete. There are palm trees, a pool, a view of water. A sign says LIDO APARTMENTS. My uncle Joe's son, about two years old, sits in a metal chair near the pool. My mother, wearing a white blouse and an elaborate updo, appears beside him in the next shot. Then the dark patch behind them lightens, and there is my father; he smiles at her, seems to remark on something funny the boy is doing. Both look terribly young. She must be eighteen or nineteen, he twenty; their doting focus on the child gives them the air of teenagers longing to be grown up.

Now my father is driving a car, crossing a body of water. Morris must be holding the movie camera in the seat next to him.

"Oh, the Chesapeake Bay," Miriam says, from the doorway. She says she'd like to stay, to watch the movies with me, but she has to finish her cooking. It's Passover, and all her children and grandchildren will soon be arriving for the seder. I'm curious about the stories the images might elicit from her, but I'm just as happy to watch alone. I can rewind the tapes as obsessively as I want.

He wears sunglasses, chews gum. The camera cuts to the highway, to a tunnel the car is entering, then to Kate in the back seat, knitting. When it cuts back again, Morris has replaced my father in the driver's seat, apparently having handed the camera to Lewis.

Now my father is building a boat. We're back in Florida. It's a little boat, a sailboat, I guess. He's wearing a striped shirt, rolled-up khakis, a white headband over his sweaty forehead. On his lip is a strange, bristly little mustache. He planes the wood in long, careful strokes. Just as he's about to launch the finished boat, painted yellow with a base of maple, the film jumps and blurs, as if the reel has sprung.

I watch for a while, my attention flagging, and I fast-forward through scenes without my father in them. Then abruptly I push PLAY. A car pulls up to the curb in front of a suburban house, and my brother, the most adorable, fat-cheeked, widest-grinning little boy you could ever see, tumbles out. So intent am I on my father that I don't even consider that there might be images of us. Or of my brother, I should say, since there aren't any of me—not surprising, as my grandfather died not long after I was born. But I am surprised that there are no glimpses of my mother pregnant, as she must have been when the footage of Peter was shot. Maybe my mother wasn't there that day or wasn't showing yet, or the cameraman was too caught up with Peter. After Morris's death, my father replaced the home movies with picture after picture of my brother and me, stills taken with his single-lens reflex—though none, it occurs to me, are of my mother while she was pregnant, which seems remarkable, because I've been told that they struggled for years to conceive.

One tape ends, and I get up to insert another. A jump back in time. Miriam's wedding at the Essex House. The men, including my father, a round-faced kid, wear white tuxes and white satin yarmulkes. Kate lights Shabbos candles. My uncle Joe, a burly, attractive guy with a heavy brow and thick head of hair. My grandfather at a construction site, directing a crane as it places a series of enormous concrete circles in the ground.

How ordinary it all is. The same scenes mimicked in a thousand backyards, in a thousand images of American family life. Except that there is that strange fake smile, my father's simultaneous resentment toward and attraction to the camera's watching eye. He's there and yet apart, a participant who never lets you forget he doesn't quite belong. It's easy to see in all those backyard gatherings, sweet as they are, what he was trying to define himself against, what all that sophisticated knowledge and esoterica, those books like Kronenberger's about middlebrow America, were about.

Of course, there's a lie at the center of the whole enterprise, as there always is in photographs or footage like this. It's not just that the observer affects the observed, but that only sanctioned moments get recorded. It's an official history, just as surely as are the "candid" photos taken of Caroline and John-John Kennedy playing in the Oval Office. But no matter what these home movies are trying to portray, the truth here is that all the Weinberger children felt unwanted, in one way or another.

"We had a problem, my mother and I," Miriam told me once. "She wanted sons. When I was born, she was disappointed. No matter what I did, it wasn't right." Joe apparently felt Lewis was the favored one: whatever he wanted, he got. And Lewis, according to his friends, seemed to feel that his parents didn't care for him much, and might have preferred it if he hadn't been born.

And then comes a sequence that makes me sit up and watch closely. My mother and father are on a beach, walking in the surf. She is wearing a white smock over a white bikini, her tanned body glowing against the cloth. My father squats down to photograph the water. Then a shot of Kate, knitting at a picnic table. They're all at the picnic table, eating. I stare at my mother. She is elegant, even at the beach. Her hair, sun-streaked and golden, is in a complicated roll on top of her head, and wisps escape to swirl around her long neck. She sits straight-backed on the picnic bench, her head held gracefully erect, and bites into her chicken as delicately and deliberately as if she were in a four-star restaurant. She's so gorgeous that I'm a little stunned.

Ethereal. My father cups her beautiful face for a moment. She smiles sweetly back at him. Next, my mother is standing by an outdoor faucet. The camera can't get enough of her. She removes her sandals, hops on one shapely leg, washes sand off her feet, and bends over to dry them with a white towel, so that we catch a glimpse of bikinied bottom. Strangely, eerily, as if a little Fellini has crept into the already dream-like mix, the camera leaves her for a second to follow a small pink ball through the surf, then returns to my mother wiping her feet with the towel. The sequence ends with another brief glimpse of my father, who says something to Kate that makes her laugh. I rewind it. Again.

And somehow it's this that affects me even more than seeing my father in motion: this vision of my mother, so young and unbelievably lovely.

EXERCISE 4: YORKVILLE APARTMENT, 1961

In both hands, my mother cradles a ceramic mug. The radiator in the Yorkville apartment has two settings: "boiling" and "off," and in winter they drink cup after cup of coffee to keep warm. My father sets his aside on the kitchen table, which is also the dining table, the mail counter, the desk, and forgets it until it is too cold to drink. Or she finds his cup, half-full, moldering on a makeshift shelf.

Magazines, bills, binders of lecture notes written in my mother's calligraphic hand cover the few surfaces. She won awards for her penmanship in grade school. Scattered everywhere are books, stacks of paper, outdated copies of the *Times*. My mother doesn't like dirtiness; she asks him repeatedly to wipe up coffee rings and crumbs. But she does like the casual messiness, the aura of bookishness. She cultivates it. They both do.

On the top board, their books tilt precariously to one side. A rock keeps them from toppling to the floor. She's read Jane Austen, the Brontës, Somerset Maugham. But what does he read? History, philosophy, twentieth-century theories of design? Does he go in for Mailer, Capote, Allen Ginsberg? Ayn Rand? Every morning on the subway to the architectural firm, he holds the *New York Times*, folded into neat quarters, at lap level or close to his face.

Their friends have begun to move away, to leave the orbit of parents and high school. My mother's oldest friend, Beverly, is living in Taos. On the refrigerator is a postcard, describing the smell of sage and how extraordinary it is to be able to see the stars at night. They must come to New Mexico, she writes.

DANISH MODERN

My mother, no doubt under the influence of her father, majored in art history at Barnard. She wasn't a good student, however, and when her grades dropped to Ds, the college administration told her that she either had to shape up or drop out. My mother claims she intended to be a museum curator and she even spent a semester as an intern for the Brooklyn Museum of Art, but she got no further than a bachelor's degree.

I don't think she cared about being a "success." My mother came from ambitious people—people who rose from subsistence to wealth in one generation, people who cherished education and professional distinction. Family history to me has always been a mantra of job titles and degrees: my grandmother, the doctor of psychology; my aunt Anna, an artist with a master's in chemistry from Columbia; my mother's brother, John, a Ph.D. in physics and an electronics engineer in the High Energy Physics Lab at Harvard; my father, the architect. I found my family's achievements an inspiration. My mother found them a curse.

My mother as a young woman was bright, creative. But she wasn't driven. Married at nineteen, she probably thought she would be a stay-at-home mother and wife. If she was at all the woman I know now, she wanted country, agrarian simplicity—the influence perhaps of summers at Lake Mahopac. Lazy summers on the water, away from everything. She just wasn't attached to material things.

When I was growing up, my mother would talk with tremendous resentment about the suite of Danish modern bedroom furniture that her parents had bought for her and my father as a wedding present. She thought it was beautiful, and she loved it, but she held it against them—against her mother, in particular. It was emblematic to her, representing the power of money to exercise control. Her parents were setting them up in housekeeping, and once they'd acquired all that gorgeous furniture there'd be no other way to live.

As a child, I was always attracted to "fancy," as my grandmother says, enchanted by linens and china so fine you could see the light shine through. My mother, on the other hand, didn't mind tree stumps for chairs. In San Luis, she used an industrial-sized cable spindle for a kitchen table. That came later, of course, after she had given up the house, the suite of Danish bedroom furniture, the classic British racing green convertible MG my father bought for her in Florida. But her cable spindle and tree stumps were about money, too. Voluntary poverty is a middle-class privilege.

There is no doubt, however, that the weight of all that furniture finally got to her. The years of their marriage that she remembers with pleasure are those in which she and my father had the least— one window and a door on Ninetieth Street.

Problems of Building

The idea of permanence has always been associated with architecture. Many problems of building are best solved temporarily. But temporary constructions are seldom as architectural in character as those built to endure.

— HENRY-RUSSELL HITCHCOCK AND PHILIP JOHNSON,
   The International Style

FORT DIX, NEW JERSEY, 1962 TO 1964
I have a belt buckle—two half-moons in a silver rectangle—that my father made during his two years in the army. He was drafted in the early six-ties and sent to Fort Dix, New Jersey, for basic training. A  stint he could have avoided, if only, as his friends begged him to do, he had signed up for the Reserves. In the Reserves, he would have done a mere six months. It was considered the worst thing in the world to get drafted, even before the possibility of being sent to Vietnam was really in people's minds. So why didn't he join the National Guard or the Reserves like the rest of his friends? He was fascinated by combat, that is true. He romanticized war. But his passion was for history, his friends claim, the strategies and heroism of old battles, not "jingoism

and nutty patriotism." He might have visualized himself as a volunteer in the Lincoln Brigade, fighting a last great cause in the mountains of Spain, but that didn't mean he actually wanted to enlist. Being a soldier was never something in which he'd expressed any interest.

Except maybe to escape Vorhees, Walker, Smith, Smith and Haines: he was bored there, he hated it. They were stuffy and conventional and he was just a draftsman anyway, a tedious, unimaginative job. "You're trained to build Rockefeller Center," Ken Schatz says, "then they put you on a drawing board." Lewis had been working on a new cupola design for Howard Johnson's. After the glory of the *College Bowl*, that must have felt like quite a comedown.

Or maybe, as Miriam thinks, he let himself be drafted to follow, once again, in his brother's footsteps. Joe had been in the Navy ROTC and won an ROTC scholarship for school; he would have served as a commissioned officer, but he dropped out of college after a few years. On the same day in 1955 that he found out his wife was pregnant with their first child, Joe had received a draft notice; fortunately, the army didn't catch up with him until after the Korean War.

When my grandmother Kate found out Lewis had been drafted, she was horrified. She asked old family doctors to write letters to the draft board to tell them that he couldn't serve, that something was wrong with him, but her efforts came to nothing.

My mother stayed in the little Yorkville apartment, alone now and missing her husband. She'd go to visit him and have to sit with him on a bed in his barracks, no privacy to be found anywhere. After basic training, he was posted to Fort Dix. They moved their things up two flights of stairs to the top story of a rickety old house in Bordentown, New Jersey. He was made a recreational instructor, assigned to teach jewelry-making to GIs. A far cry from architecture but somehow apt. He was good with his hands, and though his tastes were modern, the Arts and Crafts Movement of the nineteenth century had captured his imagination.

Clearly, he was lucky in his assignment. Men would come back from eating dinner in the mess, he told Miriam, and be ordered to pack up their kits. They were loaded onto trucks and shipped off in the night. My father believed they were being sent to Vietnam.

My mother, also good with her hands, learned to throw pottery at Fort Dix. For the most part, she was happy. Their apartment had high ceilings and a big claw-foot tub that she loved, and she got a job on base teaching general subjects to mentally impaired or handicapped children. She had no training or preparation of any kind, but the children responded to her, and she found it satisfying.

People who remember them then think of her and my father as being very much in love. When she came home from her first day of class, carrying a gigantic stack of books, my father told Stephan how beautiful she looked, all these books spilling over. And Miriam says that in the early days my parents couldn't keep their hands off each other. "Before they were married, Terry and Lewis came down to visit my parents in Florida, I remember. My mother gave them separate rooms, but every morning she'd find them in bed together. That sort of thing just wasn't done in those days, but she couldn't keep them apart."

According to my mother, however, tension between them started to develop almost immediately after the wedding. When a girlfriend from Barnard came to visit my mother in Bordentown, my father was so flirty with her that my mother was upset. They had a tendency to speak harshly to each other. "I had a *very* sharp tongue," my mother says. "We both did." My mother was reading *Madame Bovary* for the first time and remembers being mesmerized by it—this woman, Emma, cultivating a hatred of her husband.

WHAT JEROME YAVARKOVSKY REMEMBERS

"Your father was extremely funny in a wry, sophisticated way. I knew him in high school and college, and I still remember things he said. For instance, a popular expression of disdain at the time was 'pseudo,' as in 'pseudo-intellectual.' One time at RPI, Alan Hundert and this guy Serge bought 1930s double-breasted suits from a thrift shop. Dark suits with chalk stripes, so oversized they gave the impression of being a step behind the guys as they walked. We were at a Phi Sigma party when they showed up. Lew looked at them, then at me, and he said, 'Suit-o.'" Jerome laughs delightedly.

Jerome, who is now a university librarian, met up with my father again in 1962 at Fort Dix. He went to check out the arts and crafts center the first day, and there was my father in uniform, managing the place.

Jerome had signed up, as Stephan had done, with the Reserves. "It was like being propelled back to life as a ten-year-old," he says, "playing soldier." Except that at any point during his six years of service, he could have been called up again—during the Cuban missile crisis, for instance, or for a tour in Vietnam. Lewis enlisted, Jerome recalls him saying, "to avoid having a baby by government decree." But Jerome is mistaken: my father was drafted. If he had enlisted he would have had more choice in the matter of his assignment, but he would have had to serve three years. As for the quip about having a baby, it could only have been a joke or bravado anyway, because my mother had been trying to get pregnant almost from the beginning of their marriage, three years earlier.

"Your parents were a remarkable couple. Your mom was quiet, strikingly beautiful. Very creative-looking, stylish in a handcrafted way. She had impeccable taste in everything. She didn't look middle-class—too artistic."

Jerome's tone suddenly grows earnest. "You know, your parents had the most mature, loving, caring relationship I ever knew. They had an enviable closeness and affection, expressed in the largest and smallest ways. I've thought of them many times over the years. I'm so sorry to hear this happened."

THE TRIUMVIRATE REVISITED

One weekend in the spring of 1963, returning from a visit to the Barnes Foundation collection outside of Philadelphia, Irwin and Stephan and their live-in girlfriends (and future wives) stopped in to see my father and mother in Bordentown.

The next day, all the way back to New York, their girlfriends harangued them about Lewis. *What's so great about him? Why do you idolize him? What do you see in him?* On and on. Stephan and Irwin saw the venomous bombardment for what it was—jealousy and annoyance at their having put Lewis on a pedestal. But now, more than thirty years later, they recognize that the women had a point. Here was a guy with a degree from a school that wasn't particularly known for architecture, a corporal in the army, stuck in New Jersey as a recreational instructor teaching jewelry-making to GIs. Irwin had an Ivy League liberal arts education and had returned to Columbia to get a master's degree in history—the field my father had always claimed for himself. Stephan had a degree in architecture from Cornell and was working in the office of the star architect Marcel Breuer. And Lewis seemed to have given up on all the things that had distinguished him when he was young. He didn't ski, or seek adventure; he hadn't done much traveling beyond a trip to Europe on his honeymoon. Stephan and Irwin, on the other hand, were out in the world, setting off by themselves through the territory that Lewis had always led them through. He was "our man in Manhattan" no more. Since high school, as Irwin quips, his friends had "discovered Gutenberg."

They had always thought of him as heroically intellectual. An explorer, adventurer, advance man. But whatever he might have been, their girlfriends insisted, he was nothing special now.

About my mother, Irwin remarks that other women, including their girlfriends, found her intimidating: she was so well put together, so unnervingly catlike, absorbing everyone and everything with her deep, intelligent eyes, but saying nothing.

CONFESSION

My mother never loved my father. I was in high school when she confessed this to me. I would have surges of curiosity about their life and want to know what had gone wrong. Once, in response to my questions, she said, in a searingly soft voice: *I never loved him.* That voice cut through me. It struck me powerfully then, with a teenage girl's well-developed sense of romance and tragedy, as a terrible, dark secret.

But people who remember them together in those years find my mother's statement strange.

"I'm sorry," her brother, John, says. "She was pretty gaga about him as I recall."

"Everyone thought of them as the ideal couple," Miriam says. "And your father couldn't live without your mother. They got married when he was still a junior at RPI. My parents were not happy that he didn't wait until after he graduated, but he claimed he couldn't concentrate on his work without her."

In the beginning, my mother *was* gaga about my father. Lewis was bright, intense, good-looking, in a well-fed, middle-class way. A good catch, even if he couldn't dance and hated sports. She was, as my uncle John says, *pretty excited* about him. They had been dating off and on since the end of his senior year in high school. In the off phases, my mother had gone out with Joel, Stephan's roommate at Cornell, as well as Marty, a dashing jazz aficionado who had been nicknamed "Trilingual" because he claimed to speak three languages. Irwin told me that once while standing on a busy street corner in the Village, Trilingual had pulled out a brick of hashish and offered to sell it to him. Hearing that she was dating a jerk like him drove my father wild.

Not much later he convinced her to make a steadier commitment to him. It was 1959, and my mother had just finished her freshman year at Barnard College. She was planning to remain in the city during the summer, but having a male visitor in her residence hall was difficult. She had roommates, he had to sign in, and they had to keep the door open while he was there. Because it was convenient and he was in love with her, and she was pretty excited about him, she and Lewis decided that they would rent a small apartment near the school, and he would move in with her for the summer. According to my mother, that decision marked the moment when her life began to go awry. She had grown up in an environment of radical politics and liberal values. Even in the fifties, neither of her parents had believed that sex needed to be sanctified by marriage. When my mother reached late adolescence and began dating seriously, my grandmother took her aside to talk to her about birth control.

And so my mother let my father move in with her. But when my grandfather Juan found out they were living together, he was out-raged. He insisted they get married. Telling the story to me years later, my mother attributed his consternation to moral uprightness, some latent godliness—he, who had repudiated religion at the age of twelve. (He refused to go to confession in his Santiago Catholic school. "Those priests have more to confess than I do," he said before walking out of the school and away from it and the Church for good.)

My grandmother says it was the times. "Your grandfather thought, if you're that serious about each other, then get married."

They were also afraid my mother would get kicked out of Barnard if she did not—a good possibility, considering the national uproar that ensued nine years later in 1968 when the Barnard student Linda LeClair was discovered to be living with her boyfriend.

My mother felt tricked. Hadn't her mother led her to believe that cohabitation was acceptable? Wasn't that implicit in the information she had given her about birth control?

She found it absurd that fear of her expulsion from college would have motivated her father to act as he did. He didn't think that way; education wasn't a big priority with him. And besides, the arrange-ment was already ended by the time he found out about it: she had given up the apartment and moved back into her dormitory, Lewis had gone back to school, and Barnard was none the wiser.

Rose didn't, for some reason, simply tell my mother to be more discreet in the future, though that was more in keeping with her lib-eral attitudes. My grandmother and grandfather, after all, had lived together in the late 1930s—though they told everyone that they were married. This is a complicated story, involving an abandoned Chilean wife who wouldn't grant my grandfather a divorce. I'm not sure my mother knew the details, but she did know that she had been con-ceived out of wedlock; after she became a Christian, she felt deeply bitter about this. It was evidence of her mother's amorality, but also of her hypocrisy.

Her parents wouldn't even have known about their living to-gether had she not confessed it to her mother. Some uncertainty about how they would react must have remained in her mind because she kept quiet about the apartment until the end of the summer: her mother and father thought she was staying in the dorm. Then, one afternoon in the fall, my mother was sitting with her mother in her parents' living room, and she felt flooded by a sudden feeling of closeness. She decided to share this intimate secret, somehow thinking that her mother would be pleased by her daring. As my mother remembers, Rose didn't really react to the news. But she immediately told my grandfather.

Maybe a residue of Catholic indoctrination did rise up in Juan. I'm sure he was as capable of inconsistent and contradictory moralizing as the next person, but Rose's reaction is less comprehensible. She usually scoffed at conventional pieties.

My mother wanted her mother to stand up to her father, to tell him that by no means would their daughter be forced to marry. But she says that my grandmother wouldn't do it, even though she wasn't crazy about Lewis. She preferred my mother's previous high school sweetheart, Eddie, the crooner, who went to Princeton and became a doctor. There was something about my father that bothered her. He didn't always treat my mother nicely. She felt he was condescending to her, failing to value her achievements. When my mother organized the Greek Games at Barnard—a great responsibility and an honor—Lewis arrived two hours late and didn't seem to realize how much it meant to her for him to be there or how hurt she was that he'd missed most of it. As far as my grandmother was concerned, he was cold.

"Why don't you give him up?" she said to my mother. But my mother refused. My grandmother tells me she "couldn't pry him loose."

Give him up or else marry him.

My mother's parents had been "terribly permissive" all her life, my mother says, and now they were telling her that what she wanted was irrelevant. "My parents basically said, 'You're going to do this.' It was a thunderbolt. I was hoping for romance, to fall in love. I was looking forward to a man choosing me, and me him. I liked Lewis, but I wasn't sure I wanted him as a husband. I knew he was a very unhappy and mixed-up person. It seemed as if there was something crushed about his spirit. I was a very unhappy and mixed-up person, too, and not at all ready to commit to anyone. I was constantly being pushed and prodded to be someone I wasn't. But my parents were not old-country kind of people. I had had no hint that they would pick out who I would marry."

Perhaps my mother simply didn't want Lewis. Perhaps she was attracted to men who were virile and tough—like the boys in *The Lords of Flatbush*, like Vinnie Barbarino, like Wayne Reynolds.

Then my mother wanted *Lewis* to stand up to her father. But my father loved her. He *wanted* to marry her. He couldn't live without her. It drove him wild when she dated other men.

It never seemed to occur to her that she could stand up to her father herself.

"You didn't do that then," she says now. "You didn't ignore what your parents told you to do."

In a few short years, of course, many of her generation would do just that. But my mother grew up in a time when children still respected their parents' authority: they had a certain latitude in their decisions, but their parents influenced their choices of schools, careers, and marriage partners. These realities helped fuel the coming exodus into the counterculture. My mother got caught in the interstices between the fifties and sixties. She was also very young: not strong enough to express her will.

And so on January 31, 1960, in a simple ceremony performed by a rabbi at her parents' house, wearing a tea-length, white satin dress embroidered with seed pearls and looking like the perfect, radiant bride, my mother married my father. It was a small wedding, with only family in attendance—not even Irwin or Stephan was there. How she felt at that moment, smiling broadly in the candid photographs, I don't know. Perhaps even then, but certainly in later life, she blamed her mother for whatever circumstances had landed her there on Lewis's arm. Given time and the natural development of the relationship, she might have married him anyway. She liked the status marriage conferred on her. It had cachet among her friends. And she had no strong ambitions, no drive toward a career. She might as well be somebody's wife. But she felt her mother had engineered the event, and she carried what she describes as a white-hot anger into the marriage. She thought of her mother's maneuvering ever after as "the double cross."

We were sitting around the teak dining table at my grandparents' house in Queens, eating dinner and talking about Jimmy Carter. Or rather, my grandmother was talking about Jimmy Carter. My grandfather, his personality already vanishing into Alzheimer's, was sitting on her right, silently chewing roast beef. He cut it laboriously, chewed and chewed, took a sip of wine. Next to him at the long table and opposite me, my brother had already emptied his plate. He was shifting and sliding in his chair, antsy to be excused, to rush downstairs and watch television—fifteen clear channels to New Mexico's fuzzy two! I was only eleven but had more patience than he did and could sit longer. I was interested in the conversation about Carter and his education policies, though I found the issue hard to grasp. I didn't know anything about the president except that he was from Georgia and was associated in my mind with the word "goobers." But I was eager to learn. Adult talk intrigued me. Because my seriousness was not out of place with them, only charming and strange, I always preferred the company of grown-ups over that of anyone my own age.

My grandmother was perched at the end of the table—the "head" of the table, nearest the swinging door to the kitchen—and she was talking about something she'd read in the morning newspaper. Her voice was a little strident, as it often could be when she felt passionate about something. It was as if there were a pool of light around her and the rest of us were in shadow. My mother was next to her, on her left, silent. Apparently, the remarks about Carter were being addressed to her. My grandmother did not care for Jimmy Carter particularly; she thought that he was weak and ineffectual and annoyingly moralistic, but she supported him anyway. He was a Democrat and she would never support anyone but a Democrat. He had also demonstrated a commitment to Israel by brokering a peace agreement between Israel and Egypt at Camp David. That alone would win him her vote.

My mother, like her mother, was a registered Democrat and it would seem natural that Carter would appeal to her because he was so openly Christian, but she always voted Republican now. My grandmother hadn't yet discovered that her daughter, *her daughter!* intended to vote for Ronald Reagan in the upcoming election, but when she did, she would be shocked beyond all measure—and this fact as no other would bring home the full horror of her daughter's conversion.

My grandmother went on and on, so long that waves of anxiety rose in my stomach. The shrill monologue of her opinions filled my ears. I loved my grandmother and admired her for being this very thing: a strong, opinionated woman, an admiration that would only grow as I became older and learned to talk back to her, talk to her, but I could feel the tension in my mother's body next to me, the pinched profile of her lips and nose. She was holding her tongue, but for how long? And what would she say when she couldn't stand it any longer? With my grandmother, my mother always raised the name of Jesus in anger, like a club. What would it be this time? Prayer in the schools, the hopelessness of this program or that program unless we had God in our lives to make us whole, Jesus as the only solution or my grandmother's attempt to replace the power and will of God with her own humanism, which could only come to dust. I'd heard my mother talking to her father, too, about Christ, the need of God, but her tone was completely different. In it, I heard her love and genuine fear for his soul, though he would put her off in the small fretful voice of his dementia by saying, "I'm a Catholic, I'm a Catholic."

It had been a good visit so far, relatively calm, but we were nearing the end of it, and it was *impossible* to get through a visit without a blowup. The tension had been building all week, through our shopping spree at Bloomingdale's and *Cinderella* at the Met and our ritual feast at the Dynasty on Long Island, through dinner after dinner. And it was this as much as anything that prevented me from escaping with Peter to the safety of the basement: the need to be on the scene, to protect my mother and divert my grandmother, if I could, before the fatal moment. It was coming, with increasing desperation I could see it coming, the explosion that would leave my grandmother hissing with fury, dinner ended abruptly, and my mother crying behind her slammed door, while I stood in the hallway, one hand on the knob.

QUEST 16: LIBRARY BOOKS

In the trunk, which I go back to again and again now, trying to match faces and slivers of landscape in the background to words in the journal, I find a negative of my mother posed dramatically in front of a built-in bookshelf in the Florida house. A strange excitement sends me running downstairs to the darkroom to ask my husband to make a print for me. As soon as he's exposed it, I rush the sheet through the development baths, jiggling the trays, swirling the paper back and forth with the tongs so the image will develop faster: my mother is wearing a large-brimmed, artistically floppy velveteen hat and corduroys tied with a Mexican cloth belt. The hat brim covers much of her face, leaving visible only her straight nose, well-formed lips, oval jaw. Deep angular shadows slice the print in thirds. Her figure, lit from a window or a skylight above, occupies the center. She is naked to the waist. It is probably the photograph that hung on the back of my parents' bathroom door—this or one of many like it—that sent my then eight-year-old cousin, Miriam's son, Michael, breathless and awed, running for his father. "Hey, Pop. Hey, Pop, look at this." My parents were considered very avant-garde.

I was sixteen the first time I found a batch of nude photographs of my mother—a whole stack of them in a box in my grandparents' attic. They depicted a series of dance movements, Tai chi–like in their grace and precision. They weren't pornographic, but at sixteen they seemed so to me. Everything just out there. I confronted her with them.

"Oh, I'm so sorry," she said. "They're disgusting, aren't they?" Disgusting. Her word. Applying the morality of the present self to the sensibility of the past. "What a thing for a daughter to find."

No, I would say to her now. Not disgusting. Your ease, your natural poise in front of the camera, in your own body, is so impressive. Look how beautiful he must have found you. Look how beautiful you were.

Of the hundred or so in the army trunk, this photograph is one of the best, the most competently composed. I feel my cousin Michael's elation, but the thrill I experience is not inspired by the illicit. It isn't even the indignation of looking at one's own mother naked. That isn't the striking thing about this photograph of a beautiful, bare-breasted woman who is my mother. It is instead the shock of discovery, the shock, in a way, of paying attention to the ordinary. On my husband's light table, I look at the photograph through his magnifying loupe. Not *at* my mother, but *behind* her: *there they are, there they are!* The books. On the bookshelf behind her. So vivid I can almost touch their spines, almost smell the must and cigarette ash on their pages. Creased and worn softcover copies mostly, a few hardcovers, but all obviously read.

Man's Hope, The Tin Drum, The Magic Barrel. Books I've read or have been meaning to read. *Buddenbrooks, Call It Sleep, Ulysses,* Jane Austen and Simone de Beauvoir, *Madame Bovary* and *Jude the Obscure.* Books on my own shelf. *The Brothers Karamazov,* which I discovered in high school and which, along with Joyce's "The Dead," was among the first books to stir in me the passion for words. Conrad, Henry James, Pirandello, Waugh. A lot of Proust. *Native Son* and *Soul on Ice.* My father, as Miriam says, was very political. *Red China, China, The Civil War in the United States, The New Class, Gallipoli.* I assume for no good reason that the books were his. It frustrates me, in fact, that my parents' selections were clearly mixed together—my husband and I keep a joint bank account, but we separate our books into mine and his.

Proust was probably my mother's; she had a Proust phase. Flaubert, Hardy, Austen, Henry James, I know she read those. She referred to them when I was older, the loves of her youth, and now that she's taken up novels again, these are the writers whom she is most likely reading today.

I think that the contemporary titles were his. Lawrence Durrell's *Clea*. Alberto Moravia, *The Lie*. *The Crying of Lot 49* and *Catch-22*. If he were alive now, he might be reading Gabriel García Márquez, Toni Morrison, Kazuo Ishiguro. I'd send him a copy of *if on a winter's night a traveler*. *The Unbearable Lightness of Being*. I'd give him a week or two, then I'd call him up. What'd you think, Dad? I'd say. *What'd you think?*

John Berryman is the only visible poet. But why Berryman? *His Toy, His Dream, His Rest*. The one to throw himself over a bridge (though not until 1972). The same bridge over the Mississippi that I've crossed a hundred times walking from one side of the University of Minnesota campus to the other, and over whose rail I've looked more than once, not to jump, but to contemplate jumping. From the rail of the Washington Avenue bridge, it's a very long way down. And Berryman missed the water altogether.

And then, like the tempting Berryman, there are the portentous titles: *The Way of All Flesh, Lie Down in Darkness, Curse of the Misbegotten*. Even *Look Homeward, Angel*.

I've begun to feel a desire to make contact with my father so profound that it feels like a kind of worship, as if any day now I'll be erecting shrines on the unused landing outside my office in the Blaine house. Maybe I'll buy the books in the photograph, the ones I don't already have, and arrange them in the same order on my own bookshelf. Maybe I'll sit on a bench in front of them and have my husband photograph me in that attitude: dramatic shadows, floppy hat, bare to the waist.

Maybe, because it has taken me twenty years to realize I need my father, a little obsession is warranted.

DIALOGUE

You were a romantic in the nineteenth-century sense. You imagined your life unfolding like a story in a novel. Is that what you thought when you crossed into Central America to buy drugs? Is that what you thought when you put the gun to your head? Did you think of Hemingway, Berryman, of the parade of suicides through literature? Did you think of Seymour Glass, the former child star of a radio quiz show who put a bullet through his brain in "A Perfect Day for Bananafish"? Did you think, Here is a fitting end to the novel that is my life?

The first book assigned to me in my first literature course at Macalester College in St. Paul, where I'd transferred after one year at North Central Bible College, was *The Sound and the Fury.* The other students were impatient and bored with the book. I found it so stunning that I could hardly get through it. I'd read each sentence twice, then a third time, and sometimes a fourth, savoring it before I could bring myself to move on to the next. The words were crocus shoots in my soul, pushing through a hard crust of snow. A tyranny of decency ruled course reading lists at North Central, but Macalester was a whole new world. I would cross the verdant campus with the book in my hand, intoning the book's implied epigraph under my breath, "Life's but a walking shadow, a poor player / that struts and frets his hour upon the stage, / and then is heard no more; it is a tale / told by an idiot, full of sound and fury, / signifying"—a long, dramatic pause, then a whisper—"*nothing.*"

FORT DIX, NEW JERSEY, NOVEMBER 22, 1963
My parents were in Bordentown when John F. Kennedy was assassinated. My mother was teaching school. This was one of the few historical moments she reminisced about during my childhood. She remembers another teacher coming into the classroom to tell her. She does not remember what she did after that, whether she dismissed her class or went on with whatever lesson she was teaching or simply stood there at the front of the room, stricken. All that Thanksgiving weekend, through three days of unbelievable images and solemn, half-baffled announcements, she and my father and their friends, along with the rest of the nation, sat glued to the television set, its electronic pulse connecting them like a linked hand to every other household in the country: from Walter Cronkite's broken announcement that the president was dead through Lyndon Johnson's swearing in, to the shocking sight of Lee Harvey Oswald shot dead in front of the rolling cameras on Sunday morning, to the funeral cortege in which regal Jackie displayed such dignity and strength, and her little son captured the mournful heart of the world.

The thing my mother says she remembers about Kennedy's death is the sense of disintegration. Presidents left office one of two ways: they served two terms and retired, or they were voted out. Assassination was outside possibility, outside the collective imagination. Lincoln was outside memory: those were not modern times, that was history, practically theater. And who remembered Garfield or McKinley? Kennedy's death removed the nation's veil of protection. Anything could happen. Anyone could die.

DIALOGUE 2
In Company Manners, *a passage you underlined: "And with most of us the wish to understand our age is only part of the need to equilibrate ourselves, to achieve some sort of working philosophy."*

FORT DIX, NEW JERSEY, TO MIAMI, FLORIDA, SUMMER 1964
My father's stint in the army was over, finally. But what to do now? He couldn't stand the thought of going back to New York to work for another architecture firm. His father was building in Florida again, and Joe was still working for him. In fact, according to Miriam, Morris had come out of retirement *in order* to provide an opportunity for his two sons.

My mother, driving with my father through the South Atlantic states to Florida, carried a dread of the South developed from years of hearing her mother rage about the treatment of blacks at the hands of benighted, vicious whites. There could hardly have been a more disturbing time to drive through the South. Freedom Summer. Nearly a thousand volunteers were working to register black voters in Mississippi under the leadership of the Student Nonviolent Coordinating Committee, and three of them, James Chaney, Michael Schwerner, and Andrew Goodman, had just been murdered. Their burned-out car had been found two days after their disappearance on June 21, though their bodies were not discovered until six weeks later, buried on Klansman Olen Burrage's farm.

Despite the anxiety the redneck element inspired, my mother and father had taken a trip to the Smoky Mountains the summer before their move, while he was still in the army and civil rights protests were being staged across the country: more than 700 demonstrations in 186 cities, nearly 15,000 people arrested in ten short weeks. They encountered no real trouble, touring through Charleston to look at the architecture and then down to New Orleans and eventually Miami to visit his parents. Still, the tension in some places, particularly the most backwater, was frightening enough: hostile looks in Georgia diners, menacing remarks about Yankees from two park attendants wielding nail-headed trash pickers in an isolated state park in Louisiana. They avoided Mississippi and Alabama, the states issuing the most explosive news reports. Anyone with New York plates didn't go there as a tourist.

As a child, my mother was sent to Communist summer camps where they sang songs about oppression and workers' rights. My father was no red diaper baby, but his values were similar to hers. They talked, my mother says, about volunteering with the SNCC or the Congress of Racial Equality, joining all the other middle-class Jewish kids working for civil rights in the South, but they decided not to do it. It was too dangerous; they weren't prepared to get killed. In this, they were the rule rather than the exception. Not many people they knew were involved, either with civil rights or the protest movement: most of those who participated were college kids. Besides, my father had already given up two years of his life to the military. It was time to get on with it; they wanted to have a family. What had happened to my father's taste for adventure, his admiration for risk-takers and warriors, I don't know. My parents were only three or four years older than most of the student activists, and yet it was enough to make them a different generation altogether.

Of their friends, Stephan was among the few who were active politically. He spent three years working as an architect for the Harlem Education Project, an outgrowth of the Northern Student Movement, whose mission was to fight de facto segregation in the North; he marched in protests against the Vietnam War; and in 1965 he spent a week, along with his wife, in Louisiana with the Medical Committee for Human Rights—some of which time he passed crouching on the floor of the car with a bunch of whooping CORE members being followed at ninety miles an hour by a pickup full of Klansmen. His experience with CORE, Stephan tells me, was a rush; dangerous as it was, he found it exhilarating—though it sobered him when one of those CORE members, a young African American man who was in charge of the office in Monroe, was later killed in a similar car chase.

DIALOGUE 3
I was mistaken. You did not underline the passage in Company Manners. *Stephan says he did. Or thinks he did.*

ITEM ON PERMANENT LOAN FROM THE INVENTORY OF MY FATHER
My mother didn't give me her engagement ring from my father, as he had asked her to do when I was old enough to have it. When I was about to be engaged, she decided to keep it for my brother instead, so that he could give it to his hypothetical bride-to-be. Convention being what it was, this bestowal made more sense to her: the man is supposed to give a ring to the woman; the woman doesn't provide a ring for the man to give her. She asked me first if it was okay.

"Sure, Mom," I said, with only the slightest hesitation. "That makes sense. It's okay."

It did make sense, convention being what it was, especially in the church.

But it was my ring. My father wanted me specifically to have it. It was not okay, but I did not say so. I let her give it to Peter. Once again, in my eagerness to please, I betrayed myself, as I did with the trunk that I gave to Gersh.

My ring, the only direct message my father ever sent me.

HYSTERIA
I keep talking to Stuart about New York. I don't want to go as just a visitor: I want to live there, even for a short while, in my father's city, the center of my family's life going back to the turn of the century.

"We'd have to sell the house," he says.

"So what's stopping us?" I ask.

I have often talked of selling the house. Nor is this scheme the first I've proposed: let's spend a year traveling, I've suggested, live abroad, or move from place to place until we discover one that speaks to both of us. But Stuart finds such open-ended plans too threatening. He comes from a solid family of working-class Christian fundamentalists, and the notion of taking a rucksack and hiking through Europe is alien to him.

"Then how about an apartment in town?" I say. I'd settle for fewer chores, more freedom to come and go.

"But what about money?" Stuart asks. "Renting doesn't make sense when we can own. And what about the dog?"

When I get hysterical, as I sometimes do, he will agree to anything. *I'm only nineteen!* I say, sobbing. *I'm only twenty! Twenty-two! Twenty-four! Twenty-six!* Then, when I calm down, we both begin the work of talking me out of whatever plan I've concocted. It is a cycle we create together. What I want isn't reasonable. It isn't responsible. Bills have to be paid. *Yes, yes, you're right.* Paychecks have to be earned. In a year or two, when we've lived in it long enough to justify the hassle and expense, we'll sell the house. *That makes sense, of course.* I am a princess, I know, whose hippie upbringing and privileged New York family never prepared her to live in what Stuart likes to call "the real world."

Eventually, we've whittled down my plan to a month in New York after I graduate, which I hope to do in the spring. My mother's cousin Merle has an apartment in the Village; she and her husband go away every September, and my mother tells me that they sometimes let people stay there while they're gone. Or we could sublet an apartment.

"What about my job?" Stuart asks. "They're not going to let me go for a month. I'd have to quit."

"So quit," I say.

But in the end, we decide that even a month is too much. We will use Stuart's paid vacation time to go to Spain for two weeks instead. I am excited, stirred by the thought of going to a country like the one my grandfather came from.

Even so, it is not enough.

My husband and I were sitting at the kitchen table in our house in south Minneapolis, eating hamburgers. I loved this spot, tranquil and warm, especially in the late afternoon when sunlight spilled through the wide south-facing windows. Outside, a dense lilac hedge shielded us from the neighbors. It was an old house, the paint on the deep sills many-layered and chipped, the panes dirt-streaked. No matter how often I wiped them, the dirt sifted down from the old walls, crept up through the new tile we laid on the floor. However hard I scrubbed, a scum of age coated everything.

Stuart was eating his hamburger with two hands. I held mine in one hand, the other loose in the air between us. We were talking about a television commercial.

You can't tell from television commercials that there was ever a feminist revolution. They might give a woman a briefcase, but she still does the laundry, doles out school snacks. It's always the woman who scrubs the grape juice out of the brand-new cream-colored carpet.

My voice rose. I gestured excitedly.

That one ad in which the mother gets sick and her husband has to take over: he burns the shirts, wrecks the house, the children are eating Chee-tos for dinner. I hate that one.

I didn't know where these hand gestures had come from—no one in my family talked this way. It was an idea of something, culled no doubt from television, an ethnic cliché, evoking—what else? Jewishness.

But is it that the commercials are preserving the status quo or only reflecting it?

The gestures were markers of an identity that I was trying, in some utterly inchoate way, to claim for myself. I had never been to temple or even a Jewish Community Center. But once, surrounded by Jews at a poetry reading given by Yehuda Amichai at the University of Minnesota, I was swept by a rare, sweet sense of belonging. I loved the way they responded to me, the intimate banter we shared as we waited for the event to begin, as if they knew I was one of their own. I also identified Jewishness with my grandmother Rose, whom I wanted to be like more than anyone else in the world. I had been taught as a fundamentalist to disdain intellect, but I wanted desperately to cultivate her deep knowledge and fierce intelligence in myself.

Chicken or the egg?

When we watched television, I railed at the announcers, at the commercials, at the cupidity of politicians, hands raised like an exasperated New York City cabdriver. Stuart was silent through it all, sometimes amused, sometimes not. It became a joke between us. It was called "doing the hands at the television."

They must do demographic surveys. They know who buys the Tide and the peanut butter.

He liked the hand gestures, but he did not like the blood in my face, the feverish way I could talk "about nothing."

Now, at the kitchen table, Stuart set down his hamburger. "If you're going to talk like that, I'm not going to talk to you."

"Like what?" I said. But I knew like what. It was the raised voice, the flooded skin. Lying in bed at night, talking, he would say, "You don't have to yell. I'm right here." I was getting too excited again, *about nothing.*

"You're attacking me," he said.

"I'm not attacking you. I'm just talking."

"I don't have anything to do with what commercials get put on television."

For a moment, red-hot and ferocious, I hated him. I hated his bland self-control, his Midwestern calm, his Nordic stoicism. I wanted to shake him and scream, "Are you alive? Is anybody in there? Does anything matter enough to you to raise your voice about it?"

But I did not scream. I shut up about the commercials. I filed it away for next time: don't raise your voice, modulate your tone so as not to seem threatening or hostile or aggressive. Or worse, so as not to seem condescending. I knew that Stuart had a point. He couldn't get a word in edgewise; I didn't listen; I interrupted when he talked; my raised voice *did* sound threatening. My family did not gesture, but they certainly talked aggressively; they went after a subject and tore it to bits. A person could wind up like a trapped animal between the arguer and the argument.

The hatred evaporated suddenly, and yet the bitter film of it remained on my tongue. There was a moment when I had said it aloud, *I hate you*, like a rebellious child. I wanted him to see it for what it was, that I didn't mean it, not really, but it devastated him. "Don't say that again," he said. His voice was stern, controlled. And something else: the faintest tremolo. I felt terrible. *Don't say that again.* He was kind and gentle and good, but sometimes I wanted a rousing smash-up argument, vicious and satisfying. I was willing to take as good as I gave. I didn't believe a moment of hatred was the end of love.

I couldn't, regardless, seem to express clearly enough, loudly enough, the real source of the problem. Our life together was so limited, so circumscribed. Though we had begun to foray further and further from our Christian upbringings, we continued to define ourselves almost entirely by what we couldn't condone. Stuart and I didn't go to bars, state fairs, sporting events, or rock concerts. We considered this lowbrow culture and sneered at those who enjoyed such activities. And yet, we didn't exactly embrace highbrow culture, either; we scorned that just as much, deeming it empty and, worse, morally bankrupt. We didn't attend art films, dance performances, rarely went to the theater; when we visited museums, it was almost exclusively to see exhibits of documentary photography. The enjoyment of such things was not in Stuart's "programming," as he called it; it had been systematically rooted out of mine.

And yet I was always longing for something more, a wider world.

I picked up my hamburger with both hands and stared out at the untrimmed bush dividing our windows from the house opposite. We'd argued, jokingly, but with an underlying seriousness, about that, too, the trimming of shrubs. I wanted them wild, he wanted them cut into neat city-appropriate shapes. The metaphor gaped at me, obvious and exaggerated: his desire to contain *by lopping off* the branches' exuberant growth. I felt choked, enraged again, but I kept eating my hamburger.

"The bushes will be healthier," he always said, "if we prune them back. This is Minneapolis, not New Mexico." He was right, of course. This was Minneapolis. I swallowed bites of hamburger and ire. After a while, we spoke in ordinary voices, as if nothing had happened.

WASHOUT

I had a kind of a breakdown. A nervous breakdown, I guess. It started right after the move to the Blaine house. It was Halloween 1991. As we loaded up the U-Haul to make the last trip from south Minneapolis to Blaine, it began to snow, fat wet flakes that clogged the windshield wipers and forced us to creep along at half the speed limit. By the time we got to the house, there were six inches on the ground, and by morning there were thirty-one. We were snowed in, imprisoned, really, in a strange house, with its strange smells, boxes everywhere, a corner filled with things belonging to the previous owner, who couldn't get everything out because of the weather. Stuart had a job in the city; the roads were so bad that it took him two hours each way to get to work. I was alone in our new house for twelve hours a day, unable even to drive to the grocery store for fear of getting stuck. I began to cry then and continued straight through Thanksgiving. I'd be painting the walls, or standing at the island in the center of our kitchen, trying to chop vegetables so that dinner would be ready when Stuart came home, and the tears would run and run. I felt as if my face would eventually wash away, like the loose dirt of an arroyo during a downpour. Even after the roads cleared, I could not go out. I could not bring myself to answer the phone. I was not crying because of the snow or the isolation, but because, a week into it, I already knew: I didn't want that house, I didn't want to live in Blaine. I was crying because I couldn't make up my mind to stay with Stuart.

Glacial Fauna

On whatever theoretical horizon we examine it, the house image would appear to have become the topography of our intimate being. In order to give an idea of how complex is the task of the psychologist who studies the depths of the human soul, C. G. Jung asks his readers to consider the following comparison: "We have to describe and to explain a building the upper story of which was erected in the nineteenth century; the ground-floor dates from the sixteenth century, and a careful examination of the masonry discloses the fact that it was reconstructed from a dwelling-tower of the eleventh century. In the cellar we discover Roman foundation walls, and under the cellar a filled-in cave, in the floor of which stone tools are found and remnants of glacial fauna in the layers below. That would be a sort of picture of our mental structure." Naturally, Jung was well aware of the limitations of this comparison. But from the very fact that it may be so easily developed, there is ground for taking the house as a *tool for analysis* of the human soul. . . . Not only our memories, but the things we have forgotten are "housed." Our soul is an abode.

— GASTON BACHELARD, *The Poetics of Space*

MIAMI, FLORIDA, 1964
My parents packed their belongings into a car and moved to a small house in a run-down section of Miami. Their friends felt awful about this. Why would Lewis want to do that, they wondered, go to Florida to work for his father? The tough guy, the hard-ass, the materialist.

Surely there were other opportunities. Barry Fishkin says he owed his first three jobs, at least in part, to the influence of RPI alumni who had seen him on the *College Bowl*. Tom Melbert, after his appearance on the program, was offered a job at Random House by Bennett Cerf. My father made nothing of these connections. Nor did he decide, as Melbert had, to change course entirely by going to graduate school in the liberal arts. Lewis was opting, it seemed, to be a builder rather than an architect. In high school, he'd read all about Frank Lloyd Wright, the Bauhaus. He relished Mies van der Rohe's now famous dicta ("Less is more"; "God is in the details") and during his honeymoon made a pilgrimage to Le Corbusier's chapel at Ronchamp in northwest France. His vision of architecture was grand, and now he was going to design row houses and boxy bungalows for subdivisions. His friends had the feeling he'd given up on himself.

By some accounts, however, working for Morris was my father's plan all along. Jerome Yavarkovsky says my father was studying architecture *in order* to work for Morris. And Lewis once told Miriam that "instead of drawing plans for strangers, I could be working for the family." She thinks he probably went into his father's business because his brother had. My grandmother claims he went to Florida to make money: the construction of Sunbelt condos was a new building frontier and sure to be lucrative. Maybe he thought he'd be able to put his imprint on the standardized plans for the housing development. After all, his father could provide him with instant clients.

Most likely, there was a nagging voice in the back of his mind, insisting he needed to be practical and provide a secure income for his family. Morris had apparently been unhappy that his son and prospective daughter-in-law would have to be supported by their families with tuition *and* living expenses so they could finish school. He was so upset that he had threatened to boycott the wedding, and relented only after Lewis told him that if he did he would never speak to him again. Maybe going to Florida was a gesture of reconciliation on my father's part, a way to mend the rift.

On the other hand, Florida itself may have seeped into my father's psyche. Accounts of the *College Bowl* frequently referred to him as Lewis Weinberger "of Miami." I resented this tag when I first read it. If anyone was a New Yorker, it was Lewis. But then I saw it in those home movies: the sun, the sailing, the lacy white concrete around the pool.

ADOPTION

My mother, after years of trying, finally gave up hope of getting pregnant. They had tried everything, creative in their desperation: feet up, pillows under, by a river, in the woods. Tips from doctors, friends, *Ladies' Home Journal*. Nothing worked. My parents had to face the agonizing fact that they would never have a baby together.

Then Peter came into their lives. They brought my brother home from a Miami adoption agency in late October 1966, when he was six weeks old. A patch of slicked-down dark hair, dark-toned skin, cheeks half as big as the rest of his face. They stood in awe at the edge of the crib.

All the waiting and the well-meaning questions— "So, when are you going to have some kids?"—were finally over.

CONCEPTION: JANUARY 1968

A little over a year later, my parents were still living in the little house in the same depressed neighborhood, but had recently broken ground for their new house, which would be finished sometime in the late fall. Barry Klein (no relation to Stephan), a good friend of my father's from RPI, and his wife, Runja, had come to Florida to visit Barry's mother, and my parents invited them for dinner. Barry and Runja were artists living in Woodstock. They had a loose style, hip but not full-blown hippie: casual, down-to-earth, out from under all the middle-class trappings that were beginning to weigh so heavily on my mother, and perhaps on my father as well.

They talked and talked over dinner: about Antonioni's *Blow-Up*, the lackluster candidacy of Eugene McCarthy, whether Bobby Kennedy would run, and, of course, about the conflagrations across the country: draft cards being burned, war protesters putting flowers into soldiers' gun barrels at the Pentagon, Martin Luther King and the riots in Cleveland, Detroit, and Newark. Or perhaps about Israel's astonishing victories during the Six-Day War and the bizarre happening in San Francisco known as the Human Be-In. My parents spoke with enthusiasm, though current events, however explosive, had begun to seem removed from their lives. The news traveled to Florida as if swathed in layers of cotton.

Barry and Runja were relaxed and affectionate with each other. They were so clearly in love, my mother says, that it was a pleasure just to be around them. Lewis was witty and charming. He made my mother proud to be with him. They drank a lot of wine and sat at the table as the candles burned down and the little house went dark. Lewis touched my mother's hand and told her what a great dinner it was. In the kitchen after the dishes were cleared, while my mother made coffee and Runja divided the marble cake into squares, my mother didn't tell her that the marriage had started to go bad. She didn't have the courage to admit it—for one thing, they were too perfect a couple in everyone's mind. And besides, for that one night, my mother didn't feel lonely, she didn't feel things coming apart. She heard Lewis laugh in the next room and saw him smile at her as she came in with the dessert, his face soft in the candlelight, his love genuine and apparent, and for that one night she too fell completely in love. She remembers that one occasion vividly.

Later that same evening, I was conceived.

BABY CYPIE

I was named for my great-aunt Anna and my great-grandmother Cypra, both on my mother's side. Anna Cypra Weinberger. Actually, my mother once said I was not named for my great-aunt, although why she would have insisted on making such a mean-spirited claim, I couldn't imagine. My great-aunt was sitting right there, across from her in a vinyl lounge chair on my grandmother's patio.

"You were named after me," my great-aunt Anna said. "Did you know that?"

I was eight or nine at the time.

"No she wasn't," my mother replied. "Lewis and I just liked the name."

I was mortified. My mother was always starting these scrabbling little fights when we were at Grandma's. My aunt Anna pursed her lips and didn't respond. I think by then everyone was used to being baited by her, so they just held their tongues when they could manage it.

"Of course you were named for Aunt Anna," my mother says when I ask her now. "Who else would you have been named for?"

There is no argument about Cypra, though, a family legacy shared by four generations of contentious women. My middle name is Cypra (pronounced "SIP-ra"), my mother's middle name is Cypra, and my grandmother, who has no middle name at all, has always privately thought of hers as Cypra, too. Even the baby doll that my great-grandmother gave me when I was born was named Cypra. Baby Cypie, whose eyes opened and closed, and whose hair, after fifteen years of rough handling, fell out, leaving a scalp of dark pinholes, like an inverted five o'clock shadow. I tried to replace it with swirls of glued-on yellow yarn. It matted into clumps and wouldn't stay put. Eventually, I put Cypie in a box somewhere and, late in my teens, I lost her.

HOUSE TREATMENT I

Architectural Record: "All the walls are eight by eight by sixteen concrete block, reinforced with concrete and steel."

"It sounds like a prison," I say to my mother over the phone.

"It was Florida," she says. "You didn't want cozy, dear, you wanted cool."

TOOLS FOR ANALYSIS

The Florida house has entered the family mythology, like the "twenty-room" (actually eleven) summer mansion on Lake Mahopac that belonged to my great-grandparents. My grandmother, who kept the memory alive more than anyone, spoke often and bitterly of the beautiful house my parents had in Florida. It was she who saved the copies of *Architectural Record* and the *Miami Herald*.

Peter, too, talked to me about that house all through our childhood, though he was only three when we left it. I see us sitting on a dry hillside above a trash-filled ravine at Morningstar, side by side under dark pine branches, our legs drawn up into a precarious squat on the hard slope. This is one of my earliest memories. He is holding out his hands to show me how big the leaves were outside the glass doors: as big as elephants' ears.

He was proud of it in the same way that I was proud of the Mahopac house, a place I knew only from pictures and stories. These were the high-water marks of family memory. Our mother's rejection of it all had a reverse effect on us: we longed even more for what so easily could have been ours. We had not always lived in shacks. We had come from something better.

The Florida house was the place where we had been a family with our father.

1. Sneaking out the sliding glass door of the Florida house to play in his friend Brooksie's sand pile. Our mother, afraid he'd fall into Brooksie's swimming pool, tried to lock him in his room, but somehow he'd get the door open and off he'd go, trucking through piles of leathery leaves. He was two, three at the most.

2. Murdoch, the family's Great Dane. Peter tried to ride him like a horse.

3. The vintage Porsche our father bought for himself.

4. The tree house Lewis built in the backyard—which, I see from photographs, is not a tree house at all but a kind of wooden sculpture set in the grass.

5. Sitting in a pile of fire ants. When he screamed, my mother came running and hosed them off.

RECORD HOUSE

The living room (above and left) rises to a two-story height, and has a big clerestory window over the skylighted dining area. A little deck separates master bedroom (below) from the child's room.

A lawn mower starts and then shudders to a stop, a door like an air lock swooshes open and shut: small sounds contribute to an impression of complete silence. The street is wide, but curves gently around, ending in a cul-de-sac. Only residents drive down it. There are no sidewalks. Sloping lawns creep to the road edge, giving the neighborhood a freer, semi-country feel. When the children run inside, they leave their bright plastic bikes in the road, tipped halfway over.

The street has an empty, eerie quality: the tilted bikes, the lawn mower motionless on the lawn. A figure approaches, a child of eight or nine. She calls, but no one answers. She opens the door to her house, sees a pot on the stove, the flame burning underneath it. Butter or oil hisses in the pot. The child shuts off the flame. A smell of gas hangs in the air. She calls for her father, her mother again, quietly, her throat closing over her voice. But she already knows—they are gone. They have left her behind. She doesn't scream or cry. She stands in the kitchen, a whiff of gas in the air, unable to move.

Startled, I open my eyes. Stephan and I have been exchanging e-mails about my fascination with the Florida house. We've been writing to each other a lot lately, sometimes more than once a day, talking about all sorts of things, and now we've been taking the house apart together, bit by bit. At his suggestion, I am trying an exercise called an "environmental autobiography." He uses it with students in environmental design classes to explore the significance of a place or a childhood home, to help them understand the intimate connection between self and buildings, identity and landscape.

I was to close my eyes and conjure the Florida house: someone, either another person or a younger self, was supposed to come out of the house, take me by the hand, and lead me through the rooms, commenting as we went. Together, the guide and I would peer into corners, under beds, open forbidden doors, revealing, if only in my imagination, what was hidden there.

If you can take it, Stephan suggested, let your father be your guide. Let him convey his love of the house to you. It would say a lot about him, after all, his taste, how he saw himself. He didn't just find it and move in; he had it built—and he was an architect, not just any client with a design wish list. He chose it, as one chooses a painting or a car or a piece of music, even if he didn't create it himself. If you can understand his house, you might have a clearer idea of who he was.

But when I try the exercise, I don't find my father. I find myself standing in this empty kitchen, in the middle of a scene of recent and utter abandonment.

The surfacing of this image in relation to my father shocks me. I feel an anguish so intense that I can hardly bear it. And rage. Rage that this image, this terror, a child's worst fear, had been deliberately planted in me. And a rage at my father that astonishes me. My father disappeared. He wasn't raptured, he just vanished off the face of the earth.

For the first time, this under-the-skin truth registers in my mind: My father abandoned me. My father left me behind.

SO MANY

Once, on our way across the Mall in Washington, D.C., to Air and Space, the one museum I thought we'd both enjoy, Stuart and I wandered by accident into the National Gallery. We had not been getting along and had taken this trip together, hoping it would help us reconnect. We stopped in front of a sculpture of elongated dripped-iron figures. They marched eerily, looming up here and tilting off there, across the glass display case; shadows slid dramatically over the vitrine's floor. We searched for the artist's name on the placard: Alberto Giacometti. My husband took a photograph of the emaciated figures.

When I looked at the sculpture, I thought immediately of T. S. Eliot: "A crowd flowed over London Bridge, so many / I had not thought death had undone so many."

HOUSE TREATMENT 3

After a few days, I try Stephan's exercise again. I don't know why, except that I want a different outcome in that kitchen. To keep my child self from being stranded in an empty room.

I see the street. It has the surreal quality of a dream sequence on film, sunlit, but diffuse, fog-filtered. A Hollywood street. Again, a radio is playing, a lawn mower sputters and then shuts off, a door opens and closes. The sounds of the suburbs. There are birds. The hum of cicadas: a Florida sound, not one I know. I imagine grasshoppers sawing their hind legs together in the rampant weeds of northern New Mexico. It is hot.

A child approaches the house. She is nine. Her book bag bangs against her legs. Her white school blouse sticks to her shoulder blades. Asphalt sucks at the rubbery soles of her shoes. She walks slowly, book bag banging. She smells grass. New clippings like mown hay. The overripe smell of the tropics: hibiscus or rotting fruit, swollen and dropping to the ground as it did in the groves of Hawaii, where she once lived, papaya, the sour-sweet sexual smell of mango, maybe oranges. She approaches the house slowly, feet dragging.

I panic suddenly and stop writing. Where is the front door? What does it look like? Is it glass? Wood? I study the floor plan in *Architectural Record*, pulling myself out of the street dream. It is safer here, on the flat page, where the walls are drawn in black lines, and the doors are blank spaces. There seems to be a porch or a deck off the front. Lines drawn across the rectangle indicate . . . what? Open space? Floorboards? I don't know how to read the plans. My father's language is one I don't understand.

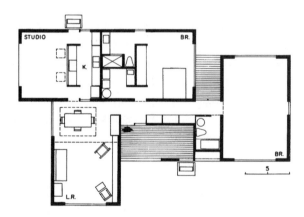

I have to move on. I have to get inside the house. A deck then. A deck and a glass door.

I stand in the street, staring at the entryway to my father's house. The door does not open. The neighborhood quiet has intensified. The jug-band cicadas saw wildly away in the bushes. A bright yellow and red Big Wheel trike has spilled on the edge of a neighboring lawn. The radio has been turned off. No one emerges. The book bag is gone, the schoolgirl blouse. I am not a child anymore. I can't see myself as a child entering my father's house. I step up to the deck. I stand there a moment, my breath a tight fist in my throat. Air will not push in or out. I open the glass door. Cool air rushes out, freezing the sweat on my arms and legs. Vivid light pours through the big square window beyond the dining table to the left. Green light. Leaf-pattern shimmery. The blur has burned off. I close the door, blocking out the cicadas. The silence is abrupt and total. Only gradually do I become aware of the white-noise hum of the air conditioner.

The house is empty. There is no sizzling oil this time. Still, my father does not appear. He does not take my hand and lead me through his house. I stand in the hallway, gazing at the gleaming teak table in the dining room, through the window to the wild growth of the yard. The walls around me are cool gray. I am tempted to reach out my hand to touch their rough, pebbly surface, but I don't. I am tempted to call out, "Dad? . . . Dad?" but I don't do that either. I fear the thin, hollow sound of my voice coming back to me, over and over.

This is my father's house, these cool bare rooms, these pebbly concrete walls, but if he lives here, he refuses to show himself.

DAD? . . . DAD?

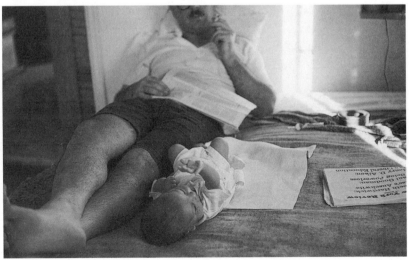

Subject: Chagrin about Interiors
From: Stephan Klein
To: Anna Cypra Oliver-Skoven
Date: 04 Apr 96 7:41 a.m.

I think I ate dinner at Lewis and Terry's at least twice when Terry cooked. Once in Bordentown. And once in Florida in the Donald Singer house. I don't remember what we ate but I do remember that everything, including the plates and furniture, was a potential conversation topic, everything a carefully selected design. . . . When I was 27 much of my life was about taste . . . so was your father's. . . . You can't believe how much of my life was about taste and design.

DIALOGUE 4

You liked fine things. Your objects were an image you were building of yourself: arty, esoteric, refined. Bentwood and Hans Wegner and Danish modern. Even the highchair for me, everything a conversation piece. The dishes, the silverware, bowls, cookware. Modernist, architectural, significant, the sorts of objects you find in glass cases at MoMA these days. De Stijl. You went after fine things with such deliberateness, constructing an aesthetic life as if from a blueprint. I bet you even read the manifestos, needing as you always did a surroundsound of discourse. Did it ever seem hollow to you? Was there ever a distinction in your mind between style and substance?

HOUSE TREATMENT 4

"What is missing from all these interior design spreads?" Stephan asks me by e-mail. "I'll tell you what's missing: people. There are never any people."

I've sent him a copy of the spread in *Architectural Record*, and we've been analyzing it together. I have become obsessed with the idea that I can know my father by understanding his house.

I look again at the *Record* photographs. No people. Almost no sign of any people: no eyeglasses folded on an open book, no stray shoes under the coffee table to give an observer the sense of someone having just left the room. Is the absence of people meant to make it easier to imagine the space as my own?

But I can't imagine myself living in my parents' house in Florida. When I look at the depopulated photographs, I don't see myself, now or then, scooting after a bright ball across the gray tile floor. I don't see my brother or my parents. I see no one. No one living there at the moment of the photographs, but not before or after either. I don't see people—us—sweeping in between shots, cluttering up the place with our presence or our voices or our objects. The room has a static, museum quality, as if the room itself—not the photograph of the room, but the room in the photograph—is a painting hung in a well-lit gallery.

"This is the point," Stephan writes. "The rooms are meant to be aesthetic objects. Without the messy taint of human lives."

The modern-art look of the place contributes to this impression. Except for the curlicues of the rocker, everything is forcefully geometric, either rectangular or square: the room itself is a narrow rectangle with the living room, two stories high at one end, and the dining room, one story high beyond it, forming a rectangular box below a large rectangular window (a "clerestory window," the caption says). Every concrete block in the walls is another rectangle, each of them strangely emphatic.

Later, I think to flip through the rest of Architectural Record, looking for rectangles and squares in other houses. And there they are, in couches and paintings, windows and walls, but it is not the same. In all the other houses, even the most modern, other shapes soften the effect: rounded chairs and footstools, curved walls, circular tables, draperies. In my parents' house, the only contrast to the rooms' hard lines is the vegetation outside. A view of giant trees fills the clerestory window. Palm fronds press against the glass in the dining room. The house, with all its windows and rectangles, is a frame for the shifting light and color of the greenery. Even so, I find it stark and uninviting.

"Have you noticed," I write to Stephan, "that the house doesn't look like it was furnished with children in mind?" The large open spaces could easily accommodate toys, a trike, a Johnny Jump Up, but there are no soft rugs, no yielding surfaces. The chairs are canvas and cane-backed wood. A fall on that floor would be hard.

"Don't put too much stock in those pictures," Stephan writes back. "It might not even be their furniture. I can show you magazine spreads of houses my wife and I designed when we were in practice together, and you'd notice that the same series of Warhol soup can prints and a certain shaggy rug appear in each one. They belonged to us."

But the truth is, I want to trust the photographs as they are, to extrapolate truths from them about my parents' lives. I'm well aware of the layers a photograph cannot reveal, the misperceptions it can accidentally or intentionally create, the messy realities beyond the tidy frame. To prove I know what I'm talking about, I describe an Henri Cartier-Bresson photograph I saw a few weeks before at the Minneapolis Institute of Arts: a snap like a found poem of a tall, crumpled man, hunched in an old mac against slashing rain, crossing a city street. An anonymous man, it looked like, down on his luck on a cold, gray afternoon, the embodiment of urban isolation and decay. But the man was no stranger. He was, the caption informed me, a famous artist and Cartier-Bresson's good friend Alberto Giacometti. Bresson and Giacometti were crossing the street to a café where they would spend the afternoon drinking coffee, smoking, and talking about art. Suddenly, the entire image shifted. I experienced a leap of recognition. Of course, I thought. Giacometti looks exactly like his sculpture: a gaunt, elongated drip figure.

And yet no matter how hard I try to grasp this house, its meaning and, even more basically, its physical features slip away from me. I have no language for the layout of a room.

Back and forth by e-mail, Stephan and I work to piece together the vocabulary. We argue. I get irritated. The thrill of argument is erotic.

"How come you don't like modern architecture?" Stephan asks me.

"Who says I don't?" I panic, as if he's accused me of turning against my father, of rejecting him, of sweeping away whole categories of culture and potentially shared interest. I don't want to lose those categories with my father. Or Stephan. I've lost too many categories with too many people already.

"It's more complicated than that," I say.

And Stephan replies, "Of course it is."

Stephan defends you. You discovered worlds. You introduced worlds to other people. You loved the challenge of hunting down the esoteric, the stimulation of discovering the theory behind objects. Art for you was a system with shape and substance and meaning, transformative, exhilarating. You believed in art for art's sake. But, fundamentally, I don't believe. The vanity of the intellect is fixed at my core. My mother has only to say, "Look what happened to him, look what it all came to."

I struggle against her voice. I want your voice. I want you to tell me that a life of the mind is not an empty life, a futile life. I want you to say that art matters. Not as pure aesthetic, but as a force in the world. I want to recover what you were. I want the you in me to come forward and speak.

Dear Lynn,

I am much too prone to share other peoples view of reality.

MY MOTHER CONTRIBUTES HER MEMORIES OF THE PAST AFTER ALL

"No," my mother says. "That's not true. I was there when those photographs were taken. That was our furniture, and they did not rearrange it. We hadn't been living there very long. It takes awhile to amass all this furniture, rugs, and stuff. The living room didn't have very much furniture in it. It was pretty raw.

"The house was in a suburban development. We were crazy about woods, but most of the land had been cleared. This was the only lot that had trees—a nursery gone wild. It had fabulous trees. There were roots and branches everywhere. We didn't want to tear any out. Singer built a walkway through, and then he elevated the house so that the foundation wouldn't interfere with the tree roots. A sophisticated solution to a complex problem. It was delightful to walk over the walkway and up to the porch. You entered the lot through the foliage over trees.

"The living room was very dramatic. Two-story height. Double-high windows. The floors were this beautiful Cuban tile, about sixteen inches. Very warm terra cotta. I hope I'm remembering that floor right—twelve-by-twelve terra-cotta tiles. I loved that color. We brought back a sisal rug from Spain, and we had beautiful teak furniture. The wood was very warm. The house was actually very warm—it doesn't show up well in the photographs. In the side yard was a playhouse that your father built. And on the wall by the dining table, I hung some of my broken mirror art. That was something I was into then. I don't know why I didn't have curtains. I was always a big one for making curtains.

"It had a front deck, and a main door with a glass panel next to it. I had some of my pottery sculpture on a stand on the porch. It was cool and dark. A huge moth flew inside the porch one winter, during the cool season. We imagined it being a South American moth traveling north, attracted by the nursery and the coolness of the house.

"The house had a galley kitchen, long and narrow, with a window through to the studio. My ideal was my grandmother's kitchen in the country, the Mahopac house. In fact, my grandmother's everything was my ideal. A big old farm kitchen, with a center table in a square room. A million doors everywhere. I always liked older homes. Lewis liked older homes, too. In Bordentown, we lived on the top floor of a ramshackle old wreck. I was crazy about it. A railroad flat with a clawfoot tub. I loved it. I've always liked old things.

"But he, being an architect, wanted to build his own house. That wasn't my ultimate dream. It wasn't on my wish list to own a home. But I was very happy to have a house, very happy to have *that* house. I don't know why he didn't design it himself. He felt Donald could do a better job. Lewis wasn't practicing as an architect. That's the basic answer: he wasn't a practicing architect. And he didn't want to chop anything down. He wanted this house to fit right in the lot. He was excited and challenged by it. I was afraid that we would end up in some conventional subdivision house. I *did not* want that.

"I loved the studio. Wow, my own studio. It had a kiln, wheel, shelves, tables. My space where I did stuff. I was actually a very successful potter. But I would make things and they would break. All this effort and then they would get broken. A lot of it got broken by you kids. Well, Peter. He broke several pieces. I was looking for permanence. And universality. When I became a hippie, I put some energy into bread baking. Dough was similar to clay, except that you bake it and eat it and everybody benefits. You don't have to worry about permanence.

"The house felt secluded. You couldn't see it from the road. The room was lit up like a cube looking in, but looking out it was a wonderful jungle. Tree frogs used to attach themselves to the windows. Very tropical. Serious spiders. It was teeming with animal life. One time, Peter was in the bathtub, and a spider about two inches in diameter—big and hairy—crawled down the bathroom door. I whacked it with a rolled-up newspaper. It fell on the ground in a little ball, a smudge. I felt sorry that I had murdered it because it was nothing. Not even dangerous."

My mother is quiet for a moment. "In my life with your father, all that mattered was either art or career. And since I had no career, all I had left was my art. It was not enough."

She looks at me, her face tight with sorrow and anger.

"It wasn't my house," she says. "It was his house. I always thought of it as his."

BROKEN MIRROR ART

QUEST 17: NEGATIVES

Searching through the trunk of photographs again, I find a packet of negatives of my father, standing on a narrow deck surrounded by three concrete block walls in the Florida house. In every one of them he is naked. He faces front, arms raised, wet, I think, as if he's taking a shower out there.

Great, I think, looking at his exposed body. Just what I need.

QUEST 18: ARCHITECTURE

I start to read books on architecture: *From Bauhaus to Our House, Behind the Postmodern Facade: Architectural Change in Late-Twentieth-Century America, Experiencing Architecture, The Poetics of Space, The Sex of Architecture, The International Style.* Stephan suggests titles to read, or I read what he is reading, so that I get complicated theory before I even know the basics. I read voraciously, looking for clues: This explains my father. Aha! This explains his house. Aha! I underline sentences. I copy out passages. If I can trace his influences I will be able to understand who he was. Aha!

THE IDEALIST TRADITION

Perhaps the centre of what is known popularly as 'modern architecture' is the idealist tradition. The architects Le Corbusier, Mies van der Rohe and Walter Gropius clearly defined a common position based loosely around certain social ideals – humanitarian liberalism, reformist pluralism and a vague social Utopianism – and the more recent architects such as Aldo van Eyck, Louis Kahn and James Stirling continue to proffer such ideals which spring from this mainstream tradition. If any particular goal may differ, the commitment to a general idealism remains. Thus these architects see it as an obligation to propose alternative visions to the existing social order. Opposed to the Marxist materialists, they do not concentrate on historical agencies for change (the working class and vanguard parties), and like the Platonic idealists they tend to carry through their buildings to perfection as if they represented some underlying cosmic order.

Charles Jencks, *Modern Movements in Architecture*

HOUSE TREATMENT 5

I am fetishizing my father's house. I know this. But I also know there is a special psychology to houses, that they express something profound about the people who inhabit them: their longings, tastes, who they perceive themselves to be and how they would like to be perceived by others. They are expressions of the ineffable, although there is no simple way to interpret them. It doesn't matter. Any reading is only one reading. Besides, outside my head my father no longer exists. I take whatever facts there are and after that I make him up. I am using his house for this purpose. Why not? He is beyond verification.

"*If I had been wiser there might have been a house. Could it have been a calm, loving house? Could we have been more loving[?]*" In his journal, my father's images of love are nearly always linked with images of a house —always that concrete word, not the more abstract "home." *A house.*

It is as if his body was not enough, as if he needed walls around him to keep himself intact. "*Such a sweet house,*" he writes, probably of the house he shared with his girlfriend Mara, though he might as easily have been thinking of Florida, "*with you / soft faced / cutting vegetables / cross legged / quiet talking / I miss you so much.*"

THE SOUND OF TREES

I send Stephan *The Book of Embraces, The Woman Warrior, A Chorus of Stones.* I love writing to him, our discussions running every which way, my mind accelerating to keep up with the exchange. He sends me "Not at Home: The Suppression of Domesticity in Modern Art and Architecture," Roland Barthes's *Mythologies*, and *Mr. Wilson's Cabinet of Wonders: Pronged Ants, Horned Humans, Mice on Toast, and Other Marvels of Jurassic Technology.* I copy out my favorite poems:

> I wonder about the trees.
> Why do we wish to bear
> Forever the noise of these
> More than another noise
> So close to our dwelling place?
> We suffer them by the day
> Till we lose all measure of pace,
> And fixity in our joys,
> And acquire a listening air.

LOSING ALL MEASURE OF PACE

Compulsive, we keep saying of ourselves; obsessive, we keep saying of each other. You are taking up all my time. We have to write only once a day. We have to allow ourselves only ten lines. I write from school, from home, in the car, memorizing sentences for him as I drive. I flag quotations, copy down overheard snippets of conversation, argue with passages in books in order, later, to offer my arguments to him. My senses are heightened, so acute that the sensation feels chemically induced. We invent a game in which we describe the furnishings and architecture of each other's houses, and I giddily launch an analysis of the results. So interiors, you might say, like photographs, lie, in that we can make all kinds of assumptions about the individuals who inhabit them, the stories their things tell about them, but we can't know what we're seeing just by looking, can we? He describes Bleecker Street for me. I respond with an ice storm that left prosaic Blaine coated in quicksilver. We talk about masks, counterfeits, doubles and doppelgangers, subjects which preoccupy me as I write about my father. His description of the 1996 *Anatomical Products Catalogue*, which he found at his health club, makes me laugh out loud. They have fake people with interchangeable sex organs. All sizes and shapes of skeletons: "Mr. Plain Skeleton," "Mr. Painted Skeleton," "Mr. Joint Skeleton," "Mr. Flexible Skeleton." Lots of brains, skulls, a lovely skull case, flexible vertebral columns . . . sorry, the "normal-knee joint" has been discontinued . . . He tells me to read the introduction to Dashiell Hammett's *The Continental Op*, about the fiction-making activity of the detective. I go to the Walker Art Museum—for the first time since I moved to Minneapolis, ten years before—in order to tell him about it. And there was *Duchamp's Leg*, sticking out from under the wall, as if Dorothy's house had just fallen on him. We play with the form of our exchanges, elaborately annotating each other's letters, sending them back and forth over several days, giggling as we work. Remember how my laugh is like my father's laugh? Well, you can hear it then. He spends two days composing a nine-page poem in doggerel about trying to buy a gift for me in a word department store. OH Goody! A Sale! / They have words by the pail! / They've overstocked gerunds / they'll give two for one / let's poke around there. This will / be so much fun! and I read it with a buzz of pleasure running up my spine. We discuss Theodor Adorno, W. H. Auden, Jim Jarmusch, the nature of memory, children playing among the trees at Yad Vashem. No one has ever validated my intelligence so completely, no one has ever encouraged my creativity to flower so explosively. "Write," the poet Adrienne Rich says, "as if your life depended on it . . . words you have dreaded and needed in order to know you exist," and I write like a drowning person, words replacing the motion of churning arms and legs, fighting upward, breaking the surface, swimming. It is the most exhilarating thing I've ever experienced. It is no less amazing for him. An architect with a Ph.D., he's written academic essays and a dissertation, but nothing, ever, like this. His letters are so imaginative and rich, I can't wait to read them; I can't wait to reply. The phone in the living room jingles whenever the modem dials in, so I surreptitiously unplug it before going upstairs to the computer; otherwise, Stuart might ask why I feel compelled to check my e-mail so often. I can't deny that, at first, I thought of Stephan as a father substitute—this man, so like Lewis in age, background, education, experience. He could give me advice, introduce me to things, let me curl into him when I needed someone. But now I'm not so sure. There's more to it than that, a smolder of connection that is being fueled into a bonfire. Stuart, only eight years my senior, is paternalistic toward me, holding my mercurial nature in check, we've both thought, with a stern warning or a "there, there," but Stephan, somehow, isn't at all this way. The thoughts that have begun to occur to me are reckless, inappropriate in more ways than one. My father's friend, and married, too, though unhappily, I bet, or he wouldn't be writing so often to me. Maybe the word "Freudian" and a tsk is all anyone needs to sweep aside the flutter I feel in my limbs. All I know is that my mind constantly drifts in his direction—and, symbolic father that he may initially have been, as Barthes says, "a symbol is an empty signifier." The meaning we pour into this vessel alters with need and desire. The fact is that he *is not* my father, but a person in his own right. I know, too, that I have touched some correspondingly deep place in him. He shares a short story with me that he wrote years before about the death of his mother when he was thirteen, and I understand it to be a gift, an intimacy that he does not often offer. I also see that time and growing older do nothing to diminish the sense of loss or longing, the need we all have to fill the gaps in our psyches, the places insufficiently nurtured. As he says, who knows what we'll be to each other. Whether we'll tire of these exchanges, whether we'll get bored and move on to something else. Who knows what we'll create out of this strange amalgam of history and leaping synapses.

SENATOR WEINBERGER AND HIS COUNTRY CLUB LADY

My father and mother hadn't made the kind of friends in Florida that they had in New York. They felt lonely, my mother says, they had no circle of peers. There wasn't much to do, either. They saw an occasional art film at the little theater in Coconut Grove, but culturally Miami was a backwater.

My father once told my mother's brother, John, that he knew if he stayed in Florida too long, my mother would leave him. He was right. My mother hated Florida. A New Yorker all her life, she was accustomed to being surrounded by her family, friends, and activity of all sorts. She felt isolated there. Irwin visited them once just after they'd moved into the new house and noticed how wistful my mother seemed.

"She wasn't prepared to be a country club lady," he says.

She had filled the house with ethnic fabrics and South American art objects like the gorgeous, Latin-looking wall hanging behind the dining table. It had been designed by her father, whose influence could be seen in everything she touched. She wanted a more artistic, bohemian life, Irwin thinks.

My mother was also finding it hard to live so close to my father's parents. She didn't like Kate very much and didn't think Kate liked her, though she usually enjoyed Morris's company. She found him warm and affectionate, and she loved to listen to baseball games with him. He was also crazy about his grandchildren, Peter and Stephan, Joe's son. There was, nonetheless, a definite conflict over how welcome my father's parents were in their daughter-in-law's home. Kate stopped by unannounced nearly every afternoon and drove my mother crazy. My mother insisted she call first.

Florida was a mistake for my father too—the biggest mistake of his life, all his friends say. He was miserable working on the development. There was nothing creative about his role in the business. His father already had an architect and, anyway, even if he'd let my father design for him, the houses were simple, low-budget affairs. My father never even bothered to get his architectural license. He was essentially a salesman, and a sleazy one at that; he once had to bribe a building inspector, an act he found humiliating. But it wasn't just being in a job he disliked: it pained him deeply to have to work for his father, to need his daddy to make a go of it. And yet he clearly wanted his father's help. Lewis's schemes for his future became so grandiose, in fact, that he apparently thought his father would enable him to take over Claude Pepper's seat as Democratic U.S. senator from Florida; he told Irwin that Morris was going to arrange it. It's impossible to know how seriously Lewis took this idea, but even as a fantasy it was both juvenile and preposterous: Claude Pepper planned to run again in the next election and went on to serve Congress for another twenty years.

WHAT MY MOTHER REMEMBERS

"Your father was away from home a lot, working, I guess, and the area around our house in Florida was pretty uninteresting, an ordinary suburban neighborhood without much in the way of cultural activity. I had this little VW Bug, and to escape I'd run down to Coconut Grove, which was the bohemian, arty area. That was where I encountered hippies for the first time.

"I'd see them hanging out in the park. One afternoon, I remember, I came across a group of them and they seemed hungry. So I went up to them and asked, 'Would you like some food?'" She laughs. "And being hippies, of course, they said 'Sure.' So I invited them to come home with me. This was in the old house. I had Peter by then, but you weren't born yet.

"So they all piled into my car, this little VW Bug. I drove to the market across the highway from the house and bought a stack of steaks, then I took them home. Lewis was out at the time, at work, but halfway through preparing the meal, he walked in. 'What is this?' He was not amused." She laughs lightly, obviously enjoying the story, as am I. "'They were hungry.' I finished making the meal, everyone ate, and then the men hitched back to the Grove. But there was a young woman with a baby, and I insisted that she spend the night. In the morning, I discovered she had impetigo, a highly contagious skin disease. I was terrified that Peter would get it. But he was fine. I took her to get some medication, and then dropped her off again in the park.

"Lewis wasn't angry, but he did not want me to do it again. Not that I can blame him. Spending his hard-earned money on steaks for a bunch of strangers in the park." She laughs again.

"Little did I know," she says, "that later I would become one of them."

MY WIFE

Under three separate portraits of my mother in a sheet of slides, my father wrote in red pen: "My Wife." The pictures are from the Florida years. The first time I saw them, I found the labels poignant, heart-rending. Why "My Wife," and not her name? "Wife" is such a lonely word, lovingly possessive and yet filled with yearning.

I realize now that he must have intended to send the sheet to someone who did not know who she was; each of the slides has his name and address printed on it. Still, under a portrait of me he writes only "Anna," not "My Daughter." Others—mostly friends—are identified by their first names. But not my mother.

My wife, he writes. *My wife*.

VANITY

She flows in her body. She exudes confidence and sensuality. She is, as Irwin says, "stunning." But after she became a Christian, she pulled her lush hair into a severe bun, stopped using makeup, wore plain, shapeless clothes, and began holding herself in the most rigid, self-constrained way.

"All beauty ever did for me," my mother said to me once, "was get me into trouble."

Beauty was of a piece with intellect and art—or maybe beauty *was* art, *she* was art, a beautiful object that men could adore. "Vanity, vanity, all is vanity," Solomon says, that soul-cry of despair, and my mother could not have agreed more. Pure emptiness, hollowness, futility. Beauty and intellect and art—ashes. They blew away.

CRITICS

"He was cold to her," my grandmother Rose says to me one day. "I saw that. She would reach out to put her hand on his shoulder and he would do this." She moves her shoulders abruptly sideways, as if flinching from someone's touch. "It sent a chill through me.

"And he disparaged her, too," my grandmother says. "He sneered at her opinions. Your mother was a very bright woman, at least as bright as he was, but he made her feel stupid."

"He disparaged *everyone*," Stephan says. "He had a need to be the smartest one in the room. He should have been a teacher. He was *always* lecturing everybody on what he knew. But if you asked him if he had read some book and he hadn't read it, he got flustered. He couldn't admit that he hadn't read it."

"Was he a nice person?" I ask.

"Oh, yeah," Irwin says. "He was wonderful."

"Was he a nice person?" Stephan repeats, drawing out the question. "I wouldn't say he was a nice person. He had a wicked sense of humor, a playful devilishness. He wasn't hostile, he wasn't nasty, but he also just . . . didn't put up with a lot of bullshit. He had this way of smiling with only half his face: from the nose up he'd have this glower, and from the nose down he'd be smiling. It was really strange."

"I had mixed feelings about Lewis," my mother's brother, John, says. "I thought he was a fairly extraordinary person. I thought of him as the older brother I never had, but he could be very condescending."

"I had an enormous crush on your father," Bobby Blender says, "but he was not the 'love of my life.' It was not passionate. There was always something distant about him."

Dear Lynn,

First the general principle I start from is that realizing who we really are flys in the face of what we were told and trained to be. Often by people who are concerned for our welfare and know its more dangerous to be who we really are than a standard acceptable version of a good person.

ART THERAPY

I picture my mother in her pottery studio in the afternoons when my brother and I were napping, sweaty and hot-cheeked in our sleep despite the air conditioning. Her hands, sturdy and short-fingered like mine, molded vases, jars, purposefully skewed bowls on the spinning wheel. I imagine her as she worked, thinking about the coldness that had begun to develop in him, his tendency to sneer at the things she said, her anger finding its way into the slippery cool mud.

MOVIES

In December 1967, *The Graduate* opened in movie theaters. My mother went with my father to see it. She has mentioned many times over the years that the film had a profound impact on her. Dustin Hoffman's Benjamin does not get to the church in time, and Mrs. Robinson's daughter marries someone else, but it doesn't make any difference. Using a crucifix to bar the sanctuary door, Benjamin runs away with her anyway, putting them both outside the acceptable boundaries of the bourgeois status quo.

Marriage vows were not sacred, the film proclaimed. It was not, as Mrs. Robinson kept insisting, "too late." They could be broken.

On January 31, 1968, at the beginning of Tet, the Vietnamese lunar New Year, nearly seventy thousand Communist soldiers swept through South Vietnam, attacking cities and towns and American military bases in a massive surprise offensive. Americans sat dumbfounded as their televisions flashed the pop and crackle of gunfire inside the walls of the American embassy in Saigon. Newspapers across the world carried a photograph of the South Vietnamese police chief General Nguyen Ngoc Loan executing a Vietcong prisoner at point-blank range, and Walter Cronkite officially pronounced the war in Vietnam to be a "stalemate," nowhere near the victory the Johnson administration kept claiming was at hand. Students swarmed to New Hampshire to support the antiwar candidate Eugene McCarthy. After McCarthy's surprisingly strong showing in the March 12 primary, Robert Kennedy, who was undecided until then, announced that he would run for the presidency after all. On March 31, Lyndon Johnson, undermined by Tet and the prospect of battling another Kennedy for the presidency, announced that he would not seek a second term in office. Euphoria buoyed McCarthy's and Kennedy's supporters. Four days later, on April 4, Martin Luther King, Jr., was shot to death on a hotel balcony in Memphis, Tennessee. Violence and looting erupted in Memphis and 129 other cities across the country. Arsonists set fires all over Washington, D.C., and thousands of National Guardsmen were deployed to police the smoke-filled streets, while soldiers with machine guns stood ready to defend the Capitol and the White House. In a ghetto neighborhood not far from the center of government, Stokely Carmichael advised an audience of four hundred people to go home and get a gun. At the end of April, students at Columbia took over Low Library, Hamilton Hall, and several other buildings, demanding that the university end its association with military-related organizations and abandon work on a gymnasium that had encroached on the African American community nearby. The Barnard sophomore Linda LeClair was threatened with expulsion after she admitted that she was cohabiting with her boyfriend, setting off a firestorm of analysis and recrimination in the press. Young people all across the country were experimenting with marijuana and LSD. Musicians filled the airwaves with songs protesting the war, celebrating drugs, and promoting free love. *Hair*, featuring hippies and full-frontal nudity, opened on Broadway. Students demonstrated in the streets of Paris, Rome, and West Berlin. On the campaign trail, adoring supporters squeezed Robert Kennedy's hands until they bled. He won the June 4 primary in California, beating Eugene McCarthy by a wide margin. Elated and confident, he gave a victory speech to an electrified audience at the Ambassador Hotel in Los Angeles. Minutes later, taking the back way out, Robert Kennedy slumped to the floor in the hotel's kitchen, blood gushing from bullet wounds ripped into him by a young Jordanian named Sirhan Sirhan. Two days later, Kennedy was dead. In mid-August, during the Republican Convention in Miami at which Richard Nixon received his party's nomination for president, riots broke out a few miles away in Liberty City, a ghetto just across the highway from where my parents were living; four people were killed. On August 20, democratic reforms sweeping Czechoslovakia in the movement known as the Prague Spring ended abruptly when Soviet tanks rolled into the capital city. Nine days later, Mayor Daley's police force clubbed protestors at the Democratic National Convention in Chicago. Hubert Humphrey won the nomination over McCarthy. In November, five weeks after I was born, Richard Nixon was elected president.

COINCIDENCES AND OCCURRENCES

When my parents moved into their new house in the middle of October 1968, it should have been a joyous occasion. They had a beautiful home, a son, and a newborn daughter, but they had begun to drift apart. My father was unhappy in his father's business, and my mother was increasingly bored and lonely, disenchanted with their life together. That's why there are no pictures of my mother when she was pregnant with me—she and my father weren't getting along well enough to bother. They carried on as best they could, but it wouldn't have taken much to push them over the edge.

And then, one after the other, my father's parents died: Morris of heart failure, and my grandmother Kate of breast cancer, just a year later.

MORRIS'S DEATH, VERSION I

One day, my grandfather Morris lay down on his bed for a nap, and died. Sleeping pills were found at his bedside. His grandson Stephan was in the house at the time. The coroner ruled the death accidental. Morris had a weak heart and badly clogged arteries; the pills triggered a heart attack. He would never have overdosed on purpose with his grandson nearby. His wife was dying of cancer. The day before he died, my mother had confided to Morris that she had been having an affair with a man named Jeremy, my father's best friend at RPI.

VERSION 2

My mother did not have an affair with Jeremy. He lived in New York. She wrote letters to him and he to her, that was all. He was getting divorced and wanted her to go away with him. She confided to Morris that she no longer loved my father.

"Love?" my grandfather replied. "What's love?"

The day before he died, Morris was told that his wife had breast cancer and would soon die. He did not commit suicide. He would not have left her to die alone. He was not that kind of man.

VERSION 3

Jeremy was in love with my mother. He was willing to be a father to her children. She was pregnant with me at the time. Her relationship with my father was deteriorating and she was desperate. She didn't know what to do. She should have gone away with Jeremy. Everything would have turned out differently if she had—for one thing, if she'd been able to find a satisfying life with a nice guy, my mother would not have become a fundamentalist.

VERSION 4

My mother's interest in Jeremy was never that serious. She didn't want to go away with him. One day, she left one of the letters out on the bedroom bureau, and my father found it. He was distraught. They borrowed money from my grandmother for marital counseling. My father thought she had left the letter out, if not on purpose, then subconsciously to bring matters to a head. Shortly after that, Morris died, then Kate. The family business went bankrupt.

VERSION 5

Morris's grandson Stephan spent the night at Morris and Kate's house. The next morning, his father, my uncle Joe, picked him up to get his hair cut. Morris was fine. When Joe dropped Stephan off later that day, Morris was dead. The day before he died, my mother had confided to Morris that she had been having an affair with a man named Jeremy, my father's best friend at RPI.

VERSION 6

In the afternoon, my grandmother Kate called from the hospital. Morris went to the hospital every day to see Kate but had not gone that afternoon. The day before he died, he had been told that the cancer had spread through his wife's body and she would die in a matter of days. Kate was so sick that she had to be brought to her husband's funeral in an ambulance and wheeled in on a gurney. She died a year later.

VERSION 7

The day before he died, my grandfather Morris discovered that his business was bankrupt. He had lost not only his money, but other people's investments as well, including substantial amounts from members of my mother's family.

VERSION 8

The coroner ruled my grandfather Morris's death accidental. He had a weak heart. The sleeping pills triggered a heart attack. Everyone accepted this ruling. Morris would not have intentionally overdosed with his grandson in the house. He would not have left his wife to die alone. Everyone, that is, except my father. He thought—and on this point several people agree—that his father had killed himself.

MORRIS'S DEATH, VERSIONS I THROUGH 8: NOTE TO THE READER

I am, of course, leaving out the good parts: who said what and why. I have to make some concessions. The details are just the usual, anyway: spite, old grievance, guilt, regret, the need we all have to tell our stories. There are a few things, however, that I can add. Jeremy, who turns out to be Jeremy Grainger, he of the violin case on the lawn at Bennington, told me his side of the alleged affair with my mother. He said that they wrote letters back and forth but no more. She came up to Queens once, and he drove down from New Haven, where he was doing graduate work at Yale. They met at a diner somewhere. This was in July or August 1968; she was seven or eight months pregnant with me. Except for this one time, over coffee, across a linoleum tabletop, they were never alone together. It seems to have been much more serious for him than for her.

After my father discovered the letter, my mother wrote to Jeremy, "I'm staying with Lewis. It's all over."

TOWARD THE END

My mother and I are looking at the album I put together. She stops at a photograph of herself in the Florida house.

"I was already very unhappy by the time this picture was taken," my mother says.

"How can you tell?" I ask stupidly. I can see how remote and sad she is. A photograph of her on a happier day sits in the background.

"I remember," she says. "It was toward the end. It was a journey in the disintegration of a marriage."

"I don't get it," Stuart says. "I don't get what I'm looking at."

We're sitting in a restaurant after walking through the Henri Cartier-Bresson exhibition at the Minneapolis Institute of Arts.

"Great," I say. "Here we go again."

Stuart doesn't like modern art. It makes him impatient. Despite the documentary style of Cartier-Bresson's photographs, something about them has turned Stuart off.

"It's all intellectual mumbo-jumbo," he says. "I don't know what I'm supposed to get out of it."

He has a right not to like it. I don't object to that. But I object powerfully, viscerally, to his dismissal. *I don't get it.* End of discussion. We've done a lot of dismissing, he and I, and I've had enough of it.

He responds to images, and I to words. But even in the realm of the visual—art, film, theater—he is usually defensive toward, even angered by, anything but the most strictly representational work. I want to experience more and more, while the list of what he doesn't like seems to be getting longer all the time.

I accuse him of being a literalist. He accuses me of being a snob.

Why does it matter? Because under the urgent talk about Cartier-Bresson, I am, of course, talking urgently about something else.

I respond calmly at first, but as I talk my voice rises. "I don't know if I can be with you," I say. I am crying now. Almost hysterical. "I don't know if we're compatible at all."

It is the first time I have said so aloud. It is spring. In June we will have been married eight years.

I know if I am patient, he will explain, in some way that is logical and interesting, why he doesn't like Cartier-Bresson. But I am running out of patience. I want conversation to dash and zip. I am tired of coaxing out the deeper response. I love this sweet, gentle man, but I am sick to death of limitation of every sort.

My letters to Stephan are in my mind.

I understand that the culture I've begun to crave feels threatening and foreign to Stuart. He has no categories in which to place it. His parents don't drink, play cards, have never in their lives set foot in a movie theater. They have never seen a ballet.

Like me, Stuart has moved away from his religious past, but his rejection has been less swift, less complete. He is a deeply spiritual man. He has a positive view of God, a good relationship with his father. For all the restrictiveness of his upbringing, he has been taught that God is love. He rejects the extremism of fundamentalism but holds on to belief, a tightrope walk I admire but cannot manage myself. Stuart wants to be open, if only to keep a gulf from widening between us, but he is afraid. Every step is a step into dark water.

Less than a year has passed since I first called my mother and Miriam to ask about my father. Before that, I wanted to be a wife and a mother. I wanted to refinish the cupboards in my sweet little house in south Minneapolis. But now I want the whole wide world, whatever that includes.

Stuart and I are friends. We love each other. These holes in conversation shock us both.

THE SEISMIC PLATE

My mother has said that she and my father felt that they were on a seismic plate. Nothing made sense anymore. Nothing was clear. They'd dabbled a bit in the hippie scene, smoking pot at parties, going to see Janis Joplin, but they were always the oldest people at those events; the loose abandon of these teenagers was something they could admire but not relate to. They thought about going to the Woodstock festival, for instance, to visit Barry and Runja, if nothing else, but decided against it at the last minute, and were relieved afterward not to have spent two days wallowing around in the mud with two little kids. They had friends who were artists and friends who were intellectuals; even so, they couldn't stand people, she says, who were fanatically left-wing. They were struggling to find a niche, while all the time values kept changing. Marriage no longer seemed sacred. Nor anything else. The lives they had chosen seemed more and more pointless. Even before Morris died, the tension in their marriage was reaching explosive levels. My father was probably right: my mother left the letter where he could find it in order to force a crisis. A black storm was building over their heads; something had to cause it to break.

As if Morris's death and the circumstances surrounding it were not bad enough, my grandfather's bankrupt business was "dumped," according to Irwin and Stephan, in my father's lap. Consensus has it that the failure was not my father's fault. Bad decisions were made, bad moves. Maybe, simply, the Florida real estate bonanza didn't pan out. But whoever or whatever was responsible, my father blamed himself. Thirty-one years old, and he had to face the humiliation of creditors, failed commitments, and the selling off of whatever assets were left. He had to ask his sister to help bail him out. He lost not only everything his father had built up, but almost $125,000 that my mother's family had invested in the development as well. He had to tell them he'd lost their money. He considered himself a complete failure.

Depressed and at sea, my father began to spend more and more time with a couple my mother describes as "seedy." They lived in an apartment in one of my grandfather's buildings. My mother thinks they were drug dealers. The woman also ran a side business: for "lots of money" she took women to Mexico, where she arranged abortions for them. My father was spending whole afternoons smoking dope at their place. He came home reeking. My mother suspected that the woman might also have been his lover. At home, he grew increasingly silent and morose. They'd begun to fight, too.

In the family mythology on both sides, it is always my mother who wanted to escape the boring middle-class life that my father created for her in Florida. She dragged him off into the counterculture, which, everyone agreed, "was not for him." That was the story I had heard all through my teenage years. She wasn't happy. She made him give up his house, his life. But there was nothing left for Lewis there: not his parents, his business, there was even some tension with his brother over the estate. And my mother was afraid of his increasing involvement with the couple in the apartment. She finally convinced him to spend some time traveling with her. And so, not long after the death of my grandmother Kate, they closed up their house, packed their two children into a VW bus, and set off for a year driving across the country.

My father left Florida, a defeated man.

SUBSTITUTIONS IN THE INVENTORY OF MY FATHER

Stephan can't find the Paul Robeson album with "Jack o' Diamonds" on it. He begins to wonder if it was Paul Robeson after all. Instead, he sends me Ida Cox, Sonny Rollins, Mississippi John Hurt, Bob Wills and His Texas Playboys, Leadbelly, Brownie McGhee. These are his favorites, not my father's.

STEPHAN

I open my eyes, wide awake suddenly at 5:00 in the morning. My husband is asleep beside me. I slip from under the covers as quietly as possible. The computer is upstairs. The blue boards creak under my bare feet. Stephan will be up. He rises early, well before dawn. Sometimes we catch each other. Are you there? But if not, there is always a message waiting. I am not usually an early riser, but I wake now, often, at 5:00, 4:00, even 3:00 A.M., my agitated limbs propelling me into the cold, still dark morning. I'm composing before the computer bings to life, before the modem's electronic chime announces a successful connection. Early, I write. The words spill. Light graying into morning. A torrent of words. I cannot contain them. I do not want to contain them. Mouth burrowing. I see him in my mind in white tennis shorts he later says he does not own, standing on the Manhasset railway platform. Tall, hawk-nosed, his curly hair more gray than black. I delete Mouth burrowing. I write Crazy. What the hell are you thinking? Thirty years, one lost father, and two marriages between us. From the beginning, I noticed that though I described my life with Stuart in some detail, trying to convince both Stephan and myself that I *was* happy, he almost never mentioned his wife. But still. Then I remember how he curled up his legs on the red vinyl seat to talk to me, a mile a minute, about my father, his intensity forcing me backward into the joint between my seat and the train window. I delete Crazy. What the hell are you thinking? An explosion of language and image and idea. I write it again: Mouth burrowing. I don't know yet, at the end of the poem forming under my fingers—Mouth burrowing / under night-tangled hair / woke me—whether I will press SEND.

I leave Stuart one night in April, walking out of the house in Blaine with just a suitcase. We have had a fight, a confrontation over my e-mails to Stephan—a parallel with my parents' life that might seem karmic or deliberate if these scenarios weren't so common.

I wait a full week before I tell my mother. I'm afraid that she will tell me divorce is wrong or that walking out is a sin or that my obligation is to trust God to help us work through our problems. I'm afraid she will say that Stuart is a good man, don't give him up, don't lose him. "Stuart," she had said to me once, "keeps you from flying apart in the universe."

But the truth is it's hard to know how she'll react. Once, in a moment of particular misery, I had told her that I often found myself attracted to other men. But the attractions were fantasies. After the infatuation wore off, I realized I didn't even especially like these guys. But what did those attractions say about me? The fact that I always seemed to be *looking*? She hadn't been shocked or judgmental; she said it didn't surprise her. This exchange took place before I'd heard about Jeremy. But when I talked about my urge to leave, she said, "But you don't want to be alone, do you?" I was twenty-six years old.

Another time, I told her I wanted Stuart to agree to sell the house so we could move into an apartment in town. I couldn't stand living so far away anymore or having so much property to take care of. I didn't talk about leaving him then; I thought the problem was my lack of commitment, and I was trying to make the marriage work. My mother and I had just stepped out of the car and were standing in the garage of the Blaine house. It was nearly Christmas and cold; our breath steamed in the unheated air. She gestured at Stuart's workbench against the wall, the tool chest I had given him last Christmas, the array of lawn equipment. "But Stuart will have to give up all this space," she said, her mouth a pucker of disapproval. "He loves it."

I was astonished. She of all people. She who had sold everything, abandoned *everything*, in the search for a more meaningful life, now valued a workbench more highly than her daughter's sanity? Couldn't she see how leaden my face was? I had asked her to come to Blaine because I was so depressed I could hardly function.

But, of course, it was only her own regret that my mother was trying to express. She didn't realize that I'd been living out the cautionary tale of her unhappiness my whole life.

That was four months before the confrontation with Stuart that sent me rushing away from Blaine, pure adrenaline in a white Saturn, knowing nothing about the future beyond my plan to show up on the doorstep of a friend in Minneapolis.

I had needed my mother's permission that day in December, for her to tell me that what I wanted was acceptable, not frivolous or irresponsible or selfish. But sitting on the futon in the room I've rented in a house with three other people in St. Paul, getting up the nerve to call her, I finally realize I don't need her permission. I just don't want her to harass me. I don't want her to try and make me feel guilty. Or regretful.

As usual, the last thing in the world I'm prepared for is the thing she actually does. Which is why when I tell her, the phone cord wrapped around my knees and a trail of sweat running down my spine, I'm completely taken aback when she says, "Maybe now you can understand what happened to me with your father."

Mozart's House

If you don't know this house here is Mozart's birthplace, you are not interested, even though you walk right past it, a great lover of Mozart.

If you do know, you stand before it filled with a number of emotions and thoughts, including awe.

On the other hand, if you have made a mistake, and are standing in front of the wrong house thinking it is Mozart's house, your thoughts and emotions are exactly the same as if you stood in front of the correct house. Are they just as valuable? You will come back from your trip abroad and tell someone about the experience—your thoughts and emotions included—and that experience will make a difference to you as your life goes on, and will perhaps make a difference to the person or the many people you tell about your experience in front of Mozart's house, and it won't matter that it was the wrong house. It won't matter unless you find out it was the wrong house. Then in your own eyes you will feel you did not really have the experience you thought you had. Your experience was false, and had no value.

The example of Mozart's house is a bad example, because it must have a plaque on it, and even perhaps colorful banners, and crowds going in and out. But there are other houses that are unmarked, the former habitations of much-loved people. And there are other places in front of which we have stood feeling awe that will never be given plaques, such as the stationery shop in Paris where Samuel Beckett bought his note cards. "That man put his foot on this very threshold once."

—Lydia Davis, "Remember the Van Wagenens"

I keep coming back in my mind to that house on Kit Carson in which my father is supposed to have died. How many times did I walk by it without ever getting close enough to peer through the slats in the gate, to see if there were footholds or gaps that might have given me a glimpse over the wall? That huddled-down house, a glint of windows, a bulge of adobe, lilacs. A house in a dream like something out of du Maurier: *Last night I dreamed I went to Manderley again.* I see myself passing it on the street. A place that doesn't contain much, that from the inside would only be someone's living space, with a couch, books, shoes; on the other side of the wall would only be someone's garden, with a wrought-iron bench under the single tree. Though who knows, maybe the bench has been there longer than the person has, maybe my father sat there smoking in the late evening, maybe I would feel his presence if I sat there, too.

I think now about going back, even ringing the bell and asking to look around. But what would I say? My father died here twenty-one years ago and I just wanted to see where he spent his final hours? And even if I did go in, what would I find? Just a house like any other old New Mexico house: whitewashed adobe, turquoise sills, a ceiling of the narrow aspen poles called *latillas*, a niche for a *santo*. Would I come away with the last imprint of his soul inside the four thick walls?

The truth is, it may not be the right house at all. My brother could have been wrong. My mother is openly skeptical; she knows nothing about it. Yet her memory is so spotty that her opinion can hardly be taken as gospel. It almost doesn't matter whether it is the right place or not. I can't separate my father from it now. It is a site of memory where no memory exists.

I could call the Taos police, ask for his record, if they still have it, and answer the question once and for all. But I don't know if I can bear the language of such a report, so graphic and clinical at once.

If he did die there, perhaps he was not the first. The houses on that street in New Mexico are old enough to contain generations of the dead, whether in spirit or actuality. Ghosts come with the property.

My grandmother gives me a copy of Allen Ginsberg's *Kaddish*, which my father gave to her in the late sixties. She also gives me a pair of earrings he made for her at Fort Dix. Each is a silver rectangle, with a silver square in the center, at a forty-five-degree angle to the rectangle. They dangle from slender wire hooks. I love them and wear them constantly.

QUEST 19: DONALD SINGER

I decide, one morning, to call Donald Singer, the architect of the Florida house. I would not have known his name if it weren't for *Architectural Record*, but according to Stephan and Irwin, Singer and his wife were good friends to my parents. His number, which Stephan unearthed for me some time ago, has been buried in a pile of papers, waiting for me to get up the nerve to use it. It is February 23. My father's birthday is three days away. I don't want my father's birthday to pass unacknowledged anymore.

When a man picks up the phone, I say, as I said to Bill Gersh, "Hi, I don't know if I have the right person, but this is Lewis Weinberger's daughter." My heart is pounding, but my voice is calm. Again, I have the sense of speaking my father into the world. I love the sound of these words on my tongue.

There is a shocked silence, and then the man says, "You don't say."

I laugh. "I guess I have the right person then."

"This is amazing," Donald Singer says. "I think about your father often. I still miss him. Right this minute, my wife, Elaine, who's here in the office with me, is wearing a pendant your father made with her initials wrought in it."

"Monday is my father's birthday," I say. "It seemed like a good time to get in touch."

"Yes, I know. The twenty-sixth, right? Our birthdays are a week apart, although I'm a year older. Your call," he says, "is like a circle closing." He asks me to call him again over the weekend so that we can speak longer.

After I hang up, I can't stop smiling.

When I write to Stephan about Donald, he sends me a flood of ideas for continuing the search. He suggests I call the *Taos News* to find out if there was any coverage of my father's death, an obituary at least. But I've already called the newspaper, and I was told I'd have to go there in person to look at the back issues in their morgue.

The question about the house on Kit Carson might be settled, he points out, by calling Bill Gersh. This idea seems so obvious that I can't believe I haven't thought of it myself. I look in the Taos phone book for his number, but I can't find it. Even more puzzling, Information isn't able to give it to me either. Has he moved? It doesn't seem likely. Maybe I'm just mixed up about which directory handles Lama.

As for where the ashes were scattered, the person who would know is my father's brother, Joe. Why don't I call him? Stephan asks. Joe was a big part of Lewis's life. He was intimately involved with the development in Florida. He went out to New Mexico after Lewis died to oversee the cremation of his remains. Maybe he even has other documents, such as childhood papers or letters. If I want information, who better to ask? But the thought of calling Joe still sends a ripple of anxiety through my body.

I call my uncle. It's my father's birthday, what would have been his fifty-seventh. There is never going to be a better time. I try to picture Joe as I dial. My memory from the one time I met him, at my cousin Michael's wedding when I was sixteen, is a mere fragment: he walks into the hall with his wife beside him, a stocky man with a round face, and someone says to me, "That's your uncle Joe, your father's brother." The face is still there in my mind, deeply tanned, creased with a smile, but I have the feeling that it is a photograph of my grandfather Morris I'm recalling.

My stomach is in knots, but Joe seems happy to talk to me. It's the first real conversation I've ever had with him.

"Tell me what you want to know," he says. His voice surprises me, nasal and a little rumbling, but still mild, almost gentle; it rises or falls only to emphasize an occasional word, and rarely registers the intensity his words seem to imply. I've been told he's a taciturn man who spends a lot of time alone. Even so, he talks steadily, without pause, about one subject, then another, as if he were a stereo set on random play. He has a blunt yet poetic way with words. He makes a remark about "Italian-American women, built like oak trees, all wearing the same black dress," and without catching the exact connection to the larger conversation, I write it down, thinking how lovely it is. Miriam has told me repeatedly how much she likes her brother, how much she admires him, and I can tell right away he's a much more complicated person than I've been led to expect: I'd formed an image of him as a working-class tough. But it's hard for me not to feel wary of him. If there has been a villain in the stories told by my mother's family and some of my father's friends, it has been Joe. In particular, it was he that they blamed for the failure of the development and the burden that subsequently fell on my father.

This time I'm prepared.

1. *Joe doesn't know anything about a house in town.* "All of Lewis's things were piled up at Gersh's," he says.

2. *Mara was Mara Andover, daughter of a Connecticut business tycoon.* She was intelligent and beautiful—tall and blond, so the photo I picked out is probably correct. She raised goats. The house Lewis helped her build or built for her was in Santa Fe. He lived with her there, Joe says, though I don't understand this assertion: in the journal, my father mentions building a house with Mara for a young couple. He made the cabinets himself and was pleased that the couple liked them. "Quite a house," Joe says.

3. *Lewis was in love with Mara, but the relationship ended: she was reluctant to introduce him to her family because he was Jewish.* "Somewhere in those papers," Joe says, "he signs his name 'Lewis Lewis,' as if to eliminate 'Weinberger.'"

"God," I say. "That's terrible."

4. *Joe is not sure about Lynn.* "She was some girl Lewis enticed into coming to New Mexico. He had a pretty heavy succession of women there for a while. She thought they were going to a ski resort, and when she found out otherwise, they parted company."

Thinking of my father's letters to her and of the words on the postcard, *I can't be with a man because I want you,* I wonder if we can be talking about the same woman.

5. *Lewis never really practiced architecture.* "Though young architects usually have a lot of ideas about their own place," Joe says, "Donald Singer was experienced with the Florida climate. Lewis had worked on designing some jail for Vorhees, that firm in New York. But that's about all the experience he had. Lewis and your mother thought they could make a lot of money on the development. My brother's dream was to get his hands on fifty thousand dollars, then go do whatever he wanted to do. But it didn't work out that way. You know, people in construction are not usually heavy intellectuals."

6. *New Mexico was not the place for my father.* There was nothing for him to do there. Joe supposes that Lewis went to New Mexico to please my mother. "He was very much in love with her. I mean, from the time he was in high school. Your mother really disliked life in Florida. She looked down on the people there. They had a lot of friends. Very nice people, but your mother was not thrilled with them. My wife and I didn't socialize with Terry and Lewis a lot. You know, there was a big age difference between us. Nine years. Practically a whole generation. And she was very standoffish. My father was crazy about Peter. He thought nothing of just dropping by the house, essentially unannounced, to see his grandson, you know. Your mother didn't like that. They had a lovely place. Very open, spacious. She made these ceramics and put them all around the house. They looked like kindergarten things."

I bristle at this remark, but then he says that my mother was taking some courses in glazing and other techniques and was getting "reasonably good" and that he doesn't know why she lost interest in it.

"To do this stuff," he says, "takes a lot of work. There's this Japanese potter named Hamada who I've always loved. He's been making these pots for eighty years and the decoration is always a sprig of bamboo. I heard that someone asked him, 'When are you going to do something else?' And he said, 'After I get *this* right.'" He chuckles with satisfaction, relishing what is obviously a favorite anecdote.

7. *Joe was not working for my grandfather when the business went under.*

My father had arrived in Florida at the tail end of Pickwick, a successful development of about a hundred homes that Morris had built when he came out of retirement; not much later, Morris began Plantation, but by then Joe had launched his own contracting business. I've heard all sorts of dark, resentful rumors about this deal, but I don't think there's any truth to them. All I know for sure is that Miriam and her brothers felt deeply depressed after the meeting in which they had to tell my mother's family and the other investors that the Plantation project had gone bankrupt. The investors, who referred to them derisively as "the Weinberger boys," couldn't help but think they were to blame.

"My father was a pretty good builder," Joe says, "but just a so-so businessman. He had spent most of his life in New York, working with the same people over and over again. I don't think they ever had contracts with each other, they just agreed on what they were going to do and then did it.

"I guess my father was under the impression that he was going to live *forever*, because at one time his partners suggested that they take out an insurance policy in case something happened to him, but he didn't do it.

"And these old men, friends of my father, were partners in the business, but once he died, they had no interest in it. You know, one of them had gotten involved because his son-in-law needed a job. That sort of thing. And to them, Lewis was just a kid. They weren't interested in doing business with him. Everything was based on their personal relationship with my father."

Even without the headache of the estate and the lack of funds, the development itself, Joe explains, was not doing well. Plantation, west of Fort Lauderdale, eventually became a popular area, but people were reluctant to buy there in those days. Morris was ahead of his time, and the sales were slow. My father was trying to finish the project and sell off the buildings; whether it was completed or not, he would be forced to repay the construction loans.

"How it actually ended," Joe says, "I don't know. It just stumbled its way through. It was a long time ago. It just *went away* as far as I was concerned."

8. *The cigar box and the several thousand dollars that Irwin says were found beside my father's body.* Just as I'm getting up the nerve to ask him about the money, Joe tells me that he and Lewis were going to invest in a land deal in New Mexico. Joe had sent him $13,000 to buy property. At the time, he was working on a project in Boca Raton. My father had asked him to come out to New Mexico.

"I told him I couldn't. I had a job. You can't just disappear on people, you know." Joe has always regretted his refusal to rush over. Not long afterward, he got the call that my father had killed himself.

"I was going through some of his things with this fellow, Bill Gersh. I don't know whatever possessed me, but I asked Bill if he had come across any money. He said he had, and then he gave it to me. He was holding on to it so it wouldn't get stolen, he said, since he was the one who had found him first. It was in the same little box that I had given it to Lewis in."

I ask him if it was a cigar box, if there were other things in it, too, but Joe says, no, there was nothing else in it, and it wasn't a cigar box; it was a little checkbook-sized thing. "Gersh gave it to me in cash," he says, "which impressed me because he wasn't flush with money, either. That was quite a decent thing to do."

I want to be open-minded. I feel surprisingly drawn to my uncle; for all his roughness, I sense that he's a goodhearted guy. I want to trust my father's brother, but after the way my mother's family has always talked about him, it's hard for me not to be suspicious. Is he offering the tale of this money as a piece of history, I wonder, or is it a preemptive strike? My grandmother Rose told me about a conversation she'd had with him after my father's death. She'd heard about the box of money and, assuming it was drug money, had called Joe and told him Lewis owed her several thousand dollars, the money she had lent to him and my mother for marital counseling. She intended to send the money to my mother. But Joe denied she had any claim to it and she never heard from him again.

This doesn't mean I don't believe the money was Joe's or that he sent it to Lewis to buy property. For one thing, my father talks about the land deal in his journal. He says he was trying to buy land for "my brother and myself."

What does seem peculiar is that Joe sent *cash*, a bundle of it, to someone in the drug trade. My mother, with a certain acerbic satisfaction, points out this oddity to me later that afternoon. I couldn't help telling her about my conversation with Joe—minus the remark about the kindergarten things—and she couldn't help being interested. I'm convinced that Joe didn't know or accept what his brother had gotten himself into. Lewis told him stories about the drug trade, including an escapade in the Gulf of Mexico, but Joe didn't believe him, thinking it was "a lot of nonsense." My father's erratic behavior may have been harder to discount, but maybe Joe simply didn't know how to categorize it. Lewis once sent Joe's son, Stephan, then about fourteen, down to the high school to buy marijuana for him (though Stephan has no recollection of this incident; if Lewis asked him to do it, Stephan says he couldn't have complied because he knew no one in high school who took or sold drugs). Another time, he drove Joe's truck into a canal. My father was fine, but "the *truck*," Joe says, with still fresh annoyance, "*sank* out of *sight*."

After the accident, Stephan drove my father to the courthouse in Stuart, Florida, to appear before a judge. Lewis told his nephew that while he was driving Joe's truck, he had heard voices speaking to him from the radio. Stephan can't remember now whether the voices had told Lewis to crash the truck or whether he had crashed the truck to stop the voices.

Lewis also had some suspicious social connections. Not long after he and my mother had left Florida for the last time, Joe and his wife, Myriam (like my father's sister but spelled with a "y"), were invited to a party at the home of one of my father's friends, a big-time developer in Miami. The place was filled with young women in see-through dresses. Heaps of powdery white cocaine had been set around the apartment in little dishes like hors d'ouevres.

"It was just not our kind of experience," Joe says, then adds, so deadpan I almost don't catch the joke, "Born twenty years too soon, I guess."

On another visit to the same developer, Joe and my aunt were sitting on the couch when a woman came out of the pool and walked casually across the room stark naked. My aunt sat there in frank astonishment, her eyes like saucers. I wonder if perhaps it was there that my father had discovered the drug that would ultimately be his undoing.

"I don't know what was going on with Lewis," Joe continues. "I actually don't know what the hell he was doing. He was telling me all these stories about being pursued, one thing and another. I had no idea what the hell he was talking about. I thought he was putting me on. It was like something you read about. I didn't actually know anybody who took drugs. It was a foreign world to me.

"Lewis," he says, "was left some money when our father died, from his personal assets, enough so that he didn't have to work. It was a disaster." Pain suffuses his voice. "I always felt that if Lewis had had a job he could go to every day, he would have been okay.

"He was a loving, affectionate person. But he didn't know what he wanted. When he went out west with your mother, he had a romantic notion of life being simpler. He expected to find something that didn't exist."

9. *I forget to ask where my father's ashes were strewn.*

FATHERING

My father, Joe tells me, had a difficult relationship with Morris, who grew up in an era when fathers didn't bother much with children. He told them what to do and when to do it and wasn't interested in their personalities or particular likes and dislikes. "My father was the type of man who, when you needed a new overcoat, would take you downtown with him so he could have you on hand for the *size* but wouldn't let you pick out the one you wanted."

When I hear this characterization of my grandfather, my father's love of esoterica—the British military-issue trench coat whose D rings had been designed for holding hand grenades—suddenly makes a new kind of sense.

Morris was strait-laced and very uncompromising, Joe says. Lewis felt unwanted. Even so, my father, as the baby in the family, had many advantages. Lewis was able to do things, like taking a trip to Europe as a teenager, that were out of the question for Joe.

Clearly, there was a tremendous amount of frustration in the family. Kate, for instance, had a lot of talent but few outlets for it. "My mother was often a driving force behind my father," Joe says. "She was more entrepreneurial than he was and pushed him into doing a lot of things. It was because of her that my father took up golf, for example, though he was never very good at it. In this day and age my mother would have been the head of some corporation." He says the same of Miriam. There was never any question that he and Lewis would go to college, but their father didn't think it was necessary for their sister.

"What was it like working for Morris?" I ask.

"*Fearsome*," Joe replies.

"'Fearsome?'" I'm impressed by the force of the word, though Joe's voice is as mild as ever. Miriam had told me that the last time she had seen Joe, at a party for his seventieth birthday, he had upset her by launching into a diatribe against Morris at the dinner table. She felt Joe didn't understand the hardships their father suffered; there were times during the Great Depression when he didn't know how he was going to put food on the table, much less pay the bills. "Fearsome in what sense?"

"My father had a personality where he expected everything to be able to be answered with yes or no. If he wanted to know why something wasn't finished, he didn't want to know there had been an earthquake that morning. He'd get fairly, I won't say 'abusive' is the right word, but unpleasant. He modeled himself on a foreman he had who was an ex-sergeant in the German army. His attitude was, If you don't like it, there's the door. But I wasn't in a position to leave." Suddenly Joe's voice deepens with fury. "Morris couldn't have treated a Mexican farm laborer the way he treated me and gotten away with it. He would have been knifed."

Knifed? I was hoping Joe would speak openly about his relationship with Morris, but I hardly expected such candid anger.

"Was that true when you were growing up as well? Did you have a difficult relationship with him when you were a child?"

"No," Joe says. "I had no relationship with him *at all* as a child. We were put to bed before he came home for dinner, so he would not be disturbed while he read the newspaper.

"And the fighting and squabbling between my parents went on *all the time.* My cousin once described their relationship to me as a wonderful love match, and I didn't know who the hell she was talking about. My father had a really volatile temper. He was an avid baseball fan. He'd have two radios going at once, two games being called at the same time. Later on, it was the radio and the TV. Then he'd fall asleep in his chair. It drove me out of my mind. I'd go to turn them off, and he'd pop up—boooom!

"But he loved my son, Stephan, and Peter. I mean, if you could picture my father—well, you never even saw him." His voice drops, expressing an amazement that is also a kind of anguish. "He would *pitch pennies* with Stephan. Here's this grown man, you know, with this little kid."

WANTED

I tell Miriam what Joe said about my father feeling unwanted.

"Oh, well," she says. "He was unexpected, yes. That was the story. People say things. They don't realize what an effect it has on a child."

She tells me a story about her mother, Kate, who was a "change of life" baby herself. Kate's mother was in her late forties or even fifty when Kate was born, and her father was in his mid- to late fifties. All her relatives used to say to her, "Poor child, you're going to be an orphan. Your parents will never live to see you grow up." It was a constant refrain throughout her childhood. "Do you know what that does to you," Kate said to Miriam, "to grow up like this?"

"She heard it all the time," Miriam says, "and her parents lived to see her get married! And then she did the same thing. I wouldn't say that my mother said anything to Lewis directly, but somehow the talk got around that he was, you know, 'an accident.' An accident!

"She wasn't an easy person, my mother, but she had a good character. I had a hard time with her, but I only wanted to be like her. I'm sure she didn't mean to hurt Lewis. They didn't plan on having more children. In those days, no one had three children. My father was *embarrassed.* My mother was what? In her late thirties, I guess."

"Why couldn't they have three children? They couldn't afford it?"

"Well, it was probably for a lot of people a matter of economics. And I guess it was just not the thing. But I remember my mother telling me that my father was very upset. He said, 'Who wants to have more children?' My mother said, 'If you want me to do something about it, you'll have to come with me.'"

"Uh-huh," I say stupidly, as if this little anecdote conveys the most ordinary information. In fact, it shocks me. The news that my grandparents had considered aborting my father is more than a little disconcerting.

At the same time, I'm struck by how common this feeling of being unwanted seems to be. Irwin and Stephan, while not expressing any sense that they were unwanted at birth, spoke frequently about feeling abandoned as teenagers, describing themselves as "waifs" and "orphans." My mother, too, thought of herself as unwanted because she was conceived out of wedlock, but largely, I think, because her mother was so undemonstrative.

"And Lewis knew this?" I ask.

"Obviously. He knew it, but they had him anyway! And he was my father's pet. My father adored him." She lowers her voice. "But there were a lot of dynamics going on in that house, you know. And in the heat of the moment, things get said that shouldn't be said, which are hurtful."

Being wanted / Being needed / Deserving above, my father writes in his journal, apparently referring to his friends in Taos, on whom he's trying to focus his energy after the breakup with Mara. And then again, in a letter to Mara, who he says does not want him as a boyfriend or lover: *starting over / proving my worth / I guess that proves my worthlessness / and general incompetence.*

The sense that he has to deserve love does seem to be a theme with him. As is the sense that worthiness for him is equated with achievement. But maybe I'm wrong to think that he had no confidence in himself because of his parents. It was only after they were dead that he felt he couldn't make it in the world.

Life's the same everywhere, that same passage ends. *And we rise or fall / according to merit / I've always had my family / built-in assurance of success.*

When I call back, Donald Singer tells me that he and his wife and another couple, the Greenbergs, whom I have never heard of, spent a lot of time with my parents.

"The six of us were really tight," he says, "like in a movie. It was dinner at someone's house, films at the art theater in Miami, and lots and lots of talk. For a while, several years in the mid-sixties, it was the kind of friendship that people write stories about."

Don met my father and mother not long after they came to Miami, introduced by Bob Greenberg, a mutual friend. They soon discovered that Barry, of Barry and Runja Klein from RPI, had been a close friend of Don's in high school.

I ask Don about the house, and he tells me that the house they built, from which I've spent so much time extrapolating deep truths about my father's identity, was not the house my parents originally wanted. They had spent many hours planning another house, much bigger and more elaborate, but when it was priced out, it went over their budget, which, as *Architectural Record* reported, was a mere $22,000. They were all crushed when they had to abandon it, but then Don went back to the drawing board and in a single day knocked out the new one. Though he and my father spent a fair amount of time discussing layout and materials, Don says that Lewis left most of the particulars to him. He would never talk much about his "architect side," though he had mentioned his less-than-satisfactory experience at Vorhees.

The concrete block, which my father loved, was Don's idea, and was inspired primarily by Frank Lloyd Wright. "We had many discussions," Don says, "about the fact that by not covering up the block, one could forever see the hand of the workman who put it there."

I hear the echo of the things I've read, about modernist architects' "truth to materials," how concrete and glass and steel epitomized the shift away from expensive, labor-intensive, overly fussy "bourgeois" building practices toward mass production and industrialization. The sculptural properties of raw materials were revered; ornament became, as Wright declared, "*of* the surface not *on* the surface." Leaving a structure exposed represented a refusal—at least in theory

—to disguise either the processes of its production or the imprint of those whose labor had produced it.

"Did you rearrange the furniture in the magazine's photo shoot?" I ask.

"Well, the rocker, that was mine and Elaine's," Don says. "And that painting over the dining table was ours, too."

I can't help smiling, a bit triumphantly. My mother was so certain, vehement even, that the shots had not been set up; but it is hard to argue with Don's claim to his own furniture. It isn't that I'm pleased necessarily to have proved my mother wrong. I'm diverted by memory itself, playing its usual tricks. Even so, however shapeshifting or biased, each person I've encountered with his or her shard of knowledge and memory, his or her perception of what happened, *does* contribute to what is ultimately a credible history. It's as if Don has picked up a misplaced tile from a mosaic I'm trying to reconstruct and has said, Oh, I know where that goes, and set it, with absolute confidence, into place. There is a term for this: "intersubjectivity." If you talk to enough people, collect enough details and points of view, piece by piece a picture emerges, a kind of truth.

Still, my mosaic seems to travel on the back of a flatbed truck driving fast over a rutted road. The painted fragments, even set in the right place, vibrate and shift position.

Don tells me the actual tile in my parents' house was two-foot-square white Cuban tile, not twelve-by-twelve terra cotta, as my mother remembered, and it was my father who designed and built the wooden walkway through the banyans. We also talk about my father's hatred of the building business and the episode of paying off the building inspector. Don tells the story as my father told it to him—as a hilarious anecdote, almost a joke.

"Something on the project," Don says, laughing a little at the memory, "hadn't been done properly, I guess, or maybe this was just the cost of doing business. But Morris told Lewis that he had to pay this guy off, and he gave him, two, three hundred dollars, whatever it was. And Lewis said, 'What do I do with this? I don't know how to do this.' But Morris just waved his hand at him. 'You'll figure something out,' he said. So your father took the inspector all around the property, this entire apartment complex, showing him every hall and closet in the whole place, delaying the payoff as long as he possibly could. Finally, they were in the very last building, on the very last floor, and there was nothing more he could show the guy. They were riding down in the elevator, the two of them standing there, both knowing what was supposed to happen next, and your father had no choice now but to do it. He pulled out the envelope. The door opened, they both stepped into the lobby, your father thrust the money at him, and said something like "Uh-ah-uh," and the inspector said something like "Uh-ah-uh," then pocketed the cash and walked away. Your father was very funny. He was amused by his own clumsiness. But it was abhorrent to him, too. He hated it."

"Why didn't Lewis design the house?" I ask him.

"Why did I design the house rather than Lewis?" Don echoes. "I never could understand that myself, although the fact that he asked me to do it was a great source of pride to me. I admired him greatly and felt his insight was such that he could have been a very good architect."

What is clear, at least as Don remembers it, is that Lewis wanted nothing to do with designing buildings.

"I kept begging him to design the house himself," Don says, "but he refused. He had put that part of his life behind him."

"He couldn't afford to fail," I say on impulse.

"What do you mean by that?" Don asks.

What do I mean? "He needed to prove something to his father, I think, to impress him, but he couldn't put himself on the line like that. He couldn't risk creating something and not have it come out perfectly. That would have been too devastating."

It seems a banal explanation, the same old boring psychology; still, it feels true: something unappeasable in Morris acted as a goad and a constraint on my father his whole life, even after Morris was dead. The only time Lewis seems to have defied his father was when he insisted on marrying my mother while they were still in college. And, paradoxically, she married him then only because she felt coerced into it by *her* parents.

Don didn't know very much about the turmoil between my parents, even though he spent so much time with them. By the time they moved into the house, they were on the verge of splitting up, and yet he had no inkling. Their friendship started to collapse when my parents began to socialize with a new crowd.

"I remember going to a party at your parents' house with several people we didn't know, and having pot turn into the evening's recreation. Neither my wife nor I felt comfortable taking part. I believe the rejection became a wedge between us. About the time that Lewis and Terry left Miami, Bob Greenberg left Betty, and the end was pretty complete."

And then he says the most extraordinary thing to me. He says, "I have a tape with your father's voice on it."

"What?" I ask. "You do?"

"Yes. I interviewed your parents after the house was built, along with other people. About the process, what it was like. It has about five minutes of him talking on it. I've used it many times in lectures to architectural students. I'll send it to you. And if you listen carefully, you'll hear yourself in the background."

I'm astonished. I will get to hear my father's voice.

"Just open the mind," the poet and essayist Albert Goldbarth says, "and the past it requires will surface."

I can't wait to tell Stephan.

COINCIDENCES AND OCCURRENCES 2

The woman who bought the Florida house from my parents when they moved to New Mexico came to see Donald Singer. She wanted him to make some changes.

"It has a bad aura," she said. "Bad things happened there."

This was 1970.

Donald Singer was not in the aura-fixing business. He wanted nothing to do with it.

FOREST FIRES

By chance, I turn on the radio one afternoon to a report of forest fires raging through the mountains of northern New Mexico. The exact location is unclear to me, but I learn later that the fire swept across Lama Mountain. A number of buildings burned down. I wonder about Gersh's house, the complex of lovely pink-tinted rooms. And then later, about the shed where my father's wooden trunk is sitting in storage. The trunk I wanted but never called to ask for.

LIVING ALONE

I have moved to a two-room studio in a turn-of-the-century apartment building in St. Paul, surrounded by forties furniture I found at a thrift shop—a yellow dinette set and a curvy rose-colored upholstered chair that fill me with pleasure whenever I look at them. The only things I took from the house in Blaine were an antique bowl I had bought in Seville, the red army trunk and the wooden box with my father's Graflex camera in it, my grandfather's art, a bookshelf, and my books. I spend my days in this sunny space, happily alone, writing. At night, I play Billie Holiday or Ida Cox on my small stereo and, suffused by their warm voices, eat takeout wonton soup in bed. My only links to the outside world are the few hours I spend at school or with Stephan by e-mail.

Subject: The Scent of Lilacs
From: Anna Cypra Oliver-Skoven
To: Stephan Klein
Date: 02 Jun 96 8:40 p.m.

It was beautiful today, sunny and breezy, though a little cool. I tore off a branch of lilac on my way across campus: I was absurdly pleased to come across bushes that were not yet done blooming, though the flowers had begun to curl and darken at the edges, and which were in a reachable spot where I could break one off without anyone eyeing me. Do you ever get the feeling you can't experience something enough? I held the branch to my nose and I couldn't suck enough of that smell into my body. I crushed it between

my fingers, so my skin would absorb it. The smell
of home to me—I used to bring them in armfuls to
my mother. The blossoms on my branch, old as
they were, fell off at a touch. I kept scooting
forward out of the shade of a nearby oak, dropping as I did a trail of purple stars behind me
in the grass. Do you know that in literature,
lilacs are a symbol of death? 'When lilacs last
in the dooryard bloom'd,' Whitman writes in his
elegy to Lincoln. . . . In Taos their smell is
almost a physical weight in the air. . .

HOUSE TREATMENT 6

The tape from Donald arrives, along with
a set of color slides and a sheet with information describing the Weinberger
House. The interior looks entirely different in color: warm and inviting. The built-
in couch against the wall is deep purple.
Circular and square pillows in bright red,
yellow, and electric blue further brighten
the room, softening its hard lines and
angles. A cream-colored rug covers the
wide tiles. The reddish wood of the ceiling glows. The house is beautiful.

And there is the tape. It says, "FOR ANNA: Play This Side."
This tape, I think, has my father's voice on it.
I don't play it. I put it away. Not yet, I think. Not yet.
I want the moment to be perfect.

ANOTHER SUBSTITUTION IN THE INVENTORY OF MY FATHER

Years after my mother gave her engagement ring to my brother—who
had it reset in a band of gold and diamond baguettes for his beautiful bride, Julie—I finally tell my mother how upset I was about the
whole incident. I'm on one of those kicks in which you start to say

all the things you've kept bottled up inside, to more or less good effect. My mother, whatever else she is or is not, is a person who owns up.

"Oh, Anna, I'm so sorry," she says. I can hear how terrible she feels, which makes me feel terrible in turn. I should have let the matter lie. "I didn't know it meant so much to you."

Shortly afterward, I receive a package of presents for my twenty-sixth birthday. She usually sends me one "big" present—a sweater, a pair of winter boots from the J. Crew catalogue—and one or two small tchotchkes. This package contains a tiny antique ceramic jar that she'd brought back from a missionary trip to China and a battered black leather box with a pair of pearl earrings in it.

These were given to me by my parents when I married your father, her note says. *I love them, and wear them all the time. I want you to have them.*

I am so touched I cry. Sometimes my mother gets it exactly right.

GONE SO SOON

I wait a long time before I listen to the tape. When I do, I am alone, in the middle of the night, sitting on my futon. As I felt on the day I first opened the journal, I am depressed and lonely. I want something from my father. I want him to appear to me. I want him to be there for me in the dark night.

It begins with Simon and Garfunkel:

So long, Frank Lloyd Wright,
I can't believe your song is gone so soon.
I barely learned the tune.
So soon, so soon.
I'll remember, Frank Lloyd Wright,
All of the nights we'd harmonize till dawn.
I never laughed so long,
So long, so long.
Architects may come and architects may go
And never change your point of view.

Then the music fades out as a man's voice emerges. I feel a moment of confusion. Is that him?

". . . people," the voice says, "about not really having been more hysterical about it, uh, more *effectively* hysterical about building it, you know, not *insisting* that things be done right. You know, like where they ran the ceiling the wrong—where they changed the direction on the wood. And I looked at the guy and he had half of it, he had half of it up, you know, and I said, 'Oh hell, we'll get used to it.' We *have* gotten used to it. But I kind of feel it *now*. I would say, 'Take the thing down and let's start over again,' you know: it really *should* run in the right direction."

His voice is deep, resonant, but not particularly smooth or well modulated. Middle-class New York. His habit of emphasizing single words in an otherwise flat sentence reminds me of Joe.

"But this is something I encounter all the time in the building business, you know, not really wanting to push people *that* hard. You know, not wanting to cause them grief and cost them money. I suppose it was remotely conceivable I could have told the block place to take all the block back, but, you know, we wanted to get into the house, too."

"But having built for yourself," another voice—Donald's—says, "I don't know . . ."

"Of course," my father replies, "the only thing I really did myself was clean the block with that wire brush, which was a really *horrible* job. And so I don't know if that's really a—if you consider that a creative contribution to the house."

There is music again, a rock instrumental this time. As before, my father's voice rises out of the chords, except this time he is laughing. The sound is a mirthless huh-huh-huh. "Yeah, I think it's important that the house doesn't really become the only thing in your entire life, you know. And it's *not*. It's a place we live, and it's a great house, and I, sometimes when people ask me about it, I deliberately sort of play it down so as, you know . . ."

I hear myself now, as Donald said I would if I listened closely. Tat-ty yah, tat-ty yeah. Bee, bay, bay. He must have been holding me on his lap. Bi-bi-bi-big, I say, a-big-big.

There is more, my father's voice still talking, but I shut off the tape. The fist has tightened in my throat. This recording is the closest I will ever get to experiencing my father as a living, breathing human being, and I can't feel enough. Maybe I expected him to speak to me. To tell me something more than that the wood should run the right way. I am numb and empty and more alone than ever. I wish I had waited to listen to it with someone else.

So long, so long, so long, so long, so long, so long, so long. . . .

ON MY FATHER'S LAP

BROKEN MIRROR ART 2

"I'm sorry you have to do this," my mother says. We are sitting next to each other, our knees nearly touching, on the couch in the spare room of my grandmother's apartment.

"What?" I ask. "Construct him?"

"Construct our whole life, instead of just having lived it."

"Oh," I say, looking away. "Well."

QUEST 23: CREATIVE CONTRIBUTIONS

At Stephan's instigation, I call my uncle Joe again.

"Do you know anything about Bonnier's?" I ask.

Stephan wouldn't tell me himself what Bonnier's was. Just call, he said, and see what Joe says.

"Bonnier's? Sure. That was a store on Madison Avenue between Fifty-seventh and Fifty-eighth, the first in the city to sell Danish modern furniture and dinnerware. I came across it one day in the early 1950s after a trip to a design show at the Museum of Modern Art." Clearly enthusiastic, he tells me that simple modern designs were not available everywhere, at Pottery Barn and such, as they are now. "This stuff was revolutionary. You know, beautifully detailed, but designed for mass production at the same time—high-class household items that ordinary people could afford. The simpler the design, you know, the more perfectly it has to be executed. When Myriam and I got married, we filled our house with it."

He mentions that he used to tell Lewis stories about architecture. He throws out titles: Lewis Mumford's *Sticks and Stones*, Henry Russell-Hitchcock's *In the Nature of Materials*. I'm a little taken aback: this is a Joe I hadn't imagined, the man behind the blunt words and bluff exterior. He and Lewis both loved the physicality of architecture, he says, the way things went together. And I remember Stephan telling me that Lewis used to talk about how much he appreciated the curve of the seat and the way the splat came up on Wegner's Wishbone chair.

"So," I say, "I guess Lewis would have seen that furniture in your house when he was a kid?"

"Oh, sure," Joe says.

Joe mentions the Singer house. In Florida everything was stucco, he says, a schmear of plaster that disguised the sloppy craftsmanship of the building underneath. But the Singer house was different: the exposed seams had to be perfect; to get them absolutely straight, Donald cut the joints with a diamond saw.

We had many discussions about the fact that by not covering up the block, I hear Don saying, *one could forever see the hand of the workman who put it there,* and it occurs to me that for my father, this notion was not the abstract philosophy of modern architecture. Joe had conveyed this respect for craft to him.

Following a line of questioning suggested by Stephan, I ask about Wilke Pipe Shop, and then about my father's attraction to things British. Joe replies that Wilke was near Bonnier's on Madison. He found it on one of his rambles in the city. And when he was young, English stuff was considered cool, English clothes, tweed jackets, overcoats, British racing green Rovers with hand-tooled leather seats. It was just after the war.

"And Stuyvesant?" I ask, inexplicably dreading the answer.

"I was very good in science and I wanted to go to Stuyvesant. I got in, but my father, in his wisdom, refused to let me attend. As far as he was concerned, one New York City high school was as good as another. I was pretty much used to doing what my father told me, but when Lewis got to be in high school, I talked to my father about letting him go there. I was afraid he wouldn't be challenged otherwise, that he'd just slide through school."

And then I finally connect the dots: Wilke, Wegner, desert boots, *In the Nature of Materials*. Sauerbraten at Luchow's after school. They all came from Joe. All those things my father was known for, his arcane knowledge, his reputation as an explorer. They were all about Joe. Joe brought the news home.

I think of the nine years between Joe and my father. Lewis may have been desperate to impress Morris, but it was Joe he admired, Joe whom he wanted to emulate. Joe, who was for Lewis a better father than their father had been.

He went to Stuyvesant because Joe couldn't. He became an architect because Joe didn't. Joe, unable to avoid it, got drafted. Lewis let himself get drafted. Joe went to Florida to work for Morris. Lewis went to Florida to work beside Joe. Even that little sailboat my father built: Miriam looked startled when I mentioned it to her, because Joe, apparently, had built a sailboat, too: it sat in the breezeway of his house in Florida.

I feel a sinking sense of disappointment. Of course my father was born with the fire and intelligence to absorb his brother's lessons. And along the way, he must have made his own discoveries. But the persona he affected, the information he used as currency, the passion for innovative design with a practical purpose and a history to it—all Joe. The things about my father that were the most original didn't come from him at all. "Lewis" was no longer "of the surface"; he was "on the surface," a schmear of stucco.

Messy Vitality

I am for messy vitality over obvious unity. . . . I am for richness of meaning rather than clarity of meaning. . . . I prefer "both-and" to "either-or," black and white, and sometimes gray, to black or white. . . . But an architecture of complexity and contradiction has a special obligation toward the whole. . . . It must embody the difficult unity of inclusion rather than the easy unity of exclusion. More is not less.

— ROBERT VENTURI, *Complexity and Contradiction*

"FLUTTERING HEART" 5

"That actor from *Jurassic Park*," Stephan says. "He always makes me think of your father."

"Sam Neill," I say. I am sitting with him and Irwin in the candlelit garden of the Bryant Park Cafe. I'm spending the summer in New York with my grandmother, having decided to get a divorce.

"He always reminds me of Lewis."

"You're right, you're right," Irwin says. "Sam Neill in that World War II spy picture. That's him."

I have a hard time computing the resemblance. Sam Neill is tall, sandy-haired. My father is dark, round at the edges. Not as conventionally handsome but more memorable, I think. And besides, Sam Neill is so, well, un-Jewish-looking.

The conversation drifts. The two of them tell me some of the same stories they had told at Miriam's: Stephan and my father calling Irwin at four in the morning from White River Junction after a ski trip; Irwin seeing a movie and eight acts of vaudeville at the Jamaica Theater with my father in the sixth grade—until wine and the humid summer night loosen us enough to talk about other subjects.

Under the table, my foot brushes Stephan's leg.

"I feel as if I've always known you," Irwin says.

I smile, touched. My father's presence flits in and out.

WALKING TOUR

The two of us start at Union Square and walk south. The Strand is our first stop, the bookstore my father and his friends used to prowl as teenagers. Stephan is excited to show it to me, this place they all frequented and one of the wonders of New York, the last of the great used-book stores that once dotted Fourth Avenue and this part of Broadway. It's a cavern of books unlike any I've ever seen, the people inside strangely overshadowed by the towering shelves and large bins, as if they might turn a corner of the labyrinth and be swallowed up. I weave a few paces behind Stephan through the stacks of books. I hover at his elbow while he browses, a little afraid that if I let him out of my sight, I won't ever see him again. When he turns to ask if I'm ready, I try not to seem too eager to leave. But this extravaganza is more than I'm ready to tackle right now; the choice of books is overwhelming. It is a relief to retrieve his backpack from the sullen, very black-haired boy at the front counter and funnel through the security gate onto the street.

Broadway seems dirty and harsh, but the June air is pleasant. There is a smell of peanuts, and a whiff of cigar. I take a deep breath and feel myself revive a little.

There's so much of Manhattan I've never seen before. Stephan sets an unconsciously fast pace on his long legs, his face animated, pointing out landmarks as we walk, and keeping up a stream of eager observations. He wants to show me everything; everything excites his interest. We look in all the windows, dip in and out of shops. He draws my attention to elaborate doorways, wrought-iron balconies with red geraniums spilling over them, the gothic tower of a church. As always when we're together, I have the impression of electrons sparking off the tight curls of his gray-black hair.

Our ostensible goal is Chinatown. I've been there once or twice with my family but remember little more than the strings of greasy Peking duck hanging in the windows. In fact, I had no idea that block by block the city changed its character so much; each neighborhood is a new world, sometimes a new universe. Stephan explains that the quickest way to Chinatown is down Broadway, but we'll veer toward Washington Square Park and through SoHo instead, because that's more interesting. He points toward the row of brownstones where Henry James lived and the building where the Triangle Shirtwaist Factory fire took place. We each buy an ice cream bar from a cart next to the dry central fountain. My grandmother said once that Washington Square was a needle park, and I half expect to see men lolling on the benches, hypodermics sticking out of their arms, but if they are there they're hidden by the chess players and skateboarders and crowds of strutting girls in itty-bitty tops.

In the few weeks I've been in the city, I've only just managed to figure out which direction is north and which south, and though I try to fix the streets in my mind as we zigzag through them, I really have no idea where we are. We gaze through iron bars into a store filled with velvety deco furniture, then turn down another street, passing a model boat shop, where Stephan shows me the ship he covets. Such stores! They're like something out of Bruno Schulz. One has whole tableaux of toy soldiers from various wars. That such fanciful places exist, much less thrive, seems extraordinary. Stephan's face is lit up and boyish as he browses. We continue through the harsher, half-cobbled streets and cast-iron buildings of SoHo, then turn a corner onto a wider avenue, treeless, clogged with honking cars, oversized trucks, raging taxi drivers. Canal Street. Bristling with cheap electronics and faux designer watches, sunglasses, scarves, umbrellas, the unrelieved concrete and blaring commerce of the street almost knocks me backward. The sidewalk is so congested it's hard to move.

The people pressing past us are mostly Chinese now. We turn onto Mott Street. A chaos of backed-up cars, delivery trucks, weaving bicyclists shrilling their bells, and pedestrians in flip-flops carrying plastic bags of goods, it nonetheless feels like a retreat from Canal's hard glare. Carts piled with fruit and vegetables, only half of which I recognize, take over what little is left of the sidewalk: bok choy, broccoli, spears of giant white radish, some huge citrus thing that looks like a greenish grapefruit. From the open fronts of stores spill bins of puckered mushrooms, dried squid and every size of shrimp, baskets of blue-claw crab, still alive, waving vicious-looking little pincers. Customers call out in Chinese to the vendors, then point across one another to what they want. Ripe melons and sweet garlicky durian, the searing smell of salt, rotted vegetable skins, oily asphalt, exhaust from the truck tailpipes, fish, fish, and more fish, all the odors stew together in the sun. We stop to buy a mango and litchi nuts. I smell the mango, sucking its sweetness into my body. The scent is so delicious I want to put off eating it for a while so we can carry it with us. Stephan zips the mango into an outer pocket of his backpack for me, and even through the canvas the fragrance wafts out behind him.

It's then that I realize that even though I'm quiet, and still responding in a near murmur to Stephan's various exclamations, there is a quickness in my limbs, a lightness. When we began the day, I felt, as I often do, blank, muted. Usually it's only afterward that some sensation starts to surface, in the recounting of details either to myself or someone else, a kind of debriefing. So it startles me to discover that I'm enjoying myself so much already. The street, the day, Stephan's comments on the architecture. I love the clatter of the city. This, in particular, just as it did on that walk uptown from Penn Station with Stuart, catches me completely off-guard.

I'm also thrilled to be with Stephan. His relationship with his wife, as I surmised, is deeply troubled; their estrangement had grown to the point that they had talked frequently about splitting up. In the recent past he's looked for an apartment of his own. Even so, I don't imagine there's any future for us. I don't even necessarily hope for one. We might spin fantasies about matching white bathrobes and breakfast on the terrace, but an actual life seems far-fetched and, in some way, too sentimental. I've already had my white wedding. What is important to me now is this day, this place, Chinatown with all its smells. For me the only essential fact is that with each step across the city with this man, each feeling of pleasure or joy or excitement that I allow to creep in, I scratch out another of the endless, life-sucking *I will nots* seared into me by Wayne, by Curtis, and, most of all, by the Church. Next to Stephan I feel electrified. He is quite simply the most vibrant human being I've ever met.

It's past noon, the heat is stifling. We choose a restaurant on Elizabeth Street with air conditioning and tanks full of bizarre sea creatures in the window. Stephan orders tiny snails in black bean sauce and clams with garlic and scallion and fat shrimp with the heads on. These are things I've never eaten, and I follow his lead in picking the snails, called periwinkles, out of their shells with a toothpick. They are black curled things, ugly and slimy, but I've decided that my new motto in life is to say yes, when my first impulse is to say no. They explode with briny deliciousness on my tongue. Stephan and I lick the last sauce from each whorled shell before chucking it with a plink into the steel discard bowl. Having grown up landlocked, I've never been much on seafood, but the slippery clams are succulent, too, and though I hesitate at the eyes, I crunch through the glassine legs of the shrimp and even into the upper body, where the guts are. A waiter brings us yet another hot washcloth for our sticky fingers and clears the midden of shells heaped up between us. Scraping the last wedge of garlic and scallion off a clamshell, I realize I hardly knew what food was before today.

When we finish, the dishes wiped clean despite how much there was to eat, we walk back through Chinatown and down the narrow streets of the Lower East Side. It's quiet enough to hear both the rush of honking cars in the near distance and the snapped air of pigeons taking wing. This, of course, is where my family lived, and Stephan's, too, when they first came to this country—or maybe farther over, near Orchard Street. I'm not clear about the exact location.

I love this area, the rusty brick wall around the oak trees growing in a churchyard on Mulberry Street, the sense of layered generations, one on top of another, but I'm getting tired, a little cranky. Stephan promises that we'll make just one more stop and then head back. He dips into a little shop where a man who's a ringer for Rumpelstiltskin sells collectible toys and miniatures. The store is odd and, like so much I've seen today, both magical and baffling: shelves filled with ballerinas, ballplayers, soldiers with pith helmets and bayonets, birds, girls in bikinis, motorcycles, ocean liners, all less than an inch high, made of painted metal or plastic, and all primarily meant for the pleasure of adults. I don't know what to make of it. Stephan buys something, and the shopkeeper puts it into a box.

"What is this?" I ask, smiling, when he hands it to me on the street.

I lift the lid to expose two tiny figures: the first is a naked woman painted in white enamel, one arm clutched across her bare breasts, the other covering her lower parts, shoulders hunched like Eve just after she's eaten the apple; the second is a flamenco dancer with black hair and a red dress whose arms are exuberantly raised in dance.

VOICE RECOGNITION

Stephan and I are sitting on a bench in Damrosch Park, across the street from my grandmother's building on Amsterdam Avenue and Sixty-first Street, a small cassette player between us. It is a weekday afternoon and, even in summer, the park is nearly deserted; the few visitors march purposefully through the precise rows of trees, on their way to one of Lincoln Center's theaters. As my father's voice leaps above the last bars of music, Stephan's eyes redden around the rims, his mouth tightens with emotion. He shakes his head solemnly as Lewis discusses his ambivalence toward the project, and his own limited role in creating it.

"Of course," my father says, "the only thing I really did myself was clean the block with that wire brush. . . ."

I watch the pedestrians, feeling almost as detached as the first time I played the interview. But this time, I recognize my father's voice. And when we get to the part of the tape that I haven't heard before, I'm startled to find my eyes are watering, too.

"I'm not just the owner of a work of art," my father says. "I'm the caretaker of it. And it doesn't sum up my whole life. And I suppose if we were designing another house right now, we'd do a completely different house. I think, you know, contradicting everything I've said already, I'd do a house that was more, uh, adventurous, I guess. That had more complicated spaces."

The interview ends, and Stephan shuts off the tape, but the sound of my father's voice continues to play in my head.

"So strange," Stephan says, "to hear the voice of Lewis as if on a telephone, almost, calling from a quarter century ago. We all went on. We all developed beyond that point. Except your father. He didn't. The foolish fuck."

Big Enough Spaces

Make your spaces big enough, man, that you can walk around in them freely, and not just in one predetermined direction! Or are you all that sure of how they will be used? We don't know at all whether people will do with them what we expect them to. Functions are not so clear or so constant; they change faster than the building.

—MIES VAN DER ROHE TO THE ARCHITECT HUGO HÄRING

LUFTMENSH
"The hip world was not for him," my maternal grandmother says of my father. My mother, she says, was always the *luftmensh*, if you know that word. It means, literally, "airman." Someone with feet planted firmly in the clouds. My mother, or so this version goes, drew them both into the counterculture.

It was a rush that began when you made the last engine-straining climb out of the canyon, breath squeezed in your ribs by the seven-thousand-foot-plus elevation, and then, just as you wondered if you and the poor car were actually going to make it, you swept around the final cliffside horseshoe curve and found yourself on the sagebrush mesa. You stopped the car. You got out and walked toward it, hushed, the great purple-green fissure of the gorge conferring on you a benediction you could never have known to pray for. The land—incredible—spreading mile upon blue mile to the mountains. And the light! Gray, purple, blue, violet, orange, red. So tangible you wanted to grab a handful, seal it in a plastic bag, and take it home with you.

Taos was like that. If you had been living, say, in the suburbs of Miami for a long time, you'd start to feel every molecule of oxygen flowing through your body, little capsules of pure air traveling up and down the nerve endings, every neural pathway from your fingertips to your toes to your nostrils to your eyeballs tingling. You'd feel fully awake for the first time in years. But fundamental as it was, the landscape was only part of the experience.

There was a tendency among new arrivals to think of this country in terms of vast open spaces and gorgeous scenery, unpopulated panoramas, empty land, all mountain and light and fierce energy radiating from the earth. A savage place, they imagined, where the spirit could soar unfettered, freed from civilization as they knew it. That was the romantic ideal many people carried, not least among them the hippies who came to Taos in great waves in the late 1960s.

It didn't take long to get their heads set straight.

There were signs on buildings: THE ONLY GOOD HIPPIE IS A DEAD HIPPIE. KILL. Words scribbled on a billboard on the way into town: HIPPIES — STAY OUT OR ELSE. Signs in windows: NO SHIRT, NO SHOES, NO SERVICE.

The town passed an anti-hitchhiking ordinance. The Taos Municipal Education Association, terrified that hippies would corrupt Taos youth, passed a resolution that declared, "As parents, citizens, and educators, we ask to be included in the fight to crush this cancerous epidemic for all time." The town council, more circumspect than the educators, created a committee to investigate the problem, deciding that communication and fair but firm enforcement of existing laws were the answers. To his credit, the police chief said that unless they committed any real crime, he would treat hippies as he treated anyone else, though how this pledge translated into practice was an open question. Letters for and against flew in the *Taos News*. Several churches attempted a dialogue with the newcomers; at the same time, they hammered together a slew of new youth programs designed to keep the hippie lifestyle from infecting Taos teenagers.

Governor David Cargo, never mentioning hippies per se, made this statement: "It is fair to say that the appearance of substantial numbers of visitors in rural areas possessing unsophisticated public services would strain New Mexican hospitality severely."

It was 1970. Substantial numbers of visitors came. Hospitality was severely strained.

Houses occupied by hippies were firebombed. Windows of hippie-owned businesses and vehicles were smashed. Hippies were beaten, one was shot. Someone threw three Molotov cocktails at a coffeehouse full of longhairs, accidentally exploding the bottles against the wall of a neighboring Hispanic residence. Some hippies stopped riding bicycles in town because young La Raza members couldn't resist opening their car doors into the spokes and sending them flying over the handlebars. One longhair didn't feel like dying for the sake of his appearance, so he cut his hair after someone shot at him. In the time-honored fashion of vilifying all outsiders, hippies were accused of having uncontrollable libidos. Claims were made that they had raped Hispanic women. Considering that a wrong look could get you punched, and a leer could get you killed, these assertions seemed questionable. A kid at the hot springs took a bullet in the leg.

It was less a land of enchantment than a battleground.

Among the locals, which included established Anglos and Pueblo Indians, the Hispanics were most vehement in their hatred. They valued tradition, religion, family, land, respect for elders, authority, and country. They had struggled for generations to achieve a margin of security, *wanted* but could never *hope* to have the kind of prosperity these stupid-ass kids so casually scorned. They hated their dirtiness, hated their laxity, hated their assumption that the land was there for the taking, like Manifest Destiny. These hippies were invaders. They were vermin. Draft dodgers while the sons of Hispanics went to war; college dropouts while the best Hispanic kids worked in auto body shops or at Moly Corp, the molybdenum mine. And they bought property, these cockroach *pendejos*, land that Hispanics had possessed for three hundred years but couldn't afford to hang on to. They bought it with the money and privilege they had supposedly renounced.

Even old hippies did not want new hippies to come. In the spring of 1970, at about the time that my parents went to Taos to live, some counts put the influx of hippies expected that summer at 25,000. There was not enough food to go around. Hunger and malnutrition were a problem, especially among children. Sanitation was inadequate or nonexistent. A lot of people got hepatitis. An article published in *The Mother Earth News* that April tried to forewarn those who were planning to go there about the harshness of the conditions, explaining that it would be wise to bring heavy work clothes, a shovel and an axe, a kerosene stove, bread—both kinds, because there weren't any jobs—and a healthy respect for the Hispanics and Indians. The Family, a group marriage commune that had moved to Taos from Berkeley in 1968, was blunter. It posted a notice on the bulletin board at its general store, a center of hippie community and commerce, advising hippies to move on or just, please, stay away: "We recommend Utah for anyone looking for a place to start a commune."

That summer, the county became one vast sleep-away camp for strung-out romping "freaks." As exaggerated as the estimates turned out to be, the actual numbers were in the high hundreds, at least, and maybe low thousands, significant in a town whose normal population was less than 10,000. Significant, too, for the communes that were trying to be more than crash pads for drifting kids. Many decided to adopt a closed-door policy, limiting visits by outsiders to one night. They did so reluctantly because it contradicted the notion of human love and connection on which they were founded, but it was essential for their survival. They were trying to create a new society and to forge new bonds to replace the traditional family, and transience and overcrowding didn't help. It strained their resources as well: too often people would crash without contributing either work or goods, wanting instead to "do their own thing," which sometimes meant they weren't willing to hoe the corn or wash the dishes after dinner. Reality Construction Company, a commune that shared a mesa with Morningstar, kept people away with a .22 rifle and a guard booth; they shot at people who tried to help themselves to their corn. But even among extremists, Reality was extreme, run as it was by survivalist radicals from a failed revolution in New York and San Francisco.

Morningstar, on the other hand, was a freewheeling place, established as an eastern outpost after the original Morningstar, one of the first communes in California, had failed. It was completely open, but because it was open and because of its remoteness it tended to attract nut cases and criminals. The FBI and local police were constantly raiding the place, looking for fugitives, a fact of life that I remember from our time of living there with Wayne. They would come in the middle of the night with dogs and roust everyone out of their beds while helicopters with searchlights buzzed over the compound.

There was, unquestionably, a lot of wild behavior, and in 1972, Michael Duncan, who owned the mesa on which Reality and Morningstar had set up camp, decided he'd had enough of the craziness and kicked them both off his land. But many of the saner hippies had already moved on.

By 1974, only a handful of the dozen communes or intentional communities established in the area remained. Those that did, such as Magic Tortoise, Lama Foundation, and New Buffalo, were more structured than most. Magic Tortoise devoted itself to building a long-term community of stable families; Lama Foundation offered courses of study in pan-religious subjects, attracting people who were committed to a disciplined exploration of their spirituality; and New Buffalo, the first commune established in New Mexico, was a collaborative farm, producing vegetables and raising goats, milk cows, and chickens on its sixty acres, loaned for the purpose by Rick Klein, one of the founders.

My parents must have known of Taos in relation to Georgia O'Keeffe and Alfred Stieglitz. It was also getting a lot of play in the national media: a spread in *Time*, another in *Newsweek*, and one in *Look*.

Maybe they had already read Willa Cather's *Death Comes for the Archbishop*, a book my mother loved and one of the few she suggested I read:

> Beautiful surroundings, the society of learned men, the charm of noble women, the graces of art, could not make up to him for the loss of those light-hearted mornings of the desert, for that wind that made one a boy again. He had noticed that this peculiar quality in the air of new countries vanished after they were tamed by man and made to bear harvests. . . . one could breathe that only on the bright edges of the world, on the great grass plains or the sage-brush desert.
>
> That air would disappear from the whole earth in time, perhaps; but long after his day. He did not know just when it had become so necessary to him, but he had come back to die in exile for the sake of it. Something soft and wild and free, something that whispered to the ear on the pillow, lightened the heart, softly, softly picked the lock, slid the bolts, and released the prisoned spirit of man into the wind, into the blue and gold, into the morning, into the morning!

After I left for college, I used to carry that passage, some sentences triple-underlined, in my wallet. Anglos and Hispanics had reconciled themselves, pretty much, to living with each other by then; in high school, I'd been called "honky" and "gringa" so many times that it began to feel affectionate. Taos had become literature to me, a place of the imagination, a place of memory, and I was as susceptible to nostalgia and bullshit about it as anybody. I fantasized, with my usual melodramatic bent, going back one day, dying in exile for the sake of it, for dusk on the mountain and the turpentine smell of sage. Even so, I never learned how to be at peace with the place, how to embrace its strangeness, how to meet its irrationality with anything besides cynicism. Whatever had originally drawn my mother there, she eventually set herself up in opposition to almost everything that made Taos what it was. I had been taught to despise its excesses, to see them as inspired by the devil and in need of exorcising. Even after I stopped calling myself a Christian, I found I could long for Taos from a distance, but I could not live there anymore.

After leaving Florida the first time, my
parents spent a year traveling across
the country. They stopped in Taos to
visit a friend and fell in love with it,
or at least my mother did. Then, after
meeting up with her brother, John,
who had been living in a communal
house in Arroyo Seco, they traveled on
to Oregon, they in their VW bus, he on

his BMW motorcycle with his current girlfriend perched on the back.
It might have been John who had planted the idea of being a hippie
in my mother's head; four years younger than she, he had given up a
graduate school fellowship to head west, though he dropped out for
only a year before going back to school to get a Ph.D. in physics. For
him, being a hippie was the equivalent of bumming around Europe for
a while after graduation. My mother, on the other hand, was looking
for change, dramatic and irreversible.

All these young people were breaking out, she told me, freeing
themselves from stifling middle-class expectations and routines. Unlike
her own family—and particularly her mother, with whom she seemed
locked in lifelong battle—they promoted a vision of self-realization
that was not based on prosperity, professional success, or the creation
of a perfect, respectable family. After my father's parents' deaths, the
bankruptcy of the business, and the near collapse of my parents' marriage the summer of my birth, that rejection of suddenly hollow-seem-
ing bourgeois values held tremendous appeal. Rather than rebuild
their lives, they could just leave them behind. And bohemia, after all,
was in my mother's blood: her own beloved father had fled an unhappy domestic situation in Chile in the early 1920s to pursue life as
an artist in Greenwich Village.

My mother, however, had no art to sustain her—and anyway, art
for her was "not enough." In fact, even as a hippie, she espoused no particular ideology. All that came through for me as a child was her intense
anger at her mother, her wish to repudiate all that Rose stood for.

That was a politics of a sort, I suppose. For all her free living and apparent freethinking, my mother hated feminism: she equated it with Rose—in her view domineering, emotionally inaccessible, more eager to work than to stay home to care for her daughter. In response, my mother, as a hippie, came to embrace an extravagant domesticity, not of the highly polished June Cleaver variety but a form even more extreme and more basic: she adopted the life of a pioneer woman, making everything she needed by hand, from scratch. She farmed, cooked, canned, sewed, dropped out to make her household a world. Other hippies did the same, proclaiming a back-to-essentials philosophy that was loosely modeled on traditional Native American life. My mother wasn't an idealist, though, and expressed no interest in establishing a new social order; if anything, she wanted to live alone with her family on the frontier, like Laura Ingalls Wilder.

In early fall 1969, my parents and John (with me, only a year old, and my brother, three, in tow) wound up at a commune called Canaan in Takilma, Oregon, where they found the residents frantically throwing up houses in preparation for winter. My father volunteered his services as an architect and introduced the hippie builders to the notion of a truss, which would span a fairly large space without any interior load-bearing walls. Unfortunately, he forgot one crucial element in the design: diagonal supports, necessary to hold the truss in place. To his intense embarrassment, the structure sagged, and the truss had to be propped up with posts to keep the roof from caving in.

My mother and father left Canaan not much later, after only a month at the commune, though my mother says they would have stayed on if there hadn't been so much poison oak everywhere; my mother, always terribly allergic to it, got such a bad case that her eyes nearly swelled shut. Instead, they left John in Takilma, returned to Florida, sold their house, sold or gave away their belongings—all of my father's Hans Wegner chairs, the bentwood rocker (which my mother still insists was theirs), and their Danish modern furniture—made a detour through New York, where they had dinner with Irwin and spent their last night with Stephan and his wife, and then headed to New Mexico again.

My family finally settled in a one-room, dirt-floor cabin on Lama Mountain just north of Taos. I was two, my brother four. There was no running water, no electricity, the walls were not insulated. We bathed in a round metal washtub filled with water carried from a pump and heated on the stove. We had a horse and a view of sagebrush plain and mountains. We had stars at night.

LAMA MOUNTAIN

FOUR WALLS
"Don't think your salvation lies in shutting yourself behind four walls like me . . . I'm too serious for an amateur . . . and not serious enough to become a professional. A life of poverty is preferable, believe me . . . to an existence protected by an organized society . . . where everything's planned, everything's perfect! . . . We need to live in a state of suspended animation . . . like a work of art . . . in a state of enchantment . . . We have to succeed in loving so greatly . . . that we live outside time . . . Detached . . . Detached."—Steiner to Marcello, Federico Fellini's *La Dolce Vita*

"We were living on East Seventy-ninth Street, and they came for dinner with you and your brother and wound up staying overnight. I had gone with Lewis to park the van in the garage, and he told me that he really felt like he'd failed. He was going out there as a kind of defeat. He had just quit smoking and was wondering if it hadn't already caused something to start up inside him that would eventually prove fatal. They left the next morning. That was the last time I ever spoke to him. I might have had a letter or a postcard, but that was the end of it."

ARTIFACTS 5

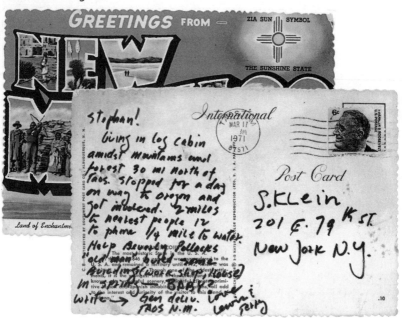

30 MI. NORTH OF TAOS

Joe and his wife came to visit us in the little cabin on Lama Mountain, a place so small and primitive that it shocked them when they first saw it. These were the conditions in which Lewis and Terry—dragging *two little kids* along with them—had chosen to live? Joe wondered what in the world his brother could be thinking. When I suggest to Joe now that maybe he considered it romantic—and it was, after all, breathtakingly beautiful—he replies that maybe this was so, but there was nothing romantic about it to him. The cabin reminded him of the kinds of places WPA photographers took pictures of in 1934.

PRIMITIVE CONDITIONS

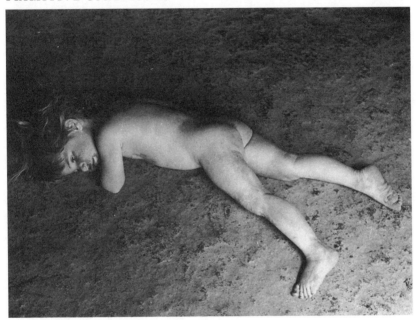

LEAVER AND LEFT 2

When my mother left my father a year later, she left him alone in the cabin on Lama Mountain.

WHAT MY BROTHER REMEMBERS 2

"It was night, and it was raining. We were inside the cabin, and Lewis and Mom were screaming at each other. I don't remember what they were saying, but I remember the screaming very, very clearly."

My mother took my brother and me and moved to New Buffalo, a commune just outside of Taos. My mother hated it. The commune was overcrowded, sleeping twenty or more people to a room, and, according to my mother, "People expected more than housework as your communal contribution."

At a New Buffalo party, she met Wayman Reynolds. Wayne had a house to himself on another commune called Morningstar. We went to live with him.

WILD ABOUT THE EYES

Some time after my mother and father split, my father went to visit my mother's parents in Queens. He had felt close to them during his marriage. They were living a cultured, apparently gracious life. He related to them in a way that he never could to his own parents. He remarked to my grandmother that his parents were more like the old-world immigrant generation to which her parents belonged. My grandparents' friendship was important to him, and he must have felt its loss keenly. My grandmother understood, but Lewis had behaved badly toward my mother during the breakup, threatening to take Peter away from her if she left him. The several thousand dollars my grandmother had lent him and my mother for marital counseling had not yet been repaid. My grandmother says she didn't really care about the debt, but his treatment of my mother made her loath to forgive it.

"Lewis," she said to him that day, "you owe me money."

My father was agitated, thin, wild about the eyes. He grinned at her, went to his coat hanging in the closet, and pulled out a wad of cash from an inner pocket. He peeled off a thousand dollars and tossed it on the table.

My grandmother knew my father wasn't working. He couldn't, she thought, have come by a wad like that honestly. From the look of him, and from the wad itself, she was sure it was drug money.

Miriam saw him the same week and found his behavior just as erratic. He stopped in to see her but told her he couldn't stay right then, promising to come back in the afternoon. A few hours later, he called to say that he had to leave town immediately: he and a companion had been at Macy's, the companion had "forgotten" to have the electronic tag removed from an item of clothing, and an alarm had gone off as they were walking out. They had escaped without getting caught, but my father was in a terrible state of panic; they were being followed, he told Miriam, and they had to get out of town as fast as possible.

My grandmother sent the thousand dollars to my mother. Later, she felt terrible for being so cold to Lewis. She never saw him again.

30 MI. NORTH OF TAOS 2

When Joe and Myriam returned for a second visit, my father was living alone. They were concerned about him and had come to see how he was doing, but when they arrived, Lewis waved to them, said he had a party to go to, and disappeared. They had no idea when, or if, he would be back. Worse than that, he'd left his truck parked in front of Joe's pickup on the narrow road so that it was impossible for Joe to turn around. The road was far too steep to back down; Joe and Myriam had no choice but to stay the night in the cabin. It was winter and bitter cold. The windows were covered with nothing but paper, the cabin was uninsulated, and the floor was dirt, with the icy hardness of frozen concrete. To keep warm, they stoked the little potbelly stove until it was so hot it was glowing red. A dog, which had just had a litter of pups in the corner, kept going in and out of a small door cut for her in the bigger door, sending in a swish of frigid air each time. On a previous visit, Joe had built some bunk beds for my brother and me because we were sleeping on the dirt floor. He and Myriam slept in the bunks, but even with the stove going full blast and all the clothes they had with them heaped on top of them, they could not get warm. They'd brought groceries with them from town, but in the morning, when they tried to make breakfast, they found that all the eggs were frozen solid.

Lewis did not reappear the next day. Instead Gersh came to their rescue. He didn't know where Lewis was either, but he invited them to come down to his house. He was having a party, and Myriam, getting into the spirit, stood at his big cookstove, which was like the one she had grown up with in Belgium before the war, and made Spanish fry bread for everyone.

"He had a really lovely house," Joe says. "It was nice and warm."

They spent the night there, and in the morning, Gersh helped Joe push my father's truck off the road. They drove away without ever seeing Lewis.

WHAT MY UNCLE JOE REMEMBERS

"For somebody who spends their entire life with books, it's not very useful living on a farm in New Mexico. Lewis was entranced with these old-timers who came as homesteaders. But I felt he was not really equipped to try and homestead that place. I mean, he didn't have *any* of the manual skills. He grew up in New York City. Anything you want fixed, you pay somebody, a plumber, electrician, carpenter, mechanic. The way he grew up, you didn't get your hands dirty. And what your mother planned to do out there, I have no idea. She once talked about joining the cowboys to help round up the cattle. I mean, I see these people work—there are cattle ranches around where we are. These are serious cattle people. It's hard, dirty work.

"Lewis had a lot of promise, but nothing ever materialized because he didn't stay at anything long enough. He played with his photography. He played with silver-making. He had no discipline. He had a flare for things, but they never got *pursued*.

"Most of these hippies—I hate to sound so blunt, but they were just a bunch of spoiled Jewish kids from Long Island."

MANIC DEVELOPMENT

In the second part of the journal, marked by the shift from poems and letters addressed to Mara to letters addressed to Lynn, my father writes excitedly about a hundred-year-old adobe house "with two-foot-thick walls, an apricot orchard, some geese, ducks, and possibly some pigs. Also an enormous woodworking shop." He says that he is taking pictures, and is "not so insane." He doesn't do drugs, he says, except when he gets them, which is "fairly rare here." This letter is followed by two architectural drawings of a long, narrow property that might be the house, orchard, garden, and workshop.

It isn't clear what happened with the hundred-year-old adobe house because my father doesn't mention it again. He switches gears, says he's planning a little communal development and trying "to buy 8 acres of pretty land, mountains all around, a row of cottonwood trees, irrigated."

He's struggling to be alone with himself, but he can't do it. He asks Lynn to come to New Mexico and "be with me for a while in a simple place."

The development, like the adobe and the land, seems desperate, unreal. He is so carried away by the idea that he begins a letter to Mara (why is he writing to Mara again?) by talking about the effect her name has on him, and then rushes headlong into a description of his latest project, which begins coherently enough, but devolves quickly into a manic list: "Energy problems water problems — space problems. Where are people going to live if not in trailers. How many roads — houses for natives — barrios — communal — sharing wells — outhouses — solar heat — methane — alcohol — sharing costs — place for animals — tradition ⟶ technology — govt. money ⟶" The rest of the page is torn off, although the list continues on the other side.

The desire to create a self-sustaining community is clearly a response to communes like New Buffalo. The difference is that the one he's imagining is a closed community that targets middle-class buyers. "Middle class hideouts," he calls them, with outhouses and "grow holes" instead of pools and tennis courts. In a letter to Lynn, he is pleased to be what he calls "a juggler again." He identifies this sense of purpose with the spirit of his father.

Once again, he is not going to be the architect on his own project, jotting a note to himself about "architectural involvement / use of professionals." He can't start over, he feels, as a carpenter or a cabinetmaker. He goes over his list of possible identities and decides to be a "go-getter." He repeatedly expresses concern about dealing honestly with people and not compromising his word. It gives him a sense of integrity, of personal worth, of self-importance. If only the pieces of this puzzle had fit together, maybe the development would have worked.

It was 1974. My father had been in New Mexico for four years, one year with my mother, three alone. Morningstar commune had broken up, New Buffalo was on its way down, hippies had begun to drift in all directions, some back into the mainstream, others farther and farther out.

He appeared scruffy in photographs taken of him at the time, his almost shoulder-length hair wiry and unkempt. He did, however, look better in these pictures than in any others: thinner, sunburnt, robust, young. All the baby fat was gone, and his mustache had been shaved off. There's no sign of the heavy black-framed glasses either. But he didn't join a commune: even at Lama, he and my mother had lived in a cabin away from everybody else. Nor did he seem to have felt comfortable "dropping out," as his preoccupation in the journal with his professional identity makes clear. Still, he was susceptible to the vibes around him. He acknowledged them almost sheepishly in a letter to Lynn, the words chopped, as is usual in the journal, into lines of poetry: "Could be just hippy bullshit / but the coincidences and occurrences / that have come down seem miraculous to me—/ and in the most uncontrolled and unconscious actions / I feel the most remarkable—well some protective influence."

He didn't say what the coincidences or occurrences were, or why the protective influence failed him in the end. He made reference in this letter to having had several crackups—as, apparently, had Lynn. "My madness," he explained, "has given me a multi-layered reality and I'm trying to enjoy it, rather than be freaked out by it." But he was afraid, just the same, that all the "insights visions and other creations" of his mind were only "figments and a defense against being engaged in the common everyday reality that we were born to work and die in."

There was no doubt that he was adrift. "Start drawing again," he admonished himself. He seemed to mean architecture—perhaps he bought the notebook for that very reason. It began with all those drawings of furniture: couches and chairs, boxy or curved, like someone wanting to be held. Page after page was taken up with the question of who he was and what he should do with himself now. "Do too little," he wrote, "with what I am."

In a long arc down one page, one word over another, in a cascade that is visually reminiscent of my father's old favorite, e. e. cummings, he wrote, "No / use / now / in / thinking / that / I / could / go / it / alone / live / there / and / work / all / day / Build / an / animal / scene / buildings / and / gardens / for / my / friends." The "now" refers to the loss of Mara. He wrote again and again about not belonging, not having a home of his own, of being alone. Railing at Mara in a letter, he referred to having "bought my way in" and accused her too of using family bucks, jobs, and social status as a way to project competence and to feel secure, an urge he understood, he said, because he'd done the same himself.

"What future is there now?" my father wrote. "Work in Arroyo Seco /—Do what / Lama? Build a house / Rollo—Bill / as an equal / work hard / goat scene / chicken scene."

"Be a carpenter," he asked on another page, "in competition with professionals? Too late."

In many of his poems, he linked the idea of lost love and loneliness with his failure to achieve something professionally.

INTERIM NOTES

I'M NOT A CARPENTER
OR AN ARCHITECT
OR A BELIEVER
OR A GO-GETTER

↘ JUST LEWIS
NOT ENOUGH

WHEN ALL SAID AND DONE
THERE'S NOTHING LEFT TO SAY.
NO EXCUSES
NO "I LOVE YOU'S" THAT WILL
MEAN ANYTHING

NO ONE GOES WITH ME
ANYMORE

Dear Louis
If you leave here its
your business
If you live here
its your business
we're trying to make
a good life
and your part of it
I'm into it and
want to do it gently
and in a good way
and not argue with
u or anyone - so if
u want to lay bricks
and get wood and
grow food and make
a solid way it is
here for you and
I offer you no threats
Gersh

COINCIDENCES AND OCCURRENCES 4

I think the land my father was trying to buy in late 1973 or early 1974 was the land that my mother eventually bought in Talpa in 1976. It had, as he said, water rights and a row of cottonwoods growing down the middle. There are not many properties in Talpa that match that description. We chose our three acres from a twelve-acre parcel. Along a ditch that ran between the first and second acre grew a perfectly aligned row of towering trees. The acreage also had irrigation rights, an even rarer commodity.

DEAD WEIGHT

For three years after my father died, my mother could barely function.

"I shouldn't have left him," she said once. "I left him at the worst time in his life, when everything had gone wrong for him."

Maybe. But how long should she have stayed, as unhappy as she was? Weren't ten years enough? Not to mention the seven years with Wayne, which have to be factored in. She wasn't just a battered woman, afraid to leave her abuser. She was a woman who felt responsible for the death of the last man she left.

When I squinted my eyes / you looked like Terry / a fantasy / and children / and a house / dead memories being indulged.

You carry the weight of a suicide with you all your life.

DIVISION OF LABOR

I am the brooder in the family. The introvert. The Jew, my grandmother says, then smiles sheepishly. "I know that's a stereotype, but still." Compared to my brother, the extrovert, the athlete, the businessman.

We have divided our father's world between us: I am the voracious reader, Peter is in commercial real estate in Idaho.

I am glad to be the Jew. I am the one who dwells on things. Who wants to consider all the meanings and contradictions and possible scenarios. Who can't let things go.

I am not the Christian my mother tried to make me into. Accepter of doctrines. Rejecter of ideas. Closed-system, closed-box, self-monitoring, self-diminishing, self-truncating, self-immolating, God-is-always-watching panopticon prisoner.

I want to do enough with what I am.

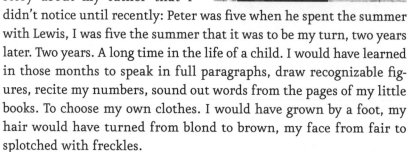

DEADBEAT DAD

There is an irregularity in the story about my father that I didn't notice until recently: Peter was five when he spent the summer with Lewis, I was five the summer that it was to be my turn, two years later. Two years. A long time in the life of a child. I would have learned in those months to speak in full paragraphs, draw recognizable figures, recite my numbers, sound out words from the pages of my little books. To choose my own clothes. I would have grown by a foot, my hair would have turned from blond to brown, my face from fair to splotched with freckles.

I would have begun, in that time, to call Wayne "Pop."

I retrieve the divorce decree, with its stark, official language and my mother's name spelled differently from how she spells it now—one of many variations on Teresa (Terésa, Teressa, Tess, Teri, Terry) that she'd tried out over the years—from the trunk filled with my father's photos. *Plaintiff and defendant shall be, and they hereby are, awarded the joint care, custody and control of the parties' minor children.* Joint custody. How is it then that I don't remember spending any time with him? Not a weekend, a holiday, a summer vacation?

I know he came to visit us when we lived in Taos. That silhouette in the doorway at Morningstar. And there are a series of photographs of me as a two- or three-year-old in a landscape that is clearly New Mexico: in several, I am holding on to strands of barbed-wire fencing, which he let me play with while he took the pictures. But what about all those other years, the nearly four years between the time she left him and the day he died? Didn't they make any arrangement to share our time? To share us? Weekends, Thanksgiving, Christmas, every other summer? Was he too unstable, too depressed, to take us?

The parties have amicably provided for the permanent care, custody and control of their minor children and their support as set forth in the stipulation and agreement attached hereto.

In his journal, we are part of a to-do list:

Spend next Saturday with the children
Pick up tools on Monday
Buy some materials, take silver and make a little concho belt
Make a chair of white select pine
The children: perhaps take them on a trip.

The entry before that, dated Saturday, March 2, says, "Today I'm going to see my children and Terry and Wayman. Try and remember that they're all there." *Try and remember.* He is having trouble because his mind is taken up with Mara, who is coming to see him for the weekend. The pages that follow are all about her. *Try and remember.* And though we are there in other passages, obliquely, in reference to loved ones and lost homes, this is the only direct reference to us in all those agonized pages.

The divorce decree is dated September 11, 1972, five days before my brother's sixth birthday. I don't know if Peter knew, as he opened his presents, exactly what had taken place. I don't know if my father was there that day, but I do know this: when my mother left him, my father threatened to take Peter away from her. *You will never see him again.* I imagine that would have made her hesitant to let us visit him, though she must have eventually decided that he would not follow through because he went on to take Peter with him on the trip to Seattle.

He did not threaten to take me.

My mother made it hard for him to see us in other ways. Two years after the divorce, when Morningstar split up and Wayne took us to live on a beach in Hawaii for a year, I don't know if she asked Lewis if it was all right, or if she just did it. Joint custody agreements prohibit one parent from moving children from one state to another without the other parent's consent. He could have taken her to court, but in that time and place the law didn't count for much, and anyway

I doubt he had it in him to challenge her. For that year, she effectively removed him from our lives. When we returned, we settled in Colorado instead of going back to Taos. We were a three-hour drive away.

In contemporary terms, "deadbeat dads" are men who don't pay their child support, but what about men who don't make themselves felt in their children's lives? Who are nothing but a silhouette in a doorway? Worse, who put themselves permanently beyond reach? Men who die. Or, more accurately, choose to die.

In one of the first sessions with the therapist that I went to after the crying episode in Blaine, I said, "I can understand that you can't live for someone else, even your children. That somehow it has to come from inside."

"Bullshit," the therapist said. "That's bullshit."

I looked at her, taken aback. I had made this statement before to friends, to my husband, over and over to myself. Since early adolescence, I had made a practice of trying to understand why people did what they did. I didn't need to forgive because I had already excused. He died because he didn't know we loved him. He didn't see us because my mother kept him away. Suddenly I felt relieved. My father died and left us, as my mother says, "holding the bag." It was bullshit. He should have lived for my brother and me.

We were reason enough.

DIALOGUE 6

Did you know that Peter died once? Briefly, anyway. Where you were, I don't know. You adored him, everyone says, and yet probably didn't even know that had happened.

It was from an overdose of LSD, during a party at Morningstar. Peter and his friend Corey were outside, exploring the contents of someone's VW bus. Peter was six, Corey five. In a box between the two front seats, Peter found a strip of white tabs that looked like candy. There were eleven in all, and he divided the paper between himself and Corey: six for him because he was older and the one who found them, and five for Corey. Peter gobbled his down, all six at once. Corey held off and so was able to go for help when Peter's eyes rolled back into his head.

Mom came running, followed by a woman she did not know who called out that she was a nurse. They rushed Peter to Holy Cross Hospital in Taos. It was more than thirty minutes away, even though they avoided the switchbacks and took the faster road straight to the highway. By the time they got there, Peter was nearly unconscious.

The story gets a little confusing at this point.

They brought Peter into the emergency room, and he was taken out of Mom's arms—or so I imagine—and laid on a gurney. Beyond that, no one paid much attention. You know what hospital staffs in that area were like: notorious for ignoring hippies, even refusing outright to treat them sometimes. Someone eventually came over, a doctor, I presume, glanced at Peter, told Mom that nothing could be done at the moment and that she should watch him in case there was any change. Then, she and Gwen, the nurse who had come with her, left Peter and went out to get a hamburger.

I learned this detail only recently—not included in the standard edition of past tellings. It struck me as outrageous. She went out for a hamburger while her son was practically comatose? Lately I've been finding in stories about Mom that once seemed amusing evidence of rampant neglect and selfishness. The hamburger detail certainly qualifies. I asked her what she remembered about the episode, and she made it sound as if this all happened within a few minutes: they arrived at the hospital, were told that nothing could be done, and went out to get a hamburger, leaving Peter lying on a gurney.

More likely, they'd been there for some time, and Holy Cross was small, maybe it had no cafeteria, no place to get a quick bite and a cup of coffee. People waiting in hospitals, even during emergencies, do go to the cafeteria. And even if Mom couldn't get the staff to pay attention, she had Gwen's experience to rely on in deciding whether it was okay to leave. Maybe it was just the word "hamburger" that made it seem so criminal.

"Why did you do that?" I asked Mom.

I'm often reluctant to ask her these questions because I feel guilty about my motives: whatever she says will be used against her.

"Because I was starving," she answered without thinking. She didn't realize yet that we were out of the realm of anecdote and into the territory of recrimination.

"But both of you *left after the doctor told you to watch him,*" I said.

She gave a rueful laugh. "*I guess we thought he was going to be okay. But thinking about it now, it doesn't sound very good, does it?*"

"No," I said, and laughed, too, trying to lighten my tone, to let us both off the hook.

We changed the subject, and I swallowed the other question on my mind, namely, why wasn't she banging on the desk, running up and down the ward, demanding that the doctors do something? She knew their attitude toward hippies. But maybe it was her middle-class background interfering: even then, she had implicit faith in doctors; she was scrupulous about getting me and Peter vaccinated against measles and polio and hepatitis at the Free Clinic, and later, when I was in high school, she would take me to be examined by our family doctor if I had anything worse than a bad cold. She believed in doctors. If they said there was nothing to be done but wait, then that is what she would do. Or maybe she was stoned. She was never much into drugs, not even pot, but this was Morningstar, after all, and she was so hungry that she left her six-year-old son alone in a hospital during a drug overdose. I know at least one person who claims that Mom has admitted to taking acid a couple of times, though she's denied it to me.

Or I may just have a need for her to be culpable, if not for neglecting my brother in the hospital, then for bringing us into an environment where such a scenario could unfold: a six-year-old kid swallowing six tabs of acid he'd found in some hippie's van. This is the trouble with trying to be rational about the facts and people's motives: there's no place for your anger to go. Corralled into ever smaller pens, it doesn't vanish; it blows up even the most casual events.

Later, Mom wanted to correct the impression I had gotten from her first, impulsive response to my questions. She and Gwen had been in the hospital for hours, she said. She was terrified but felt that Peter must have been stable because the hospital staff seemed so unconcerned. She was faint with hunger, which was why they left, but so disturbed that she could hardly eat anything. While she and Gwen were outside, a hippie came up to them and held out a pressed-tin medallion with what appeared to be a lung stamped on it. "I just felt I needed to give this to you," he said, and Mom started to cry.

She couldn't explain why they didn't go out in shifts, but I was relieved to know she took the crisis seriously.

When she and Gwen returned, they went up to see how Peter was doing and found that he wasn't breathing. Gwen gave him mouth-to-mouth resuscitation, which revived him, and then she started screaming at the staff. Everyone finally scrambled over to see what was wrong. I'm not sure what they did then, nor is Mom; they didn't have him hooked up to any machines, even to monitor his vital signs, and were reluctant for some reason to pump his stomach. My brother, Gwen said, was dead for a full minute before her efforts brought him back to life.

This is one of our great family stories, one of those anecdotes Peter and I like to tell at dinner parties, or when people express skepticism about our counterculture credentials because we dress so conservatively. Good one, isn't it, Dad?

"Dead for a full minute," we always say.

I am the best me there is.
If that's not enough
am sorry
So sorry
Be happy
Be whatever you
are
God damn
God damn
Shit

WHAT WAS REALLY WRONG?
Self-absorbed, preoccupied with the loss of home and career, his journal showing little of the fire and intellectual curiosity that made him a hero to his friends, my father came to the end of himself. I don't know where he got the gun, but I don't think he planned it. It wasn't a rational act. The journal suggests that he had achieved a degree of calm, a false calm maybe, chiefly resignation, but not only that. There

are the sketches, the excitement implied as he details his ideas for a communal development. And then, what? A downward swing, depression overtaking him as swiftly as winter dark?

Something snaps, and after filling page after page with architectural designs, loaded on cocaine, his children and his wife and Mara all mixed together in his mind, he dies.

WHAT WAS
REALLY
WRONG

THERE ARE
A THOUSAND
GUESSES

GO LIGHT
GO LIGHT

SAD TO BE SO
SERIOUS
SO LIGHT
ALL FINE
FLOWING SOFTLY

NO I BREATH
? READ
AND GO ON
TOMORROW LOTS OF THEM. PEOPLE TO LOVE
I SUPPOSE.

THINGS TO DO ENOUGH TO OBLITERATE THOUGHT
I HOPE
THINGS TO DO
SUPPORT MYSELF
THAT WILL DO
COMMON ENOUGH
ANXIOUS ENOUGH.
REALLY EASY

SUCH A NICE HOUSE IT WAS. DID YOU LOVE ME? YOU SAID
YOU DID
DID YOU HATE ME? MAYBE TO
DID I LOVE YOU?

I WAS SO GLAD TO BE INSIDE
AND ANGRY

THAT I HAD BECOME A DOG.

BUT INSIDE
TAKEN CARE OF
FUTURE BEING PLANED
IF I COULD HAVE BEEN A:
    CARPENTER
    CONTRACTOR
    ARCHITECT

YOU WOULD HAVE
GETTING FUCKED
SO MANY TIMES FURIOUS
RAPING
PILLAGING
SO MANY TIMES
 SCREECHING PULLING OF YOUR HAIR
        CLUMSY

OH GOD!!
REALLY
THE GOOD WAS ONE OR A NUMBER OF ILLUSIONS
THE BAD BLISS

AND MAGICAL ME CALLING THE TUNES
    CALLING THE MAMA OF THE DAY
      MAD AS THE HATTER
        JEALOUSY ON ORDER
          SELF PITYING DEMAND DAY
           INTROVERSION
             EXTROVERSION
               ON AND OFF

WITH YOU TO PLAY WITH.
TO PLAY MY GAME
AND YOU
    I DONT KNOW ALL OF YOU
      ONLY PART
        ANGRY THAT THE PART I DIDNT WANT TO
        SEE WOULD EMERE

THEY WERE YOU
I SHOULD HAVE HELD YOU WHEN I THOUGHT YOU WERE
CRAZY

THEN I WOULD HAVE BEEN HELD.

SATURDAY, MARCH 2

No, wait. Those few references to Peter and me are
not the only references.
There is that page in the
very center, taken up with
a child's drawing, which
I'm sure is Peter's. Saturday, March 2. Oval clouds,
a sun with spindly rays

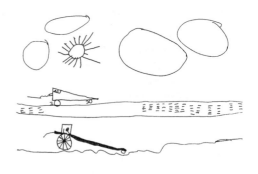

poking out on all sides, two cars, one over the other, positioned on
squiggly lines of road. A boy's drawing. There in the middle of those
tormented poems, those curved-in chairs, this child's drawing of a
race on a sunny day.

I see Peter at the table, his sneakered feet kicking through the
space under a metal and vinyl kitchen chair, intently marking in the
spokes on the big wheel, carefully inscribing my initials in the window
of the upper car.

And then, on the other side of the page, are a half dozen cars,
much more elaborately drawn, by an adult hand. My father took the
pen after Peter finished his drawing, pulled the sketchbook toward
himself or leaned over Peter at the table, and drew sleek, old-fash-
ioned cars, one like a Rolls, another like a car out of a Sam Spade
movie. Peter pressed close to his arm, delighted to see the cars emerge
under the quick-sketching pen. Several big flowers are also drawn
around the cars. The flowers are upside down on the notebook page,
the cars upright. I was probably sitting opposite them.

The flowers must have been for me.

And what about Sydney, the blue and yellow bear? Maybe my
memory is right after all. I remember being in a toy store with my
father beside me. I remember tinny music and bright florescent lights,
a wire bin full of hard rubber balls. I could have my pick of the toys.
What did I want? The bear was huge, it seemed to me, crushed plush
with a big bow. Peter did not bring it from Seattle. My father bought
it for me that Saturday. I'm sure of it.

There we are. Two pages in the middle of his last testament.

In the last few years of his life, my father had been so seriously involved with drugs that he took trips to Central America and brought back cocaine. There was nothing dramatic about being a developer in Miami, but the cloak and dagger of drug dealing must have appealed to his romantic soul. He returned several times to Florida, where he took out little boats to meet bigger boats in the Gulf.

"His operations off the coast," as Stephan calls it.

He became paranoid. The cops were onto him. The FBI. He claimed that the workmen on his brother's construction site in Miami were plotting against him. Pacing wildly up and down in Donald Singer's apartment one afternoon, he told Don to whisper because the workmen could hear everything they were saying: they had planted a microphone in his belt.

Acid flashbacks tormented him. One day a tree he was lying under turned into what he called a "superanimated being" and attacked him. But before that, before the creeping fear had set in, before he got crazier and crazier, the drugs in some perverse way had made him feel validated. He didn't care about the money. He met Irwin one evening in New York and boasted that he was giving the money away to anyone who asked. He told Irwin that it was the only time he ever felt successful. If he put his mind to it, he, like his father, his dead father, could make money, too.

Donald Singer thought he should be hospitalized. He called the psychiatrist whom my father had seen for marital counseling with my mother, but the doctor didn't return his phone call right away. By the time he did call, my father was gone.

DIALOGUE 7

"Start drawing again," you admonish yourself in your journal. And then you doodle buildings, flowers, exploding spiral stars. You scrawl a frenzy of numbers across blank pages, calculating.

What were you calculating?

My mother was right. Art for you became the art of forms. In the end empty, insubstantial. You created an aesthetic life, a tasteful life, a hedge against bourgeois suburban Florida, the creeping ordinariness of your choices, but not a creative life, a passionate life. You did not direct your passion or intelligence into work of your own.

"I become manic," you say in the journal, "because I do too little with what I am. Get going my brain screams, start making connections between things, start producing and creating."

The only thing you did yourself, you said, on the house of which I have been making so much, was clean the block with a wire brush.

There was a contradiction at the core of you. Between the artist-intellectual and the entrepreneur-businessman. You did not know how to integrate the two or bridge the gap between them. You did not know how to please your father and be yourself. How sad that the only time you ever felt successful was when you were selling drugs. That you needed that wad of cash in your pocket to feel like your father's son.

You had a heroic sense of yourself. And yet you gave up, almost from the beginning.

Your two irreconcilable sides pulled you apart. I know what that feels like, although for me the contest is between the Christian and the Jew. I know what it feels like to have no place to stand in the middle.

You drifted into the army, you drifted into your father's business. You trailed my mother into the counterculture. You crossed the border.

You died.

Lynn

I dont know what I can tell you about myself — I'm shaky but trying to hang in there. Going to buy land and slowly and carefully build a house — do fine work I hope. I have passed through strange spaces including an approximation of death — and feel I want to keep going largely because of the love my friends have given me and the love I can give them.

DEAR LYNN,
    THIS LETTER IS WRITTEN SEVERAL HOURS
    TO YOU ON THE PHONE.
    I'M REALLY DRUNK
    I'M THIRTY-FIVE
    (PED 260 PICAS)

DEAR LYNN,
    I'M GOING TO WRITE THIS, SEVERAL
    HOURS AFTER TALKING TO YOU, EVEN
    THOUGH I'M QUITE DRUNK

DEAR LYNN.

Inert Stone

Passion can create drama out of inert stone.

— Le Corbusier, *Toward a New Architecture: Guiding Principles*

Dear Lynn,

This is the morning after talking to you. Without being able to see you or touch you it was good to find that people really do not change much, although outwardly they create new forms.

It may seem strange to say it but, I was reassured about you, reassured at your telling me about a crackup — both because I have had one (or even several) but because crackups occur when our bodies revolt against the excesses of our ~~minds~~ minds. Places we shouldn't be things we shouldn't be doing. Things we are not doing.

I become manic because I do too little with what I am. Get going my brain screams start making connections between things, start producing and creating. That doesn't stop the blockages that prevent me from being truly creative in this world but they do give me a short speeded up movie of what is possible.

You seem to get the reverse effect. Complete slowdown when your body revolts against too much activity which for some reason loses its meaning.

Now I haven't changed really. I revolt against the reality games people play. Solar heating fanatics are the rage here. Photographs as a reality supposedly better than the one we see with our eyes. Any enthusiasm that seems a substitute for pure undiluted reality. But I know now that this view can only lead to a ~~the~~ termination of existence. If I want to continue to exist I must find a game to play, either with myself or with others that will enable to be in contact with — well lets say energy.

. . . .

I don't want to know any more about my father.

I can't absorb any more. I can't digest one more detail. Stop, I want to say, when people start to tell me another story. Everybody is eager to tell me now. Everybody is ready with anecdotes. But I don't want to hear them. Stop, stop, stop! I want to get on with my life. I want to get out of the head of a man who killed himself at the age of thirty-five.

Things to do enough, I keep thinking, *things to do enough, things to do enough, to obliterate thought.*

But then Stephan turns up Mara Andover's phone number. "It was in a directory on the Internet!" he exults.

QUEST 24: MARA ANDOVER

I send Mara a letter first, afraid that a call out of the blue might shock her. Stephan can hardly stand it. "It was twenty-three years ago," he says. "Just call her."

"The woman was his lover, after all," I tell him. "It's not like calling Gersh or Donald Singer."

It may be just another one of my delaying tactics. Each of these calls takes so much out of me. But I'm excited, too. I want to speak to her. Amazing, I think, my father's lover.

"Do it your way," he says. "Just get in touch with her." He's proud of his detective work.

The letter comes back: "Addressee Unknown."

"Will you just call her?" Stephan says.

"Well," Mara Andover says when I identify myself on the phone, "I've gotten some strange phone calls, but none as strange as this." She doesn't sound disturbed. She has a rich, lively voice.

"You don't need to worry about anything you might tell me," I say. "I already know about the drugs and everything. I know he died on cocaine."

"He did?" Mara asks incredulously. "Who told you that?"

I'm blank for a moment, surprised by her surprise. Who did tell me that? No one. It's just something I've always known. It is one of the givens: my father, the architect, who killed himself high on cocaine. "That's what I've always been told," I say. "He died loaded on cocaine."

"What, early in the morning?"

"In the morning?" I ask, genuinely confused now. "He died in the morning?"

"Yes," Mara says. "Right after breakfast."

CONNECTIONS FROM THE OLD KNOWN UNIVERSE

Mara met my father at a party in February 1973 at the Mabel Dodge Luhan house, a sprawling adobe set on a small rise among cottonwoods just south of downtown Taos. Georgia O'Keeffe and Alfred Stieglitz spent a lot of time there in the twenties. It may have been a party given in honor of my father's thirty-fourth birthday. Someone, Mara remembers, baked him an outrageously rich chocolate cake. A few days later, my father and his friend Art Ross showed up at Mara's house in Arroyo Seco.

"Ostensibly," she says, "to hear about my recent trip to Africa."

Mara grew up in Connecticut. Her father was a corporate lawyer; her mother was in book publishing. She graduated from Vassar, was active in the antiwar movement, and lived for a while on an East Coast commune, then made her way out to New Mexico. When she met my father, he had been involved, as everyone knew, in the "import-export business" and was just coming out of what she called a dark period. He was tired of the adventure, of sneaking across borders, risking his neck on trips to Central America. That sort of thing. Mara was also interested in building and architecture; her grandfather was an architect, too. My father might have been attracted to her, she says, because she was "fresh from the old known universe of eastern ways." She turned twenty-four that March.

When she met my father, he told her that he had tried once, about fifteen months earlier, to kill himself by driving a truck off the road in Florida. She must be talking about Joe's truck, I think. As she recalls, it rolled several times and landed in a swamp. My father was dazed but otherwise all right. He pulled himself out of the cab and stood there in the thigh-deep water, wondering what to do. The police would be there soon. They were closing in on him. He had carved a secret compartment for hiding cocaine in his belt buckle; he couldn't let them catch him with it. So he pulled off the belt and threw it in the swamp. Drugs and erratic eating habits had made him so skinny that his pants wouldn't stay up. Finally, he made his way back onto the road, clutching his pants around his waist.

"He might have embellished," Mara says dryly.

Joe and Donald Singer had thought my father's truck wreck was caused by drug-induced craziness and was not a suicide attempt, which, from Don's description of my father's behavior in his living room that same week, makes sense. But it's impossible to know: maybe my father *had* meant to kill himself, if only to silence the voices speaking to him from the radio.

At the time Mara was introduced to my father, she was living in a long, narrow adobe house in Arroyo Seco at the base of the mountain that cradles the Taos Ski Valley. The road from Arroyo Seco to the valley runs in a straight line toward the edge of a small cliff; below it are the houses and willow-lined creeks of Valdez. At the cliff, another road meets the first at a ninety-degree angle. A tiny gas station, no more than a battered wooden booth, hangs over the cliff's edge, shored up on that side by stilts, though it wasn't there in Mara's time. The house was just opposite where the gas station is now. I know the spot well, though I don't remember a house. In Taos, we always referred to that road as the Rim Road or just the Rim.

When Mara moved to Santa Fe in the fall, my father moved with her. A friend of hers had bought a small adobe on a remote, several-hundred-acre piece of land, and Mara was going to remodel it for her. My father followed her there.

"He seemed to believe that things had gotten too hot in Taos and he needed a place to hide out," Mara says. "Now this could simply have been a good line, since in 1973 we all had semiromantic visions of being outlaws. Or it could have been his paranoia."

If he was doing drugs when they were together, she wasn't aware of it. He wanted to put that life behind him, she says. They spent four months working on the house together.

"We had a fairly idyllic time there for a while."

On her birthday Lewis embarrassed Mara by dancing on a table in a restaurant. He was a generous, bighearted person, she says. Extremely bright, loving, outgoing, he liked people and was liked in return. He had bought a Graflex camera, which he fitted out with a Polaroid back. At parties, he would sit people down and take their portraits. All of their friends. People loved it, especially because they could see the pictures right away.

"I used to call him the 'Yiddish actor,'" Mara says. "Always doing this unbelievable shtick."

He had all these "theater bits," takeoffs from vaudeville and the radio shows of his childhood. He and Mara had a running gag from *The Shadow.* My father was Lamont Cranston, the Shadow's alter ego, and Mara was modeled on Margo, the lead female character. "Stay in the car, Margo," the Shadow would always say and, of course, she wouldn't. She'd land herself in all sorts of situations from which the Shadow would have to rescue her.

"Stay in the car, Mara," my father would say. "Stay in the car."

He collected facts, peculiar histories. He was an extraordinary storyteller. He could be flamboyant, too. One day he climbed partway up a windmill and, clinging to it, belted out a song as if he were delivering an aria. "This was strange stuff for a girl from a strait-laced WASP family," Mara says, laughing.

My father also had quite a temper. He didn't direct it at Mara, but he would get enraged at minor things. If he hammered his thumb, he would throw a tantrum: hurl bags of cement, bursting them, and work himself into a fit. Mara would take the dogs for a walk until he calmed down. "He was very theatrical," Mara says.

Mara and my father were together for about a year. They split up in late winter, January or February 1974. The months they spent together gave him stability, but he was gradually returning to the state he was in when they first met.

People really do not change much, although outwardly they create new forms.

A trip to Florida that winter to see Joe had left him unsettled and depressed. Mara felt out of her depth. He had asked her to marry him. She thought that she loved him, but she turned him down, afraid of spending the rest of her life propping him up emotionally. It had nothing to do with his being Jewish—she'd had Jewish boyfriends before, though her family had been less than happy about it. She suggested they go their separate ways and offered to turn over the lease of the house on the rim to him so he would have somewhere to go. She told several of their friends that she thought he needed watching.

Crackups occur when our bodies revolt against the excesses of our minds. . . . I have had one (or even several).

"Lewis," Mara says, "suffered an enormous amount of guilt." Some of it was the times, the recent political upheavals and the resulting liberal guilt.

A good person of course gets defined by standards which we have seen change remarkably in the last 20 years. So they're getting a little shaky to go by.

But my father "developed guilt to a fine art," she says. According to Mara, some of it related to his inability, at first, to have a child with my mother. Their struggle to conceive left him with a profound sense of failure.

Starting over, proving my worth. I guess that proves my worthlessness and general incompetence.

As for my brother and me, he talked about us often, but he made no real effort to see us. He and my mother were not getting along, for one thing.

He had other troubles, too. My uncle Joe came to visit him and was picked up at the Albuquerque airport by the police and held for questioning. Dick Bannister, an "associate" of my father's, had just jumped bail and apparently fled the country, and Mara thought that the police were checking out anyone with a possible connection to the drug trade in Taos. The police released Joe and put him on a bus to Questa, the nearest town to Lama. Mara met him there.

My father was paranoid, but Mara isn't sure that it was caused by drugs or any real trouble with the police or FBI. "The drug trade in New Mexico was ridiculously out in the open. You could tell deals were being made by whose car was parked in front of whose house. Lewis was perfectly capable of feeling paranoid from just a cup of coffee. He drank enormous amounts of it. He was sort of jittery all the time."

"As I think about it now," Mara says, "he was probably running from the sadness of being separated from his family."

But it wasn't only that. Something was seriously wrong with him. Mara didn't have the skill to recognize it then, but she thinks now that he might have been mentally ill, possibly with bipolar disorder. She didn't know how to cope with him.

During the week of April 9, 1974, my father came to Santa Fe to see Mara. He wanted to retrieve some things that he had given her: a necklace, a concho belt. And a gun he'd wanted her to have "for protection." He was in bad shape. He hadn't been sleeping or eating; he was deeply unhappy. He spent the night pacing Mara's house. In the morning, she offered to give him a ride back to Taos, but he refused and hitchhiked instead. As soon as he left, Mara called some friends in Taos to tell them about the gun and to urge them to get it away from him. They didn't take her very seriously. *Cool*, they thought, when she tried to tell them that Lewis had gone over the edge, *far out*. Two days later, they called back to say that he was dead.

The day before he died, another friend, Lee Driver, saw my father building a bonfire outside the house on the rim. He was throwing piles of photographs into it. There was a stack of portraits of Mara, and he was burning all those Polaroids, too, all the portraits of friends that he had taken at parties with the Graflex. Lee, Mara says, asked my father what he was doing.

"I'm destroying the evidence," my father replied, "that any of us ever knew each other."

Lee thought Lewis was distraught over the breakup with Mara, but Mara thought Lee had missed the significance of my father's act. She thought Lewis was afraid that people might be linked to him. That the police or the FBI might use those photographs against his friends.

The next morning, my father went out for an early breakfast with two or three friends at Michael's Kitchen, a local restaurant. Afterward, he went home and killed himself.

ARIA

Something about Mara's account has elated me. It makes me feel as if the man who recited "The House of Morgan" and sang Paul Robeson songs off-key had not, even at the end, been wiped out. Mara describes his remarkable intelligence, his sense of humor. The "Yiddish actor," always doing "this unbelievable shtick." There he was in the desert, acting out the vaudeville routines he had picked up with Irwin at the Jamaica Theater in sixth grade. Her description restores an earlier sense of him to me.

Though, truth to tell, this man too is a strange man. Her description is of yet another Lewis that I haven't encountered before.

"He was exactly the type who *wouldn't* dance on tables," Stephan says.

"That's not the Lewis I remember," says my grandmother, shaking her head.

Maybe Mara brought out the dancer in him.

JUST GEOGRAPHY

I'm still trying to sort out the drug issue. Mara says he didn't use drugs regularly when they were together.

"Maybe occasionally," she says. "At parties. They were around."

"But in one letter to you in the journal," I say to Mara, "he says 'I'll finish writing this if I don't come down'—?"

"Maybe he meant 'Come down to Santa Fe,'" Mara breaks in. "We went back and forth a lot. You know, just geography. North and south."

I shake my head at the simplicity of this explanation. I had assumed he was referring to a drug high. Partly because there was so much visual slurring of the words, and partly because of all I'd heard about the last days of his life, I had read the journal—everything in the journal—with the assumption that he was heavily into drugs at the time he wrote it.

"Well, what about the bonfire? That sounds drug-induced."

"That could have just been theater. He was *very* theatrical. Big into the dramatic gesture."

I see him in my mind, frenzied by fire, flinging photographs, one by one, and then in stacks, onto the pyre. The flames light up his face, his sweat-oily skin. Shirtless, perhaps, in early April. *I'm destroying the evidence that any of us ever knew each other.* The faces blacken and curl; Mara's large, sultry eyes are the last to disappear.

It is pure theater.

It also means he planned to die.

And here am I, your daughter, compiling all the evidence you failed to destroy, piecing the record back together, furtive handshakes and all.

As soon as I get off the phone, I dig out the journal. Sure enough, there it is. In a clear, unshaky hand, he wrote: "I'll write this and send it if I don't come down. You can read it with me if I do. They will be notes." There it is, simple geography. The "notes" were the ones I described as "devolving into a manic list." The list is, I still maintain, manic: his hopes and expectations seem inflated and unreal. He did, after all, kill himself only days or weeks later. But the second sentence and the steady handwriting had never registered with me. I had wondered why he was writing to Mara again because their relationship seemed to be over. I had assumed he was speaking to her as if to an imaginary figure in his head, but no. They may not have been lovers, but they were still friends. She saw him just days before he died.

When I see those sentences now, I feel like laughing. My father is dancing away from me again, but I don't mind. He shifts, he moves, he feints.

QUEST 25: NOT HIS NOSE

I go back to the metal trunk of photographs. "A good thing you retrieved that trunk when you did," Mara tells me. "A lot of the houses at Lama were destroyed by wildfires that swept up from San Christobal last spring." I sift through all the images again. At the bottom of the trunk are the Polaroids: a stack of a hundred or more. It's as if I've never seen them before. (I send several portraits to Mara for identification; she writes back that none of them are of her. The blonde with big eyes is someone named Pam.)

So they were not all destroyed.

All these people my father had photographed at parties. These friends who had helped him travel through strange places, even if they could not sustain him in the end. I also realize that several of the photographs of me and Peter are Polaroids from the Graflex. I am about four or five, shaggy-haired, dramatically freckled. In each, we are wearing different clothes, so we must have spent more than Saturday, March 2, with him.

You have to know how to read the record.

I find many unfamiliar pictures of my father. I didn't recognize him the first time I sorted through them. In one, he resembles the Marlboro Man, a cigarette dangling below his bushy mustache. In another, he wears a cowboy hat and holds a rifle upright in one hand. He looks like Robert Redford as the Sundance Kid. A third shows his shoulder-length hair combed over his scalp. It is thin and stiff: he might easily have gone bald on top. With long hair and a silver chain around his neck, he looks like a different person.

Strange, I think, how unstable his identity seems to have been. People even remember him in a refracted way, frequently in terms of somebody other than himself. A piece of Fields, of Mencken, of Sam Neill (whom he does, it turns out, clearly resemble). Not to mention the roles in which he cast himself: peasant boy in leiderhosen, World War II bomber pilot, drug smuggler with exquisite taste in furniture. My father is like a man patched together from the spare body parts he and Stephan found in the back of the limb salesman's Fiat on the road from Bruges.

I arrange the pictures from Marlboro Man, which related photos suggest was taken by my mother, to hippie to cowboy, as Mara says she knew him, and which was, of course, nearly the end. My father is a man of transformations, every picture a new incarnation, though in each I see a similar sweetness in his face.

Studying these photographs, I see that I did not inherit his nose. His eyes and eyebrows, his jaw, yes, but not, as I have always thought, his nose.

Among the portraits are photographs of my mother taken at Lama. She looks hard-edged and sad. But more than that, the portraits themselves have a disintegrative aspect. My father, as he does with none of the other pictures, distorts her image in the darkroom. In one, processing chemicals eat toward the center of her face, accidentally perhaps, but her head is strangely illuminated against a deliberately hard black background. In another, her face emerges from the bramble of another image, superimposed around the edges of the portrait. In several, the face of another woman is printed over her nude body, captured in sleep. There is also a print of the original, unmanipulated image, before and after: my mother's body under the strands of the other woman's hair resembles a cello or an Edward Weston pepper.

At Mara's suggestion, I call Lee Driver, the man who saw my father burning the Polaroids.

"My name is Anna Oliver," I say after Lee identifies himself. (Is that my name? I wonder, as I say it. What is my name? After leaving Stuart and in spite of my search for my father, I've followed my brother's lead in taking "Oliver" in honor of our maternal grandparents.) These calls are getting easier, the lag time between them shorter and shorter. "I was born Anna Weinberger."

Lee doesn't say anything, but his breathing changes. I know he recognizes the name.

"I think you knew my father?"

A pause. "What was his name?"

"Lewis Weinberger."

Another brief pause, an intake of breath. "I did," Lee Driver says.

"I understand that you saw him the day before he died?" I ask.

"I was living in the same house," Lee says. "I had to clean up the mess."

The intake of breath, this time, is mine.

BLACK MAGIC

Lee Driver knew my father through his brother, Rocky, who had taken over the cabin at Lama when Lewis moved out to live with Mara. At the time Lewis and Mara broke up, Lee was living in the house on the Rim Road, which Mara had leased before him. In early 1974, Lee was looking for someone to rent it because he was about to move to Lama himself. Lewis needed a place to stay, so Mara asked Lee if he could live there. She was worried about Lewis. He had no place to go. Lee agreed but said that there would be some overlap between the time Lewis moved in and he, Lee, moved out. They lived together for about ten days before my father killed himself.

In those ten days, my father was in a constant state of anxiety. He'd become involved with big-time players—people who packed guns—on the West Coast. They were in San Francisco, where Lewis traveled occasionally. Or maybe Seattle. He found it exciting, Lee says. And he was loaded with cash. But a cocaine smuggling operation that he was funding had gone sour. He was clearly in trouble. He may have been using as well as dealing. Lee thought he had psychological problems, too.

Lee and my father made several meals together during that time. In the evening, they would sit and talk. They didn't know each other well. The conversations were stimulating, wide-ranging and philosophical, running long into the night.

Several days before my father died, Lee came home in the afternoon to find him kneeling beside the woodstove in his bedroom. It was a long, narrow house, and Lee had to walk through Lewis's room to get to his own. When Lee passed, he saw a stack of photographs of Mara in a pile. The one in Lewis's hand had been glued to a stick. There were black marks all around the edges, and the photo had been slashed. Lewis was burning it in the stove. Lee doesn't remember asking him what he was doing or seeing any other photographs. Just Mara, marked by Lewis's voodoo.

Lee had to go to Albuquerque a day or so later. The night before he left, Lewis was different. He seemed completely relaxed. All the tension and anxiety had dissipated. He and Lee talked for a long time. Lee thought that he was going to be all right. My father's insights into Lee's own life and character amazed him.

Lee returned to Taos in the late afternoon, but instead of going home he stayed overnight with his girlfriend. The next morning, as he was making the turn at the blinking light on his way to the house on the rim, he saw Bill Gersh driving toward him, flagging him down.

A man named Simms had discovered the body that morning. He had a record and was afraid to call the police himself. Simms was my father's connection to the people in Seattle. He may have been there to pick up drugs. Simms called Gersh.

When Lee arrived, the police were there. The body was still in the same position in which it had been found. Something keeps me from asking what the position was.

After the police removed the body, Lee approached an officer. "Who cleans this?" Lee asked, indicating the gore in the room.

"You do," the officer said.

Lee and his girlfriend mopped up the blood and dumped the basins of pink water into the garden. Then they burned cedar and lit candles. They said prayers. They wanted to purify the place and to "do right by Lewis."

"We were kids," Lee says. He was only in his twenties then, but I can tell that he would do the same today.

He wasn't scared. He didn't feel "diminished." He didn't feel guilty. He and Lewis weren't in a "karmic situation" in which they owed each other anything. He had done what he could to be a friend to a brother in need. Afterward, Lee had to field a lot of calls from friends who were shaken by my father's death. Lee had long conversations with my uncle Joe, too. "They called me to talk it out," Lee says, "just as you're doing now."

Lee thought that my father had probably killed himself the night before he was found, but it could have been early that morning. Over the ten days that he and Lee had lived together, my father had gone several times to see a friend of Lee's who lived down the road. This friend, Leonard, was an astrologer and read tarot. That week, Lewis brought a .22 pistol with him and asked Leonard to keep it. At first, he refused. He didn't want a gun in the house. But when my father said that he didn't know what he might do with it, Leonard agreed. A few days later, my father came back for it. This time, Leonard refused to return it. But when my father insisted, he gave in. Perhaps he felt, as Gersh had said to me, that a man has to choose his own way.

The cards Leonard read for my father, he told Lee, showed a powerful conjunction of forces on the day of his death. He felt terribly guilty for having given the gun back to my father. If Lewis had been able to put off his decision for one more day, Leonard thought, it might not have happened.

LAST CALLS

"He had called me to come out to New Mexico, but I was working. I couldn't just take two weeks and disappear to New Mexico. Later on perhaps. The construction business is seasonal."

"Bob and Miriam had a memorial service for Lewis, and afterward I couldn't leave. I sat there with them for hours and hours, talking about him."

"I had no idea how deeply involved in drugs he was. Everyone seemed to know."

"He was a sweet and intelligent human being, and I learned a lot from him. I did not have a clue as to how to help him."

"He called us, he wanted us to come out to New Mexico and see him. But I had three kids, Bob was working. I just couldn't come. I didn't know how serious it was."

"I called the psychiatrist, but by the time he called me back, Lewis was gone."

"He came to see me when he was in New York. He thought of us as friends, Juan and I, but I was very brusque with him. 'Lewis,' I said, 'you owe me money.'"

"That was the last time I spoke to either one of them."

"Now I visit people when they're *alive*."

He died because he didn't know we loved him.

THE HOUSE ON THE RIM(?)

ALL THE LITTLE DETAILS
It was definitely cocaine, Lee tells me. And he didn't put the gun in his mouth. My father had a small .22-caliber hole between his eyes, just above one eyebrow, slightly off-center. I feel as if I've crossed the ropes into a boxing ring. I don't fault Lee for telling me what I asked to know, but every detail is a blow.

THE SEDUCTION OF STORY
When I get off the phone, I feel shaken. Lee Driver has given an account of a man unhinged. Terrified and terrifying. My father, practicing black magic on the photograph of his ex-girlfriend. I think of the box of mementos found beside his body.

It has disappeared; there is no verifying its contents. But Irwin remembers hearing that it held a Boy Scout badge and memorabilia from P.S. 134, my father's elementary school. He carried it all into the desert, but in the end, he was terribly, desperately alone.

I never expected to get this close to the bottom of my father's story. Each time I follow a thread, I think it will only confirm or add some small detail to something I already know: the photographs in the trunk will be variations on the photographs I already have; Stephan and Irwin will tell me, as my mother and grandmother already have done, that my father was bright and well read; Lee Driver will repeat the line Mara attributed to my father via him: "I am destroying the evidence that any of us ever knew each other."

I am never prepared, after my mother's lapses and refusals, after the silence surrounding my father's existence for twenty-odd years, for the vividness of other people's memories, the shocking immediacy of their stories. For Gersh's fluttering heart, or for Lee and his girlfriend mopping up my father's blood.

I don't think I wanted to get this close to the bottom. I wanted to reanimate my father. I wanted to bring life to the vibrant, intensely intellectual man that he was in his early years. That was the father I needed to carry me through my own self-discovery, my emergence from the dark ages of Christian fundamentalism. I wanted the sophisticated "Weinberger!" of the GE College Bowl and Mies van der Rohe.

But my effort to assemble my father contains, at the heart of it, a denial. Somehow I have believed at every stage of his life that my father is not a man who dies at the age of thirty-five. At every stage there is the hope that he might be held there and, by the effort of my will, prevented from ending up dead in that room.

And I wonder if it isn't this denial that has made me ambivalent about my quest for so many years: the fear that I would wind up here, confronted with the vision of his actual body in an actual room. That someone would say to me, "I had to clean up the mess."

QUEST 27: INFORMATION PLEASE
I call Information and ask for a listing for Bill Gersh.

SPIRITS AND PRESENCES

2/6/97

Anna,

Like I said, I don't take inquiries like this
lightly, and think they are important. And I think
it's important that I give you every shred I have,
regardless of whether it satisfies whatever expectations you may have or not.

On opening the door and entering the house, that
day, my exact words were, "Oh no, Lewis, not this
way." His body was still draped in the exact position
in which it had been discovered; precariously balanced
over a half tipped-over bench, his knees held by the
underside of the table, his head arched to the floor.
It was like some kind of sculpture. There was a look
of utter peace on his face, as if he were greatly
and deeply relieved (this is in relation to the way
I had seen him being over the past several days).

The gun was still on the table. A little chrome
thing that could fit in the palm of your hand.

He seemed an old man. 35 seems very young to me
now. He was very old then. And brittle.

They took him away, wrapped in a stretcher.

When I asked the policeman who was going to
clean up, and he said I was, I was as surprised as
anyone would be, confronted with such a situation. I
guess I had always thought that just someone came
along after and took care of that sort of thing.
And then, there was no one else to actually do it.
It fell to me, and my friend Diane, to just handle
it, as best we could. And so we did.

I had met Diane (for years she has gone by some Hindu name) at the Lama Foundation, which you must know at that time was a community focused on (to shorten a long story, let's just say) spiritual matters. The structure of our friendship was based on trying to do right by God, by mankind, and by the earth. We lit incense, we sat for a long time before we did anything, we prayed out loud, we prayed to ourselves, we tried to allow the-right-thing-to-do to occur to us . . . and we went to work. It is a very vivid memory. There was scrubbing. I prayed each time I emptied the washpan over the garden. I remember kneeling there, and trying to talk to Lewis. We spent a long time trying to leave that place, and didn't, until it, somehow, felt all right to do so. We felt it was our job to smooth over a hurt on the physical plane. To clean the place so that life could go on, if we at all could.

We felt good about what we had done later on, not in a prideful way, but in the way of having tried to do something, and been satisfied with how it had gone. To this day, I would say.

Tucker and Nellie are around, and probably approachable in this matter. I couldn't tell, but I guess you know that Bill Gersh died a couple of years back.

Lee Driver

MISSING IN ACTION
Bill Gersh is dead.

The wooden trunk I left at Gersh's was most likely burned in the wildfires.

The roll of undeveloped film, which I decided I should try to develop after all, disappeared in the move from my house in Blaine.

One of the silver earrings from the pair my father made for my grandmother, and which she gave me, I lost in an airport on the way to visit my mother for Thanksgiving.

The tape with my father's voice on it, I seem to have misplaced.

The story is erasing itself behind me.

COINCIDENCES AND OCCURRENCES 5

Before any more threads can disappear, I decide to call the Harwood Library in Taos. It's a little early in New Mexico, only 9:15 in the morning, but maybe someone will be there. I'm too impatient to wait. If I don't act when the impulse strikes, I may not act at all.

A man answers after two rings.

I feel a little flustered. I hadn't figured out what to say before dialing.

"Yes, hello," I say. "My name is Anna Oliver. I'm calling from New York. I'm looking for an item in the *Taos News*. I have no way of getting to New Mexico any time soon, and I was wondering if someone there could look it up for me."

"Sure," the man says. "I could do that."

I rush on. "I'm looking for an obituary. For my father. His name was Lewis Weinberger. He died on April 9, 1974." I wonder if I've spoken too quickly. If he'll ask me to spell the name.

Instead, he says, very quietly, "I knew Lewis."

His words take a moment to register. "You did?"

"Yes. I lived in the same house he did, out on the rim. That was a sad time for all of us."

"You lived there after he died?"

"Yes. With my girlfriend. And I lived in that cabin on Lama for a while, too. The one he and your mother lived in. My name is Tracy McCallum. I'm sure I've met you, but I can't remember what you look like."

A sense of connection floods through me. I tell Tracy what I'm doing. The search for my father. I ask him if he knows Lee and Mara. He does.

"He was trying to pull it together," Tracy says. "To keep himself busy. I was working on some doors for a rich man's house, and Lewis offered to help me. I think he just wanted to keep his mind off things. He was broken up about your mother."

"Still?" I ask. "It was four years later."

"I think so. He really thought he had blown it."

I struggle to think of other questions to ask him. What might he know?

"I know your mother, too," he says. "Well, since you're looking for information, I'll tell you this. Your mother used to come into the library. This was before I knew who she was. One day she came in, and I went up to her and said, 'Do you know Mara Andover? You look a lot like Mara Andover.' She looked at me in this completely stricken way. 'I was married to Lewis,' she said. I felt so stupid. I wanted to crawl under a table. But she did, she looked a lot like her."

There it is, I think. The other shoe.

When I squinted my eyes / you looked like Terry / a fantasy.

Tracy tells me that he is now the library director. "It's strange," he says, "that I would have answered the phone. I wouldn't usually. I picked it up because no one else is here yet." It turns out that I was mistaken about the time. It's 8:15 A.M. in Taos. I wouldn't have called so early had I realized.

I promise Tracy I will look him up if I come to Taos. He plans to retire, he tells me, at the end of December. It's mid-November now. If I'd waited much longer, he would have been gone.

Tracy promises to send me the obituary if there is one. I'm gratified that my errand is not in the hands of some indifferent clerk, but undertaken by the library director, yet another friend in my father's constellation.

When I find out later that he is unable to locate any obituary, or even a reference to my father's death in the "police blotter" published by the paper for the week of April 9, it almost doesn't matter. He's already given me so much more than I expected.

I WONT THINK ABOUT IT ANYMORE
HOW CRAZY AND ANGRY IT GOT.
WE'RE FREE TO RISE AND FALL
FIND WHATEVER LOVE THERE IS
I GUESS I MIGHT GO DOWN
ROCK BOTTOM
NEVER COME OUT
YOU MAY GO WAY UP
EASY AND FREE
ON YOUR OWN.

ILL SMILE WHENEVER
I SEE YOU.
EVEN IF IT BREAKS MY
HEART.
ITS LATE FOR ME TO START
MY MIND WANDERS INTO THE PAST
OTHER HOPES.
WHEN I SQUINTED MY EYES
YOU LOOKED LIKE TERRY
A FANTASY
AND CHILDREN
AND A HOUSE
DEAD MEMORIES BEING INDULGED

ITS BEEN SO CLEAR FOR
SO LONG IM GOING
TO HAVE TO BE ALONE
CARE SO LITTLE FOR MYSELF
BUT FOR 4 MONTHS YOU
LET ME PRETEND
THAT I WAS IMPORTANT
THANK YOU.
THAT I WAS HOME
CARED FOR.
THANK YOU.

SHAM SUICIDE

"We had this fantasy for a long time," Irwin says, chuckling, "that he had faked his death and was still alive down in South America somewhere."

SHAM SUICIDE 2

"Might he have been *murdered?*" Miriam's voice drops to a whisper as she utters the word. "We always wondered, your uncle Joe and I, if he might have been murdered. I mean, it's not an easy thing to do, to shoot yourself between the eyes. And he'd damaged his trigger finger, I remember. He'd accidentally cut the nerve on a sardine can in Florida. He used to joke about that, how he hoped he'd never have to shoot someone because he wouldn't be able to get his finger to perform the action."

QUEST 28: TRUTH MACHINE

It takes me a very long time to call Art Ross. A year, almost, after Mara sends me his number. In the meantime, I've gotten divorced, and with the help of the writer and professor for whom I worked as a research assistant at the University of Minnesota, I've landed a job in New York as a publicity assistant at a major publishing house. I quit the job after all of five months, unnerved by the always ringing telephone and the endless rounds of high-priority deadlines, not to mention my general unfitness for the position—since leaving Stuart, I have not owned a television set, a fact that makes my boss's mouth drop open. I've moved into a tiny studio on Greenwich Avenue in the Village, a place divided into three successively smaller triangles—bathroom, kitchen area, and front room—which my friend Elissa describes as looking like the dough that's left over after the cookies have been cut.

Stephan lives three blocks away down Seventh Avenue, in the high-rise apartment he rented after he and his wife finally separated.

I spend most of my nights with Stephan, then walk back in the morning to my desk in the front triangle. The light is good, though the jackhammering on the street constantly rattles my computer keys. The city simultaneously exhilarates and exhausts me, making it hard to concentrate on anything.

When I finally call Art, I leave a message first. I'm getting beyond the pleasure of shock value.

"What can I tell you?" Art asks when he calls back.

"Well, I'm interested in the drugs." This seems like an odd statement to make to a stranger, but I plunge ahead. "Mara said that you and my father were 'cocaine cowboys' together."

Art gives a short, derisive laugh. "Yeah, well."

He laughs often, amused or nostalgic or wry, and his voice radiates a wide good humor about his exploits.

"I knew Lewis—'Louie' as I called him—in San Francisco." Art pauses, and laughs again. "I hope the statute of limitations has run out," he says. "We were connected by a guy called Simms. Do you know that name? I knew him from my years at Berkeley. Your father had met him in New Mexico, and Simms introduced us around 1972 in San Francisco." He pauses, laughs again, ruefully this time. "I guess you could say we were 'cocaine cowboys,' like Mara said. There was a lot of idealism and confusion. We thought we were countercultural heroes. It seemed 'romantic.' In fact, Lewis once pointed out that we were involved in a criminal activity, and I couldn't believe it. 'What are you talking about?' I said. 'We're about freedom! We're about evolution!'

"Simms introduced us to the Deaver brothers. They were surfers from the Carmel area. Mickey was a small-time surfboard manufacturer. He figured out that he could hollow out surfboards, go down to Baja, and bring back kilos of marijuana inside them. After a while, he expanded the operation to cocaine. Cocaine was a new and exotic drug. In the early seventies only a few people knew about it. The Cole Porter lyrics—'some get a kick from cocaine'—are probably about as close as any of us had come.

"The Deavers would load up on raw cocaine paste from dealers in Bolivia or Peru, ferry it to refiners in Colombia, then meet inflatable motorboats—Zodiacs, they're called—off Venezuela, running for Miami. This was before serious counterinsurgency by the Feds. It was all very loose and cowboy-like. We wanted adventure, and it was seductive, the idea of being a smuggler. I mean, it was like being a rock star. You had fans and groupies, influence over people, energy flowed to you. You could inject dollars into the culture. Give money to some little candle-making venture, or commune, or whatever. If a person is, how shall I put it, 'vulnerable' to being some sort of megapersonality, this was stardom. It had glamour. We all got caught up in it."

I can't believe what I'm hearing. Even Art's language assumes the glib lingo of a movie script: "running for Miami," "counterinsurgency," "the Feds."

Before ending up in the counterculture, Art tells me, he had been a Freedom Rider and a sixties activist. He was the son of American Communists. In the early seventies, he and his companions, including my father, weren't involved in any political causes, but they thought that living an alternative lifestyle was itself a form of political action.

"It was a passionate period, but very few got through it unscathed. Your dad was more scathed than most. He was extremely imaginative, creative, with deep feelings and emotions. He was not an addictive personality, but we were all doing a little bit all the time. We took cocaine, peyote, acid, pot. Everything. We saw it as mind-expanding, mood-altering, and intensifying, not harmful. We were connoisseurs of the shit. But over time, it deforms your personality, loosens the bonds with what is really going on."

"How did you pay for all this?"

"Lewis had some capital—"

"Do you know where that came from?"

"We assumed that he had a trust fund or investments. He seemed to be well provided for, without having to work."

Lewis, as Joe had said, had inherited something from his father's personal fortune, despite the bankruptcy of the business.

"Lewis bankrolled—well, no—*invested* in operations. Simms invested some, I invested some, Lewis quite a bit. He'd invest about ten thousand dollars per, and realize about three times that amount in profit. He did about three deals of this size, each about ten kilos. Ten kilos is around twenty-five pounds of coke—small-time these days. It was the Deaver brothers' operation. Basically, all we did was wait around for the Deaver brothers to show up. An operation took six to eight months to put together and pull off."

During that time, Art and my father lived in a house on Carl Street in Haight-Ashbury. The house had individual apartments, but the front door of the building was always unlocked.

"It was like one big happy commune," Art says with evident nostalgia, "everyone sharing dope, food, kids running all over. The backyard was filled with trees and an inflatable swimming pool. And no one, of course, seemed to be working."

My father was older than anyone else in the house, and the others looked up to him as a kind of big brother. He was skeptical of religious mysticism, which he thought was naïve, Art says, and not very tolerant of bullshit; his insights into other people were direct and incisive. At thirty-three, he was only four years older than Art, but Art considered him much more mature and worldly, far less credulous than he was. He admired my father's mind, which was "always crackling." Lewis would buy books all the time—he was obsessed with Doris Lessing for a while, devouring everything she wrote—and read late into the night.

"We had to keep busy while we smuggled, so we enjoyed the arts," Art says, and I almost laugh, the image of these art-loving, book-reading, community-spirited criminals is so incongruous. "Simms introduced us to silver-making. He was at least half Indian. He got me and Lewis into it. The Mabel Dodge Luhan House in Taos, which was called the Big House and owned by Dennis Hopper at the time, was a jewelers' cooperative. Lewis and I both hung out and lived there for a while."

The Mabel Dodge Luhan House was where my father met Mara.

"Did you know," I ask, "that my father learned jewelry-making when he was in the army? He taught jewelry-making to GIs."

"Did he really? No, I didn't know that."

"He's left a trail of jewelry across the country."

Art responds warmly. "We all left a trail of jewelry with the people we knew," he says, "Women especially—wives and girlfriends."

"Did you know a woman named Lynn?"

"Lynn? I knew a Lynn Pratt in San Francisco."

"A thin blonde with octagonal glasses?"

"Yes! That's her! How do you know her?"

"I think she was involved with my father."

Art laughs delightedly. "Really? I didn't know that. I had no idea."

"I've tried to locate her," I say, "but so far, I've had no luck."

Art asks me how I got interested in finding people who knew my father.

"Well," I say, struggling to formulate an answer. It should be easy by now, but the discoveries of the past few years jumble together. "I went to get this trunk of photographs that Bill Gersh had—"

"Is that what happened to those photographs?" Art exclaims. "I'm sure there are a number of photos of me in that trunk: a wild-haired, freaky-eyed guy with a mustache." He laughs again. "Which describes one of about fifteen characters. After his death, everyone was *totally* paranoid. If anyone were to get busted, everyone Lewis knew would be implicated." He laughs ruefully. "Of course, a lot of the paranoia was chemically induced."

I tell him about the bonfire and the undamaged stack of Polaroids that I'd found at the bottom of the trunk. He whistles at the description of my father making his crazy marks on Mara's portraits and burning them.

"Your father," he says, "was a lot more in love with Mara than he was willing to admit. They were trippy together, both so bright, intellectual. But she was a very independent-minded person—too much so in some ways."

He offers to get together sometime, if we're ever in the same city, to go through the Polaroids.

"So do you think the FBI was actually onto my father, as he thought?" I ask.

"That was mostly delusion, I think. Many people, including me, were *observed* by the cops with a view toward busting them. I know for a fact that I was observed. The police would sit in a car in front of my house, bluntly out in the open. Warning me, I think, that they knew what was going on, giving me a chance to clean up my act. Lewis never wanted to be directly involved. Maybe one time he was part of one leg of an operation, but that was it. He was an investor. No crossing borders with a lot of dope strapped to him. He was way too sophisticated a guy for that.

"But paranoia knew no limits—it wasn't just the Feds who might be onto you. It's what your girlfriend was doing, what your friends were saying about you. This is a well-documented symptom of cocaine psychosis. Everyone I knew who was in contact with cocaine suffered some major deformation of personality for some period of time. Cocaine can unhinge relatively healthy people, let alone someone vulnerable."

"And this 'one leg' of the operation? What was that about?"

"I think it had to do with Zodiac boats in the Caribbean. Lewis met up with the Deavers when they hit the shore. They were shipping drugs from Colombia to one of the islands by plane; the packages would get dropped in the water, then the Deavers would pick them up and load them onto Zodiac boats to Florida. Your father was just coming off the high of that adventure when I met him. But that was as close to the action as Lewis ever wanted to be. This was before the Coast Guard and the Feds developed a mass assault and before organized cartels. These were really hippy-dippy independent operations. Mostly, we hung out in San Francisco, waiting for the Deavers. When the drugs showed up, we'd check into a hotel carrying a false-bottomed suitcase lined with bags of cocaine."

"A false-bottomed suitcase?"

"Yeah. We'd go up to a room, cut open the suitcase, then weigh out the coke into smaller bags that could be sold on the street." Art chuckles. "We'd be handling the coke, scooping it from one bag to another on a little scale, and the powder would seep into our skin. Our hands would be shaking from it."

I don't know whether to laugh or simply shake my head. My father was far too sophisticated a guy to cross borders with a lot of dope strapped to him, but he wasn't too sophisticated to haul false-bottomed suitcases full of cocaine into hotels. I picture him in a tan British military-issue trench coat and Austrian chamois hunter's cap, pulling open the door of a seedy SRO, some place where people come and go by the hour with not too many questions asked. A foggy night, a ring of cloud around a sliver moon.

A poem by John Ash about a drug-addicted tribe surfaces in my mind:

> It was discovered that the hallucinations affected
> only their perception of themselves. Sometimes
> they saw themselves as tall giraffe-like creatures
> and sometimes they were no higher than lap-dogs.
> On tall days it was not uncommon for them to die of their
>   extravagances,—

I've never taken hard drugs, so the whole scenario sounds incredible to me, comic and bizarre and outrageous and a little appalling. It's hard for me to understand the appeal of that kind of loss of control. I hate even to be drunk. I love to drink, it's not that; being tipsy seems sexy, smokily erotic. It's the grasping for balance, struggling to bring back the clarity of a still mind, that I find unbearable. Everything he suffered makes me want to be sympathetic, but I hate that my father died like this.

"Of course," Art says, "if we'd really been professionals, we would've worn facemasks and gloves. We wouldn't have let the stuff seep into our skin."

Apparently, they hadn't gotten so far into it that they actually knew what they were doing.

"Lewis was a very talented photographer, by the way. Read about it all the time. He particularly liked W. Eugene Smith, as well as Paul Strand, Imogen Cunningham. He thought that photography was magical. He had a very special camera—"

"I have that camera. A Graflex."

"Right. A Graflex with a Polaroid back. It combined instant printing with wonderful optics. It was very entertaining, but there was a particular purpose to that camera. Lewis thought that it could capture your soul—or lack of soul. He thought it was a truth machine. Your father had two things about him: one, a beleaguered idealism, and two, a strain of deep cynicism. He could also be judgmental at times.

He had this thing he did that I called the Greed Test. The Hundred-Dollar Greed Test. He'd pass out one-hundred-dollar bills to people, just to get their reaction—ingratiating, desperate—when faced with a quick hundred. He wanted to see what it brought out in people. It wasn't the best idea. More often than not, his cynicism got reinforced.

"On the other hand," Art says, "he seemed happy—not euphoric in the way of manic-depressives, just happy in the ordinary way of people enjoying their lives." He was muscular and lean, a fitness that Art attributes to working in the garden and chopping wood—and women loved him.

"What happened after San Francisco? Were there more operations?"

"Mickey Deaver took a one-way plane trip to South America."

"What do you mean, a one-way plane trip?"

"He owed the wrong people money," Art says. "Rumor has it that he got on the plane, but he didn't get off when it landed. This was a notorious way to get rid of people: throw them out over the jungle somewhere."

I'm startled, though in Art's retelling even this story sounds light, amusing. Later, someone else will tell me that my father took the news of the killing hard: following that, the drug smuggling business didn't seem like such an exhilarating game anymore. After his suicide, people speculated that Mickey Deaver's brutal death was one of the things that drove my father over the edge. Listening to Art, I think for the first time that had he not killed himself, Lewis might very well have wound up in prison, disappeared into South America, or been murdered.

"Last I heard," Art continues, "Mickey's brother, Dwayne, was tending bar and waiting tables somewhere in California. There was another associate of ours, Adam Worker, who packed himself into a body cast lined with cocaine. One of the bags started to leak." Art chuckles again. "The cocaine was seeping into his leg, making him jittery, so he was taking downers to counteract the effect, getting crazy from both. He flew from Panama City to Mexico City, where he had to change planes. In Mexico City, he was observed limping on the *wrong* leg. He went to jail in Mexico, then busted out three years later and wrote a book about it called *Escape*. A couple of years ago, it was made into a movie of the week."

There you go, Lewis. You could have been a movie of the week.

Art also mentions Dick Bannister, the "associate" that Mara referred to, the man who was thought to have fled the country not long before my father moved with her to Santa Fe. Bannister, who was staying at Lama at the time, was arrested for importing cocaine in the hollow bottoms of plaster of Paris statues. The FBI swooped down on Lama one day with drug-sniffing dogs and an arsenal of weapons. Bannister was picked up, but then he jumped the bail posted for him by the people at Lama and disappeared.

"People thought he'd gone to South America, but amazingly enough, I just came across an article about him in the *L.A. Times*, headlined 'Community Activist Runs from Law into Folk-Hero Status,'" Art says. "The statute of limitations never runs out on an open warrant, and the U.S. Marshals Office had just tracked him down to a little town in Colorado, where he'd been living for twenty-five years under the name of Richard Neil Murdoch. Someone tipped him off that the marshals were closing in, and he got away again before they could arrest him. The townspeople staged a big parade, with costumes and skits, celebrating his escape.

"The marshals kept insisting that there was a 'major distribution ring' and that these people were glamorizing a drug smuggler, but as they said, Bannister, alias Murdoch, was no different from a lot of people in the sixties and seventies, experimenting with life, running from something. I thought this one guy put it really well: 'We're all Murdoch in a little way. We're all old refugees from somewhere else.'"

I wish for a moment that the story could have been about my father, living under an assumed name, escaping at the last minute. In a way, each of the men I've met represents a different possible outcome for my father's life — Stephan, Irwin, Donald Singer, Jeremy Grainger, Art, Dick Bannister, Bill Gersh, men like him in various ways, presented with many of the same choices. All Lewis in a little way (and he them), but able to keep from stepping off that final ledge.

Then again, another part of me wishes he could have been the kind of person just to sit on the porch, down in the valley, and play casino.

"By the way," Art says, "there's no problem shooting oneself between the eyes: simply turn the gun around and use the thumb as a trigger finger. That's just from my imagination, but it seems logical enough."

Art tells me that his own father killed himself. That was in 1969; Art had been estranged from him at the time.

"There is that moment of despair," he says, "that the person is unable to hold out against. And if the means is close by and no one is around to minister to them, anything can happen."

Clearly, my father was a man for whom all the safety nets were gone.

"He didn't talk much about your mother, except to say that once they were very deeply in love, and they had a horrible breakup. There were a lot of disillusioning events. Vietnam, Kennedy, Watergate. You couldn't trust the world that was given to you. You could try to find a new way, or die a strangulated, ossified soul-death. We did a lot of experimenting, attempting to evolve into a new form of human being, but there was tremendous confusion. Often we had the best of intentions, but we were cut loose from our moorings."

Art pauses. "I haven't felt that alive in twenty years."

He describes the bonds between people in the community as being similar to those among soldiers in war. "We lived," he says, "exaggerated lives."

"Was it my father's death that got you out of the drug trade?" I ask. Art is now an antiques importer, and a successful one, judging by his prestigious business address.

"In a way. That and a series of successively harder taps on the shoulder."

Following my father's death, Art tells me, he'd taken a trip to Peru. They had been getting coke from Peru for some time, but the quality of the most recent batches had been poor. The suppliers suggested that Art come down, tour the labs, and select his own materials. He flew from Miami to Guayaquil, Equador, where he rented a car with a driver to cross the border into Peru. In Lima, Art and his Peruvian contact stayed in a house until the drug suppliers were ready for them to visit the labs. With time to kill, Art wandered the city. At one point, he was approached by a young man whom he knew immediately was a policeman; the guy attached himself to Art, following him around until, finally, Art managed to shake him off. It was a warning: he was being watched.

"There were only two reasons for young Americans to be in Peru," Art says. "They were either tourists, who were mostly hippies, or they were doing business—and there was only one kind of business to do there."

That was the first hard tap. The second came when Art went to mass in a nearby cathedral. After the Benediction, the parishioners all hugged one another. Art described it as a wave of hugs moving through the congregation toward him. He wasn't particularly religious, and it was the kind of thing that my father would probably have dismissed as bullshit, but Art experienced it as love. He was deeply moved by it, as well as unsettled. Was it some sort of message?

Walking back to the house, a black limo pulled up to the curb next to him. "I half expected men with Tommy guns," he says. But then a little girl and an old man got out. The little girl was clutching a picture of Jesus, which she held up to Art. Her grandfather tugged at her arm, trying to pull her away, while Art stood there riveted by what he could only perceive as an omen.

His contact perceived it as an omen, too. "It's a sign!" he said, after Art described the three events. "From now on, man, we're tourists in Peru."

They abandoned their plan to tour the labs and drove to the Altiplano instead. Art then took a bus across the border into Quito and flew back to Miami. On the flight over, he noticed a guy in a tan suit watching him attentively. Art wasn't carrying anything, but that would have been the case even if the mission hadn't been aborted. Nevertheless, the thought that he was still being shadowed was unnerving. When he got off the plane, the man followed a few paces behind him. Then an announcement crackled over the intercom: "TAN agent, call your office." The man's head shot up, and, with a last reluctant look at Art, the man, Treasury Agent, Narcotics, veered off, leaving Art to walk out of the airport alone. The drug enforcement agency had known about his operation all along.

Those "signs," Art says, had protected his life.

On the day in 1973 when the FBI
arrested Dick Bannister, a.k.a. Richard
Neil Murdoch, for cocaine
smuggling, my uncle Joe happened
to be sitting on the crate that contained
the statuettes in which the
drugs were hidden. He had gone
up to New Mexico to see my father
about the land deal, but when he
got to Lama, Lewis was nowhere to
be found. No one knew where he
was. Joe wanted to call his wife,
Myriam, to let her know what was
going on, and Dick Bannister was
the nearest person at Lama who
had a phone.

When he walked up to the
house, he noticed that Bannister had a bunch of boxes in the trunk
of his car, stuff, Joe thought, for the tchotchke shop he ran in Taos.
Joe helped him unload. Just as they were finishing up, the FBI, brandishing
shotguns and shouting at them to get their hands in the air,
surrounded the house. They arrested Bannister, Joe, and two kids who
had shown up hoping to buy a little dope. Joe and the *Los Angeles Times*
say that there were twenty-six pounds of cocaine stuffed into the
hollow bottoms of the statues.

All four were transported to Albuquerque, where they were
thrown in jail—each in separate, isolated cells because, as Joe dryly
remarks, "We were such dangerous criminals."

Joe's cell contained a ten-year-old *Reader's Digest* and a steel toilet
that flushed automatically every twenty minutes. When he was allowed
his one phone call, he called his son, who was going to school
in Boulder at the time. His son laughed when he heard that his father

was in jail, and said, "Dad, you've been busted!" He said he'd get his father a lawyer if he wasn't released by Monday. Finally, after two long days, Joe and the two kids were let out of their cells. Bannister had apparently convinced the police that they had nothing to do with his drug business. Joe asked the police how they were supposed to get back to Taos.

"That's your problem," he was told. Joe sprang for Greyhound tickets for him and the two boys; the bus dropped them off in Questa. He never did find my father.

FINAL GIFTS

Mara sends me a CD of Bob Dylan's *Pat Garrett and Billy the Kid*, which she says she equates with my father and his romantic visions of being an outlaw, living on the fringes, waiting for the sheriff to show up to arrest or kill him. She also sends me a beautiful silver cuff bracelet that my father made for her. It's about a half-inch wide with a pattern of tiny triangles pressed into it.

COCAINE PSYCHOSIS

After I speak to Art, I look up bipolar disorder in the *Diagnostic and Statistical Manual of Mental Disorders*, the bible of psychiatric illnesses. Psychomotor agitation, depression, preoccupation with death, euphoria, dysphoria, feelings of worthlessness, and excessive guilt are all among the symptoms. However, the manual specifically states that none of these can be regarded as evidence of bipolar disorder if the effects can be attributed to drug abuse. It seems more likely that Art's first guess was correct: my father was suffering from cocaine psychosis, a condition that some doctors liken to paranoid schizophrenia. Delusions of persecution, unpredictability, excitability, garrulousness, anxiety, insomnia, hallucinations, and violent actions, including self-destruction: nearly all his behaviors in those last weeks are on the list of symptoms. Even the free-floating philosophizing and apparent calm that Lee Driver describes might have been evidence of psychosis or of a phase of withdrawal.

As for cocaine itself, one study estimates that in 1974 as many as

5.4 million people took the drug at least once: not a huge number considering that by 1985 it had increased to 25 million, but still significant. My father, you could say, was one of those who helped introduce the drug to this country.

But maybe that's an exaggeration. No doubt I'm being a little priggish. By the early 1970s, recreational drug use, as Art says, was already becoming an accepted thing. It had entered the popular culture: it was in the music; it was in the movies. *Easy Rider*, for instance, opens with Captain America and his bum of a sidekick, Billy, snorting cocaine in Mexico. My mother says she and my father saw the movie together in Florida, in 1968 or 1969, when it first came out.

NOTES ON EASY RIDER

Oddly enough, I watched *Easy Rider* for the first time with my mother. She had been sick in bed for several days, so I rented a stack of films to keep myself occupied. Then she came downstairs in her bathrobe and sat next to me on the little wicker couch in her TV room. She watched the whole film without a sigh of disgust or a flinch at the nudity, the f-word, the murder of Jack Nicholson in the forest, the drug-happy characters cavorting around the tombs in New Orleans. But when the two hippies were killed at the end by a bunch of hooting rednecks in a pickup truck, her lips tightened. She got up from the couch and stormed into the kitchen. Here we go, I thought. I followed her.

"What's the matter?" I said. "What didn't you like about it?"

I didn't quite like the ending, either—it was too easy somehow, a little amateurish, a banner-headline ending: BRUTISH CONSERVATIVE FORCES WON'T ALLOW FREE SPIRITS TO LIVE. I was also trying a new campaign: to respect her point of view even when we disagree. I could see that she, in turn, was trying to respect mine. As a result, we had been getting along better.

"I found it manipulative," she said, still seething. She was making tea with jerky movements. "Here are these two basically despicable characters, and I'm supposed to feel sympathy for them because they got killed. Well, I resent that. I resent it!"

She simmered down enough to ask if I wanted a cup of tea, and I nodded, thinking I understood what she meant. Hippie culture wasn't something she could bear to see glamorized. She couldn't stand having those men turned into romantic heroes. She knew what it was all about, what had happened to her, to my father, to so many of her friends and acquaintances. There were few visionaries in our milieu, but many freaks and addicts and anguished souls. I saw her point, though in my mind it was a question of the chicken or the egg, whether the counterculture had damaged these people or whether these were damaged people who were naturally drawn to extremes. Perhaps it was both: in an environment with few boundaries, a fragile or volatile person could easily go haywire.

I used to be infuriated by people's nostalgia for the counterculture. For me, that period meant turbulence, drugs, booze, violent death. Most people had no idea. But it was the violence within my own family that was the real problem. I have hippie-kid friends who look with gratitude on their parents' far-out way of living. The difference between us is that their families, however unconventional, led relatively stable lives. They didn't have a drunken slob of a stepfather sweeping the dinner plates off the table or suffocating them with his huge hand. And that, of course, you can find anywhere.

Most social critics equate the end of the counterculture with the end of the sixties; for us, it began in late 1969 and continued, in a degraded form, into the mid-seventies. We drifted out of it only after my mother built our house in Talpa, when I was eleven.

By the time my mother and father arrived in New Mexico, the communes were already in decline, overrun by self-indulgent young dropouts who treated them as crash pads, by weirdoes and criminals who wanted a place to hide out, and by men and women who just found it difficult to function, in the mainstream or anywhere else.

The lack of structure was devastating to many people. My mother, unprepared for the reality of life without rules, ultimately reached for religion in order to survive, going from total chaos to something so organized that she no longer had to think for herself. And if my father, who had followed my mother into the counterculture primarily in the hope of hanging on to her, had simply had, as my uncle Joe said, a job, or if he had returned to New York, where he had family for support, or if he had gone to graduate school and done something to engage his "crackling mind," he might have been able to weather his despair.

Naturally, I can't help but think that my mother's anger at the movie has a lot to do with him. Suicide is a manipulative ending, the worst kind of string-pulling. It is impossible not to resent it, not to feel enraged. I think of Mara, who says that she has never married because for a long time after my father's death, she couldn't let herself get close to anyone. I think of Miriam, with tears in her eyes whenever she speaks of her brother, and of the anger that seems to seethe in my uncle Joe even now. I think of my brother, who loved Lewis so much, and of my mother, fundamentally derailed by his death. I think of myself, growing up with a hole in the center of my being. For most of my life, I experienced my father as a void; he had abandoned me, refusing to offer his love or his protection, or to share any of the things he knew: his stories, his love of architecture and books. He had not thought it worth living to pass those things on to me. He had not considered it worthwhile to have my love in return. No amount of rationalizing would erase those truths. Every one of us carried this burden of loss. Every one of us had been hit by the shrapnel of his act.

SALVATION

Three days after my father's death, my mother was sitting alone in the melting adobe we occupied in San Luis, Colorado. Wayne had taken my brother and me across the pastures to check on Elias Lucero's cows.

The house had two stories, with two long rooms below and a single large room above that you reached by a pole ladder. In a daze, my mother sat on the bed she shared with

Wayne. My father's death had immobilized her. She simply sat and stared.

Suddenly my mother heard a voice. It came from the ceiling.

"I am God," the voice said. "And I am real, and Jesus is my son."

When she left my father, my mother thought, I'll be fine, he'll be fine. Then he killed himself. "Everything I had known and believed," my mother says, "was no longer valid. His death destroyed all my philosophical underpinnings. I was brought up with the idea that you can do whatever you want. Just apply yourself and do it. You'll succeed. His death proved that to be false."

Until the moment she heard God's voice, my mother didn't believe that there was a God. Her family was Jewish and atheist. They believed in nothing that wasn't verifiable.

"I am God," the voice said. "And I am real, and Jesus is my son."

My mother, until that moment, had experienced everything as contradiction. "Things didn't meet," she says. "My mind felt split apart. There was my family, Lewis, his parents, the people at art school in Miami, where I took pottery classes."

I know what my mother means: the contradictions in her parents' lives, their bohemianism and her conventional suburban upbringing; her feminist mother's chilliness; the petit bourgeois values of Lewis's parents; her intellectual (increasingly cold and angry) husband selling stuccoed boxes in a desolate Florida housing development; the elevation of art as the holy grail; the reverence for material success; the lack of a moral center—or any center whatsoever.

When His voice spoke, my mother felt everything knitting together. She felt healed.

She had been at a picnic with Pam and Klea, her two closest friends, just days before my father's death. They were talking reverently about Christ. My mother thought their belief ridiculous and mocked them to their faces. Then, after my father died, she overheard some women talking at a party, wondering if she was "going to make it." She remembered Pam and Klea's conversation, and understood it as divine intervention, paving the way.

I'm going to make it, she thought. She had the assurance of Jesus in her heart.

IN MEMORIAM

No one seems to remember a funeral for my father.

My mother says that she missed it somehow.

There was a ceremony of some kind at Lama, my uncle says.

Joe's son, Stephan, remembers a sort of wake, though he isn't sure where it took place. He had been close to my father, his beloved uncle, and when he heard the news had ridden a Greyhound bus down to Taos from Boulder, where he was going to college. He was dropped off on the side of the highway near Lama and walked up the hill to find his father. It was very cold, he remembers, and he felt unbearably sad. He isn't certain, but he must have gone to the coroner's office in Taos with his father, Aunt Miriam, and Uncle Bob. "It was the first time I had seen a dead person, and I remember thinking, He doesn't look like he's sleeping, he looks dead. And I wished I hadn't seen him."

It was Joe who made the decision to have my father cremated. Miriam vividly remembers my father's body lying on a steel table at the coroner's, a terrible black hole between his eyes. When she expressed dismay about the cremation, Joe asked her, "Where are we going to bury him—in that great swamp, Florida?" She couldn't argue with him. Though her parents were buried there, it was not the place for her brother. In different ways, Florida had indeed swamped each of their lives.

Bob read the Twenty-third Psalm over the body, *Yea, though I walk through the valley of the shadow of death, I shall fear no evil*, but none of them remembers any other kind of service.

Lee can't remember a funeral, either. "That's strange," he says. "I don't know why I wouldn't have been there."

No one remembers a funeral for my father, but there were rituals.

Miriam and Bob held a memorial service.

Lee and his girlfriend purified the house on the Rim Road so that people could go on living in it.

Mara and Art Ross, as Mara writes to tell me, "took his ashes and spread them at Lama underneath a piñon tree that Art and Lewis liked to camp under. The spot had a beautiful view of the sunset over Wind Mountain."

I am trying to build a house, if only of language and memory, in which my father can live in peace. I don't want my father to be the caretaker of a sculpture anymore.

Or to be a sculpture himself, forever caught in that final startling pose.

REMAINS: AN UPDATED INVENTORY OF MY FATHER

1. A handful of photographs of him, including his high school graduation portrait and some taken in Florida by my mother.

2. A silver belt buckle.

3. Photographs taken by my father of my mother in her twenties, and of my brother and me when we were children.

4. *Architectural Record*, Vol. 145, No. 6: "Record Houses of 1969."

5. *Miami Herald*, "Dwelling Is Designed for Family Living," May 25, 1969.

6. One handmade wooden case with a 4x5 Graflex camera in it.

7. An exposed, undeveloped roll of film [ITEM LOST].

8. A piece of soft white cloth embroidered with red thread in an exploding-star pattern wrapped around a spare lens.

9. A forty-year-old Leica.

10. A red metal army trunk full of my father's photographs, including many of my brother and me and my mother right up to the time she left him.

11. Transaction receipts from a photo shop and two construction suppliers in Florida.

12. A divorce decree.

13. A postcard to my father from a woman named Lynn [ORIGINAL MISPLACED].

14. A tin lithograph that says LIBERALS FOR NIXON.

15. A photograph of my father's eighth-grade graduating class at P.S. 178, class of June 1952.

16. A sleeve of slides of my father and Stephan on a youth-hostel bicycling trip to Europe the summer they were seventeen.

17. Copies of Louis Kronenberger's *Company Manners*, *The Vintage Mencken*, and *Hornblower and the Hotspur*.

18. A postcard from my father and my mother in New Mexico to Stephan.

19. A photograph of the Jamaica High School Senior Prom, Hotel Biltmore, June 6, 1956.

20. My father's journal.

21. Photographs of my father in elementary and high school, sent by Miriam.

22. Articles from the *Rensselaer Polytechnic* about the *GE College Bowl* team of which my father was captain and in which my father is quoted.

23. Titles of the books my father read.

24. A copy of Allen Ginsberg's *Kaddish*.

25. A pair of silver earrings that my father made for my grandmother when he was in the army [ONE MISSING].

26. A sleeve of colored slides of my father's house in Florida.

27. A tape with my father's voice on it [RECOVERED].

28. A letter from Bill Gersh to my father, inviting him to stay on at Lama and participate in the life being created there, sent by my uncle Joe.

29. Bob Dylan's *Pat Garrett and Billy the Kid*.

30. A silver cuff bracelet that my father made for Mara.

31. A photograph of my father in San Francisco, sent by Art Ross. Also photographs of Mara, Art, and Mickey Deaver, who took a one-way trip to South America.

32. My mother's pearl earrings. Also, a silver pendant made for her by my father, which she polished and strung on a silver chain for me when I completed my MFA.

33. The sound of my father's voice in my head.

QUEST 29: MY FATHER'S CHEST

"It's really beat up," Iris, Bill Gersh's former common-law wife, says when I call to arrange a time to pick up my father's large wooden chest. I'm in Taos for five days, and retrieving it is my first priority. "You might not even want it. And the road is really bad, with all the snowmelt," she says. "Do you have a four-wheel-drive? If not, I don't know if you can even get up here. The ruts are really deep." Her breathy, ethereal voice sounds at odds with her practicality—a fairy talking about mud and the possibility of getting stuck.

She is not just trying to scare me off. It is mid-April, and warm enough to thaw the ground, but not enough to dry it.

"Maybe it's one of those things," Iris says, "you just need to let go."

For a moment, I think that maybe she's right.

I do not have a four-wheel-drive. I have a rental car from Albuquerque. A Mercury midsized V-6 for which, at the rental agent's urging, I paid more money at the last minute. I had thought at first that the agent was just trying to jack up the cost. But the four-cylinder compact I had originally asked for would not have made it out of the canyon between Santa Fe and Taos, much less up Lama Mountain. I have been living in New York without a car for less than two years.

How could I have forgotten the most basic relationship between engines and elevation?

No, I think, I'm going to get the chest. I'm not making this mistake a second time.

QUEST 30: ASHES

The night before meeting Iris, I invite myself to dinner with Beverly and Rollo, but I don't do it in order to ask questions or collect more stories. I call them because I simply want to connect with the people who were in my father's world. I had lunch with Lee Driver. I planned to spend the night with Mara on my way back to Albuquerque. Mara and I and Mara's business partner, Carole, who was Bill Gersh's live-in companion before Iris, will have dinner together in Santa Fe. These people had touched my father's life or had been touched by him. I want to gather them into my own history. Once again, however, I get more than I bargained for.

Beverly's daughter and son-in-law drive up just as I get out of my car: their truck wheels are caked with mud, as are their shoes and pant legs. They have just been at Lama. The ruts, they say, are two feet deep in places.

After a tour of their newly rented house and while we are waiting for dinner to be ready, Rollo says to me, "There were signs I would recognize now that he was contemplating suicide, but I didn't at the time." We are standing in their bedroom. The last sunlight on the stubbled fields and the blue of the mountain in the distance fill the big window. "I would have tried to help him."

"Signs?" I ask.

"He was giving things away. He gave me his winter coat. Sort of military style, very warm, with a fleece lining and a striking fur collar. And other things." Rollo has a high round forehead, strong mouth and chin, a nose like a spade in a deck of cards, dark, penetrating eyes. "I know now that's something people do, when they're thinking about killing themselves. They give things away.

"I saw him a few days before," he continues. "I was having breakfast at Joe's Cafe, and Lewis came in. He sat down across from me. He was very agitated, chain-smoking one cigarette after another. He took out the pack and waved it in my direction.

"I said, 'No thanks. I haven't smoked in years.'

"And he said, 'You're right. I'm quitting, too.' He stubbed out the cigarette—then immediately took another one out of the pack and lit it.

"After breakfast, he led me out of the restaurant to his car, took a box out of the trunk, and handed it to me. He said, 'How would you like to have twelve thousand dollars?' Then he got in the car and drove away. I opened the box; it was full of money. When I got home, I counted it. I wanted to know exactly how much was there: eleven thousand six hundred. I decided to hang on to it for six months and see what happened. I put it in my safe-deposit box at the bank. A week later he died. I felt like he had given it to me to take care of because he knew he wouldn't be able to do it himself."

The money again. "What happened to it?"

"When your father's brother was here, after Lewis died, he took me aside and asked if by chance I knew anything about twelve thousand dollars." Rollo chuckles. "I said, 'No, but I know something about eleven thousand six hundred.' He said it was his money, for some land he and Lewis were planning to buy, so I handed it over to him."

So it wasn't Bill Gersh, as Joe thought, after all.

Suddenly, Beverly, leaning on the doorframe, says, "You know we scattered your father's ashes at Lama."

I shake my head. I hadn't mentioned that I was wondering. The gods, I think, are on my side.

"Mara Andover," I say. "Do you know her? She told me she and Art Ross scattered them under a tree at Lama. A tree my father liked to camp under, facing west."

"I don't remember Mara being there," Rollo says, "but maybe she was. Lewis's brother might have been there, too. I don't know an Art Ross."

It doesn't surprise me that even this detail is wrong, or at least uncertain; we remember what we need to remember, what sustains us.

"We scattered them around the Ice Cream Cone Tree," Beverly

says. Her eyes are fixed on mine. She projects the same unnerving intensity as Gersh, though her soft voice and gentle manner radiate an almost transcendental calm. "That's what we call it, because it's shaped like an ice cream cone." She is a small woman, blond, oval-faced, with the unadorned look of someone who has spent most of her life in the country. In high school, she and my mother were always thought to be sisters, they looked so much alike. "We all gathered around the tree —me and Rollo, the kids, Gersh, Iris, Mara, I guess. We each took a scoop in hand, said a few words, and scattered the ashes around the base of the tree."

Beverly smiles, her fierce eyes shining. "It's also called Lewis's Tree."

A tingle of excitement spreads through my chest. "Really?"

Beverly nods, still smiling. "The kids used to play there. I can still hear them calling out to each other, 'Let's go play at Lewis's Tree.'"

QUEST 31: THE HOUSE ON THE RIM

A part of me doesn't expect to find it. I've driven past that spot a hundred times on my way to the ski valley and never noticed the house. But as soon as the gas station hanging over the cliff appears on the left, I see a dirt road leading off the highway to the right. And there, almost hidden, behind a hump of field and a leafless spray of cottonwood and red willow, shines the tin roof of a long, squat house. I pull off the highway and park on the shoulder, one wheel deep in the weeds. I am on my way to see Iris and don't expect to take long. But I want to walk toward the house on the rim, slowly. I also want to keep from announcing my presence to any people or dogs that might be around.

My chest is tight. I draw deep breaths through my nose, then expel the air through my mouth in a rush. What do I expect to find —or feel—coming here? Finally, with the fist still squeezing my lungs, I pull my camera from my bag, shove the bag under the seat, and get out of the car.

The first thing that strikes me as I walk up the road is the beauty of the scene. The house is surrounded by fields and trees. A haunch of Taos Mountain rises dramatically behind it under a brilliant blue, cloud-filled sky. Foothills, dark green with piñon, spread almost to its door. A small orchard crowds its far wall. Every few yards, I stop to take pictures: the house from the highway, barely visible above a line of brush-choked fence posts; the sheer, long, peaked roof between the mountain and a band of stark trees; the slanting huddle of gray walls from the front yard.

In town the day before, I had walked past the house on Kit Carson Road where I once thought my father had died. It has, it turns out, no wall around it at all, just stone gateposts and a slatted wooden gate, painted turquoise. The house is a gallery now. The gates are swung open, more for decoration than anything else, and only low posts and barbed wire line the perimeter. Everything, trees and yard and front door, is perfectly exposed to any passerby.

I take another picture of the rim house's long front, its two windows and three doors. There would be no mistakes of memory this time.

The house is not at all the tumbledown—or abandoned—heap I expect to find. It is obviously and lovingly cared for. Roses grow on one side of a wide flagstone pathway, and on the other, stone-bordered flower beds overflow with green shoots of iris and poppy and mats of just blooming grape hyacinth. Yellow daisies in dusky blue pots sit on either side of the dusky blue front door. Wooden birdhouses and the dark red rope of a chili ristra decorate the cracked gray exterior walls. It is lovely, more lovely than in my father's day, I am sure, but whatever the house was like then, the orchard and the willows and the mountain are the same.

A van is parked to one side of the driveway, and a wheelbarrow full of potting soil sits in the front yard. But when I knock on the door, no one answers. I want whoever lives there to be home so that I don't feel like a thief creeping around on the property, but if anyone is home, what will I say? Not that my father killed himself here. Not unless the current occupants already seem to know.

I stand in the driveway with my eyes burning, hating my father for dying. I hate that I will never really know him. I hate that he had been in such pain and so alone. But I am glad that he spent his last days in such a beautiful place.

"FLUTTERING HEART" 6

I continue the journey to Gersh's that I first made with my friend Fielding; it's now almost four years later, and this time I'm alone. Since that trip, Fielding has married her Peruvian boyfriend and had a child; together they opened a hotel outside of Cuzco. I feel good driving to Lama. I have changed my life—gotten divorced, discovered my history and launched a book, moved to New York, found a man I dearly love (whom I live with now and who will, in due, completely unanticipated, course, become my husband)—and suddenly that seems heroic. I can understand now my mother's need to transform her own life. Whatever else, I am not bored, I am not suffocating. My mother, too, after seventeen years alone following her divorce from Curtis, has gotten engaged to a lovely, kindhearted man; her happiness with him has brought a fresh beauty to her face that is wonderful to see. And Stuart, whom I feared would be as devastated by my departure as my father was by my mother's, has recently gotten a job as a photographer for an advertising firm in Minneapolis. To my relief, he seems to be managing, maybe even flourishing, without me.

The road is dry enough, I find, so I am able to pull right up to Iris's house, which sits in front of Gersh's workshop, instead of parking in the small lot above it.

When I call hello through the open door, Iris comes out and, without saying a word, gives me a long, soulful hug. Her thin frame presses into me, shoulders foremost. I turn my head to keep my nose free of her short red curls. She seems to be trying to transfer a store of sympathy from her body to mine. It is a tender gesture—she loved my father, too ("it was a tossup," she said on the phone with a laugh, "between him and Gersh")—but it is all I can do not to flinch. Except by a lover, I'm not a person who likes to be touched.

Inside, Iris introduces me to Martin, a tall, thin young man whom I know from town gossip to be her boyfriend, and Nina, her two-and-a-half-year-old granddaughter, a beautiful child with big, clear eyes and dark curls. Iris is baby-sitting.

The little girl's presence reassures me. She climbs onto Iris's lap, folds herself into her grandmother's arms for a moment, then sits bolt upright to see what's on the table. Only a teapot and two empty cups. The tea is still steeping. She wriggles off and drags a puzzle over to the floor at our feet. Iris and I both watch her try to wedge part of a rabbit into the wrong space. Iris smiles dotingly at her.

"What about there?" I say. "Does it go there?"

"I can do it," she says. "I'm smart." With her fist, she whacks the rabbit into the wrong space and then, when it won't go, slides it into the opening I pointed out.

"Gersh told me a story about my father," I say, turning my attention to Iris once more as she pours us peppermint tea from the ceramic pot. I am glad Iris's fidgety, freckled hands are wrapped around the wicker handle, because when they aren't they keep touching me. "I was wondering if you might remember. About his spirit trying to get into bed with you and Gersh after he'd killed himself?" I hadn't planned to ask her this question, but sitting at Lama with her, I think, Why not?

"That sounds familiar," Iris says, squinting with the effort to draw the memory from the depths. "Yes, I remember something like that."

I wait, but nothing more comes. Iris smiles at me between sips of tea. I look at her incredulously. It seems to me that a man's spirit trying to get under the covers with you would have made more of an impression.

RECLAMATION

Squatting on the floor so that her freckled knees poke out from the folds of her dress, Iris opens the lid of my father's chest to see what's inside.

"I used to keep my daughter's baby clothes in it," she says, turning to give me a wide, warm smile.

The chest is pushed against a wall of record albums, exactly as it was before. Nothing has moved since my first visit with Gersh. Except Gersh, of course, who died three years earlier of cirrhosis of the liver. If I had come even a year later to retrieve the trunk of photographs, I would never have heard the story of my father's fluttering heart.

The mountain has changed entirely in that short time. The fires and a dispute over privatization of communal land have driven Beverly and Rollo into town. Charred ground is all that remains of their circular house. But Gersh's place—masks, shadow boxes, record albums, labyrinthine rooms, which my father helped build—looks exactly as it did before. I am lucky. Gersh is gone, Beverly and Rollo's house is gone, but the chest is still there.

QUEST 32: LEWIS'S TREE

Before I take my father's chest and drive back to a lunch of green chili stew and beer at the Taos Inn, a fire in my hotel room, and a date for coffee late in the day with Fielding, who happens to be staying at her mother's house, there is, of course, one more thing that I have to do.

"Lewis's Tree," I say aloud, but softly, rolling the words in my mouth. As I walk across the road, I feel Iris's sympathetic eyes following me from the doorway.

The tree is just as Beverly said: an ice cream cone on a bare slope, its one scoop tightly packed but pushed back precariously. Cedar, fragrant wood from my childhood. Dense gray-green, silver shards of bark, purple-red wood inside. In winter, my mother burned cedar shavings in the woodstove.

I stand in the field below it for a long time. The ground under my feet is muddy. The heels of my boots are caked with it. A brilliantly sunny day, but raw anyway. I've come too early for the lilacs that I thought would be blooming all over town. Two weeks too early, at least. My disappointment at first was keen. Lilac season is the time of year I love most in Taos. But I see now what I've gained: a rare chance to stand in the seam between winter and spring.

I think of taking a piece of the tree away with me. A twig, a branch, not as a souvenir, but as a talisman. Something strikingly gnarled, like the sculptured driftwood my grandfather Juan would carry from beaches to his attic studio. Even from this distance, I can see tree limbs on the ground. Saturated with resin, cedar is favored as a construction material because it doesn't rot.

I don't move forward. Not long before, Stephan had given me a sketchbook as a gift; taking it from the trunk of the car, I stand there with the book and a pencil box in my hands. There is only this one opportunity to walk toward this tree, to approach for the first time the ground that has received my father. Only this one last chance to feel enough.

When I was in high school, I asked my mother to have a carpenter from our church build me a hope chest. I planned to fill it with embroidered pillowcases and tablecloths. But the chest was a disappointment. It was beautifully crafted, but instead of using oak or even pine, the carpenter made it from varnished plywood. Only the lining suited my imaginings of what a hope chest should be: closely fitted cedar boards, blood-colored and pungent. The wood pulsed inside the cheap box like a hidden heart.

I open my sketchbook. I want to capture the color. Not just of the tree, but of this landscape that is in me. My father's landscape, too, although I've spent so long refusing to grant it to him. He, an exile, a refugee. Me, a native because he—they—chose it. This, not Florida, not New York even, is my home country. For the first time, I realize that among my parents' gifts to me are these: this rush of yellow weeds beyond the bare earth at the cedar's base, these wands of red willow, this mountain, this sky, white with clouds behind it.

No use. I could never transfer that wild palette to paper. I take out a pencil. If nothing else, I'll draw the shape.

It must seem strange to Iris and her lover that I just stand there in the muddy field, holding a sketchbook. We each need to discover our own rituals. For me, that in itself is a discovery. But I worry. Am I experiencing or merely recording? Engaging or distancing? It disturbs me now that I took so many photographs of the house in which my father died. I'm glad to have a picture or two to remember it by, but did I need a whole roll? I was capturing it in order to preserve it, but also to defer its impact. I was holding the lens to my eye to dam a flood. The pencil moves quickly, lightly, over the page. I hold it loosely, as my grandfather taught me. If I concentrate too hard, the lines will come out crabbed and wrong.

The first tree is misshapen, but not in the right ways. It isn't an ice cream cone. I try again, thrusting the form from the page against graphite wedges of weed, bush, mountain, cloud, sky.

I say the name again as I work: "Lewis's Tree." I love that the children of Lama mapped it into their games. The chorus of their voices echoes in my mind: "*Let's go play at Lewis's Tree.*" They are in their late twenties now, as I am. But no one forgets. In the court battle over

the land, Beverly and Rollo have claimed this tree as the outermost boundary of their parcel. It is the burial place of a dear friend, Beverly had said, and they wouldn't give it up. My father has entered the folklore of the landscape. He has become a sacred site.

The branches on the ground could have grown from the part of my father that leached into the soil. The cedar contains him. The cedar is him.

I darken the mountain and shade the sky. The sketch is finished. I'm satisfied with it:

I title it "Lewis's Tree, Lama, 4/27/98." And then it strikes me: my father died in April. Light in New Mexico is as seasonal as leaves. I've sketched my father's tree in light similar to the light my father might have seen on the day he died.

And yet, I still don't know how to grieve.

I walk around the tree, touch its bark, surrounded by the smell of cedar. I try to quiet myself, to be open to whatever comes. I don't cry. I don't speak aloud to my father. He doesn't speak to me. But the clenched fist in my throat loosens enough for my breath to rise, even and slow. Then, with the tree a solid presence at my shoulder, I become absorbed in a sketch of the mountains cresting in blue waves on the horizon, the view from Lewis's Tree.

Martin is watering flats of seedlings in the front window of Iris's house when I come back to say good-bye. He wishes me good luck. Iris presses another long hug on me and gives me her wide, loving smile. Then, with her hands still on my arms, she says, "You know who I always think of in connection with your father?"

I shake my head no.

"*The Flying Dutchman*. It was an opera and a movie, too. An old movie with James Mason, I think, but it was based on a legend. He's this mythical character who has to wander the world until he finds a woman who will stay with him. I thought of that a lot when Lewis died. He was in search of a soul mate. Like all of us, I guess."

I stare at Iris, struck by her insight. It seems so right, so true. My mother, Mara, Lynn, the "heavy succession of women" my uncle had mentioned, and now—me. I have come to break the curse.

I am here so that my father's fluttering heart can come to rest.

A DREAM ABOUT MY FATHER

He sits on a barstool, knee bent, one foot resting on a lower rung. Behind him, the lacquered curve of the bar. Orange light glows up from below. He wears tan pants and a white shirt open at the collar. He is young and clean-shaven. He laughs heartily. A black clump of hair falls across his forehead. He leans forward and gestures with his hands as he talks. His black eyes sparkle with wit.

DIALOGUE 8
I should forgive you.

NO MORE SUFFERING

Ai! ai! we do worse! We are in a fix! And you're out, Death
    let you out, Death had the Mercy, you're done with your
    century, done with God, done with the path thru it —
    Done with yourself at last — Pure — Back to the Babe
    dark before your Father, before us all — before the
    world —
There, rest. No more suffering for you. I know where you've
    gone, it's good.

—Allen Ginsberg, from *Kaddish*

AND SOFTLY LIKE A
STONE
DROP DOWN AND DOWN
IN DEPTHS
WITHOUT BOTTOM

SLIDING WITHOUT SOUND
FILLED ENTIRE
DENSE WITH IT
SHATTERED OR
WHOLE
THERE WILL BE
REST

CREDITS

The author and publisher gratefully acknowledge permission to reprint the follow-ing: Steen Eiler Rasmussen, *Experiencing Architecture*, MIT Press, copyright © 1995; "The Sound of Trees" from *The Poetry of Robert Frost*, edited by Edward Connery Lathem. Copyright 1944 by Robert Frost, © 1969 by Henry Holt and Company. Reprinted by permission of Henry Holt and Company, LLC; Don Mochon, *Liberals for Nixon*, circa 1960, courtesy of Christina Mochon; "Varsity Scholars" from *Rensselaer Alumni News*, March 1961, Institute Archives and Special Collections, Rensselaer Polytechnic In-stitute; Professor Ernest Livingstone, *The Life Story of Ernest F. Livingstone*, Institute Archives and Special Collections, Rensselaer Polytechnic Institute. Courtesy of Teresa Livingstone; Joseph Molitor, photographs of the Weinberger house, Miami, Florida (page 204), Avery Architectural and Fine Arts Library, Columbia University in the City of New York. First published in *Architectural Record: Record Houses of 1969*, Mid-May 1969, vol. 145, no. 6; Donald Singer, architectural elevation and floor plan, Wein-berger house, Miami, Florida (page 4). Photographs of "Broken Mirror Art," "Weinberger house, living room" (page 254), "On My Father's Lap," and "Louie 2"; Charles Jencks, *Modern Movements in Architecture*, Penguin, 1973, 1987; Lydia Davis, "Re-member the Van Wagenens." Reprinted by permission of International Creative Man-agement, Inc. Copyright © 1999. First appeared in *Southern Humanities Review* (Spring 1999 ed.); "So Long, Frank Lloyd Wright," Copyright © 1969 Paul Simon. Used by per-mission of the Publisher: Paul Simon Music; John Ash, from "According to Their Mythology," *The Branching Stairs*, Carcanet Press Limited, copyright © 1984; "Kaddish" from *Collected Poems 1947–1980* by Allen Ginsberg. Copyright © 1959 by Allen Gins-berg. Reprinted by permission of HarperCollins Publishers Inc.; "Louie" photograph, courtesy of Daniel S. Cohn; Bill Gersh, handwritten letter, courtesy of Rachel and Georgia Gersh; Seymour H. Linden, "Ideal Couple" photograph, collection of the author. "Barely visible behind the arrayed might . . . " photograph, *Rensselaer Alumni News*, March 1961, Institute Archives and Special Collections, Rensselaer Polytechnic Institute; "Team Gives Personal Views . . ." article by Jack Titley, photographs by Sey-mour H. Linden, *The Rensselaer Polytechnic*, vol. 86, no. 20, April 19, 1961. "Student draft-ing" yearbook photograph, *Transit*, 1961, p. 71. "GE College Bowl Biographical Data," 1961. Institute Archives and Special Collections, Rensselaer Polytechnic Institute; "The Homecoming" paper doll soldier, from *Jack and Jill*, copyright © 1944 by Curtis

Publishing. Used by permission of the Children's Better Health Institute, Benjamin Franklin Literary & Medical Society, Inc., Indianapolis, Indiana; A. Aubrey Bodine, "H. L. Mencken" photograph, copyright © 1950 Jennifer B. Bodine. courtesy of AAubreyBodine.com; "W. C. Fields" film still, *The Big Broadcast of 1938*, copyright © 1938 Paramount Pictures, Inc. Courtesy of Universal Studios Licensing LLLP; "Greetings from New Mexico" postcard, distributed by Southwest Post Card Co., Albuquerque, NM; "Bon Voyage." Photographs of Lewis Weinberger in Europe, 1956. Photographs of Anna Cypra Oliver (pages 80, 311), courtesy of Stephan Marc Klein, Ph.D.; "Exercise 3: GE College Bowl," reconstruction drawn from articles in *The Rensselaer Polytechnic* (February–April, 1961), the *Albany Times-Union* (February–March 1961), and the *GE College Bowl* program guide (Spring 1961), Institute Archives and Special Collections, Rensselaer Polytechnic Institute. Action modeled on "GE College Bowl, University of Templeton v. University of California at Santa Barbara," hosted by Robert Earle, September 22, 1963, archives of the Museum of Television and Radio, New York City.